A Daughter's Peace Corps Journey
through the Eyes of Her Mother

I Am Me Because of You

KAREN LAWRENCE
with JENNIFER NELSON

ISBN 13: 978-1-59298-886-0
Library of Congress Catalog Number: 2015902694
Printed in the United States of America
First Printing: 2015
19 18 17 16 15   5 4 3 2 1

Book design and typesetting by Dan Pitts.

Beaver's Pond Press
7108 Ohms Lane
Edina, MN 55439–2129
(952) 829-8818
www.BeaversPondPress.com

Contents

———•●•———

DEDICATION

This book is dedicated to my grandson, Bekett.
His mother gave him a name from the country
whose people she served.

Her journey changed us and taught us lessons that
we didn't plan or even expect to learn.

Thank you!
Jennifer Nelson

Karen Lawrence

FOREWORD

I remember, as a child, being taught two songs: the first was "Jesus Loves Me—This I Know," and the second, "Twinkle, Twinkle, Little Star." Little did I know how significant those two songs would be in my adult life. They helped me through a very difficult time: when my daughter Jennifer said, "Yes, I will serve." The Peace Corps responded and assigned her to Central Asia.

Everyone was supportive and praised her unselfish choice. In many ways, it was no big surprise. She had always wanted to change the world. At the age of ten, when asked what her New Year's wish was, she nonchalantly responded, "World peace." Even before she could drive, Jennifer eagerly volunteered for many organizations. She graduated from college with a major in theology, and a minor in human services. But why the Peace Corps? Wasn't that something that young people joined in the 1960s and 1970s? It didn't make sense to me, and therefore, I didn't like it. But her choice became easier to sort out in my heart when my son said, "Mom, you have to let her go. This is what she is called to do."

Before I knew it, Jennifer received notice that her choice to serve in Kyrgyzstan had been accepted. On the cover of the paperwork she received were the faces of three cute Asian-looking children. The population of Kyrgyzstan is influenced by the peoples of surrounding China, Mongolia, and Russia. She could accept this location or reject two other assignments, but would then be forced to take the third. She accepted the first.

Jennifer received a Russian/Kyrgyz cassette with plenty of phrases to get her learning process started. Her favorite phrases were "Where is the toilet?" and "I have an earache," and "I don't want any tea." Also included in the package was her address for the first three months; she would live with a Russian family that did not speak any English, but she would have daily Russian language lessons.

I looked at the Peace Corps headquarters address: *Jennifer Lawrence, Peace Corps/Kyrgyz Republic, 304 Chokmorov Street Bishkek 720010, Kyrgyzstan.* But it still didn't seem real to me. How was it that an airmail letter would take two to four weeks to reach her? Sending her a care package would take six weeks! How could such everyday things take so long, in such a fast-paced world? It didn't make sense to me, and therefore, I didn't like it.

On September 15, 2004, we stood at the airport as a family of five, saying good-bye. Jennifer; my husband, Dan; our son Dominic (age twenty); and our daughter Heidi (age eighteen) held each other arm in arm, in a circle of tears. I was upset that airport security kept us from taking her down to the gate. We stood in a busy aisle in front of the security check-in and people stared as they walked by. In keeping with her giving spirit, Jennifer handed each of us a handmade beaded chain with a Chinese charm on the end: the character for "peace." Each of us took turns hugging and saying good-bye in our own way. We had twenty more minutes to spend together. Unfortunately, her leaving became harder the longer we stood there, so Jen said, "I just need to go." Everyone understood, but I began to realize how much I would miss her physical presence, to be able to touch her or hold her and make things all better. I still needed that, no matter what her age. As I stood there, my mind raced. She would be gone too long. Why had I agreed to this? I had to do something, so I shouted, "Wait... just one more kiss good-bye!" I rushed to her, squeezed her tight, and kissed her cheek over and over again. For as long as I live, I will never forget that embrace.

alone. The neighborhood is made up of mainly "hobby" farms, which here are basic survival farms. My family has two cows, some sheep, and chickens, and my mom makes everything we eat from scratch. The meals have been very carbohydrate focused, with the occasional meat, milk, and eggs. I have a room of my own with a lock on the door and the family has done a lot to make me feel comfortable and acclimate me into their way of multicultural life. I wish I could send you pictures of everything and everyone I have met, but I am still trying to figure that out. I must get going but I am glad to have this chance to let you know that I am doing well and that, although I am still going through the adjustment period, I'm already falling in love with the Minnesota-esque surroundings. Know that all is well and that I have met some wonderful people and look forward to the first conversation where I do not have to act out the sentence, use my hands, make animal noises, or get out my dictionary! I hope all is well and know that I have thought of you all often, as the nightly entertainment for my brothers and sisters is showing them all of my photos and cracking open my laptop.

Peace and love,

Jenny

CHAPTER 2

Her New Life

It was a relief as a parent to hear about Jennifer's adventures and how she was adjusting. My struggle, however, was being in the same place with the memories of the person who had left. Each time I walked past her room, I blew a kiss and made the sign of the cross. This soothed me, and helped me to remember that she was gone, but not forever. And for that I was thankful.

October 16, 2004

Dobrae Utra! (Good Morning!) It's so good to have a chance to write you again. Through some miscommunication I was not able to get to an Internet spot last week, so believe me, this email has been building up for some time now. I made a list of all the areas I should highlight. Trust me, there is so much more that I could only describe in person!

Food—Yes, first and foremost, the food. Like I said before, every meal is carbohydrate loaded. Between the fried breads, Hot Pocket-style meals, pasta, and potato-laden soups, I think my body is starting to adjust to the low level of protein. Not to worry; I depend on my trusty multivitamin to keep me moving. The walnuts here are excellent and there is always plenty of fruit from the neighborhood pear and apple trees. I have splurged a couple of times and bought a chocolate bar and Coke. I have even begun eating hot dogs again because it is often the only meat I see during the week. Also, I have become a major tea drinker and have even learned how to turn my cup of chai into a tasty cappuccino.

My family—They are great. My mom asked if I could relay their names, if they weren't too hard to spell. Dad is Isvandi, Mom is Filora, brothers are Ilham and Ilimda, and my sister is Denara. The dad is interesting, as he likes to tell me about how much he had to drink at the most recent neighborhood wedding. My mom smiles and laughs with me more and more. This morning she made fun of my accent, which even caused me to bust a gut. My fifteen-year-old brother is my guardian and social calendar manager. He is always thinking up things to do with other volunteers and their siblings. My sister has earned the nickname "Mama-dva" (mom #2), and bonds with me over things like washing the dishes and clothes, as well as cleaning and ironing. And my youngest brother is a little devil. He is so sweet, but there is something mischievous in the way he smiles. He always offers to carry my backpack in his bike basket, so that's a plus. When showing them pictures of my family back home, their gaze went straight to Uncle Bill. "Is he Turkish?" they asked. Sorry, Uncle Bill. But you do have blackish hair, a larger nose, darker skin tone, and a big mustache!

Daily grind—Up at 6:00 a.m. to get some quiet study time in (this Turkish family is a loud one!) before getting ready for the day. Some days I stay in the village and have Russian classes; other days, my group travels to the hub site for technical or other training. I am always in bed around 9:00 p.m., or falling asleep in front of the television with the kids at 8:30 p.m. We walk everywhere we go in the village. That, plus the fresh air and taxing language classes, keep me busy and tired.

Climate—I've begun living in my long johns. We've had frost the past couple of days and even the middle of the day has a chill to it. The cold isn't severe yet, but with all the outdoor walking and lack of efficient heating in buildings, it's easy to be cold and stay cold all day. On an average day, I wear four layers of clothes on top and two on bottom. My thermal socks have come in handy, as has the Peace Corps-issued heater.

Language—My experience learning Russian reminds me of the lead character in the movie *Rain Man*. "Sugar, sugar, sugar... sugar, sugar!" I simply take each day at a time. Some lessons are grammar heavy and I need a nap after we're done, and some lessons get me more energized to talk with my family and study when I get home. My family already knows when I have had a rough lesson by the number of times I have to say, "*Pafta ree, pashalsta*," which means, "Repeat again, please."

Media/Music—The television is on a lot at my house, usually playing Turkish news, local Kyrgyz shows, or the movie channel. On the public transportation we hear anything from "Buffalo Soldier" to Turkish pop. It really is a melting pot here of different cultures, ethnic heritages, and languages.

Faith—There are new mosques popping up everywhere and from certain parts of my village you can hear the call to prayer. It is the third day of Ramadan, which my mom and sister are observing. I told them that I wanted to participate, which only lasted one day. By the end of the only day I fasted, I announced to my mom, "*Mama, zaftra, ya ne Mussleman*." This means, "Mom, tomorrow I am not a Muslim." That whole experience is a very long story, as is the list of reasons why I wanted to participate. But I am glad that I at least tried and that my family knows I want to support them and become a part of the family as much as I can. There are a few Christians in the group and we are still trying to figure out how to get to some English services in the capital.

I've had a couple of signs that reaffirm my decision to serve here. One is a huge wheat statue outside of our village. I have no idea why it's there, since we're not known for our wheat production, but it makes me smile every time I pass it.

Also, after another volunteer made some negative and insulting comments about Catholicism, I saw a car with a fish bumper sticker when I left the hub site. That's not a common sight here, so I took it as a God wink and smiled as I watched the car drive away. To explain the mentality I've adopted, here's a quote from a volunteer who came with me to the Internet spot. After our computers shut down for the third time and he couldn't get online, he turned to me and said, "What do you expect? We are in Kyrgyzstan!" and we both laughed.

And it is so true. I always have to keep in mind that just because you are at the post office during office hours doesn't mean they will have postage available. Just because you are at the Internet café doesn't mean the power will be on. And just because you are at the bank during office hours doesn't mean the clerks will interrupt their tea break to get your cash. Patience is a virtue! I hope all is well. Thank you so much for the individual emails and the updates from home. I look forward to writing you again with news of my upcoming Peace Corps visit to a volunteer in the field and my placement information.

Peace and love,

Jenny

October 17, 2004

Hello again. I'm in a different Internet café now, since the previous one suddenly shut down again. I just wanted to pass along a wish list that my Americanski mama suggested I make. Many of you have relayed that you want to know when I need anything. So I figured it would just be easiest to send it to the whole list. Here we go: Febreze, spot remover, gum, candy, canned chips/plastic-jarred fruit, DVDs, blank CDs, Christian music, cocoa, peanut butter, ketchup, pens, *Time* and *People* magazines. Here's some more info that I forgot to relay in the last email: for anyone interested in calling me, I do have a phone at my house; there is a cheap and easy way to do it. Go to www.uniontelecard.com, click on Kyrgyzstan, and you can buy a calling card: three hours for twenty U.S. dollars. My contact info is: International Code: 011; Kyrgyz Code: 996; City Code: 3132; Home: 44270. Also, if you're sending letters through standard mail, they're taking a little over two

and raw fish to setting out candy, fruits, and lots of bread, there was plenty to do. I didn't get any compliments on my hard work until I changed out of my jeans and into a skirt. Only then was I one of the women. Traditionally, people arrive at sundown and eat first, and then there is a half hour of readings and prayers, sung by a male family member. To get an idea of how many people attend, just imagine the four largest rooms in your house filled with food in the middle and many squished people sitting on the floor along the sides of all four rooms. The men are in the largest room, and then the women and children fill the next three rooms. After the meal you can hear the Suras echoing throughout the house... indescribably beautiful!

About a week ago, two trainees and I went to the International Church in Bishkek. It is nondenominational with services in English. It wasn't the same as going to a Catholic Mass, but it did the trick. This visit was just before we were given our permanent assignments, and the message of the day's service was "God is the boss!" I couldn't have timed that visit better if I tried.

From the time that I arrived in this country I was told that I would be learning Russian, working eventually in an orphanage. One of those facts remains true. A week ago my program manager informed me that the orphanage near Lake Issyk Kul in which I was to be placed could not find me housing off site, which is one of the Peace Corps policies. Therefore, I will be returning to the Talas Oblast to live and work in a small village outside of Talas. The village is called Pokrovka, population 3,500, and it is directly south of Taraz in Kazakhstan. I could literally walk to the border in thirty minutes.

There will be two other volunteers in the village with me: Ian (twenty-four, not my current neighbor) will teach at the boarding school and Kathryn (twenty-three) will teach at the public school. Kathryn will live across the street from me with an Uzbek family, and because she is a self-defense instructor, I couldn't have asked for a better neighbor. I will be living with a Kyrgyz family: Venera (mom, forty), Madim and Kadim (boys, eleven), and Aisalkyn (girl, three). They are a wonderful family and my new room is spacious and private, because I am in a separate part of the house from the rest of the family. I look forward to living with them.

The NGO that I will be working with is a public fund for women. Basically, there are six women who repair or make clothes and, along with the profit from four handicraft groups, they keep the money in a fund for battered women. Bride kidnapping and alcoholism among men is a problem in the village, and so the NGO was started. My job, once I arrive, is to assist in the start-up of a crisis center for women, supported by and run by this NGO. I have met my director, who is a wonderful woman and former host mother of a Peace Corps volunteer. She speaks a little English, so between my broken Russian and her English, we manage to communicate. Now, I did say that I wouldn't mind moving to Talas (which is about an hour drive from my future village); however, the thought of going through border crossings four times during a one-way trip is not something I look forward to every time I travel in the next two years. I have already made two trips to Talas Oblast and in those few crossings I have been referred to as Jennifer Lopez by the guard who was supposed to be taking down my visa info (he never did; I guess having the first name of a celebrity helps in this country); I have been asked if I am married (at this point in the trip I was tired and snapped back in Russian, "No, I'm not married! What does it matter?!"); and I have been saluted and welcomed to our beautiful country by a Kazak guard. Other than the annoyance of the borders, I am really excited to be working and living in Pokrovka.

I should close this up. You will hear from me again after my swearing in (the president of Kyrgyzstan will be there!) and moving to my site. I look forward to hearing from you. I wish you a belated Happy Halloween and an early Happy Thanksgiving.

Peace and love,

Jenny

P.S. Every time I walk past the bus station, I am the topic of conversation. I look Russian. Well, I certainly don't look Kyrgyz, so people assume I am Russian, and the drivers all try to lure me into their car or *marshutka* to get me where I belong... the capital!

CHAPTER 4

Holidays without Her

It has been forty-four days since we said good-bye and now comes the time when we all come together as usual and celebrate the holidays. How will I be able to do it without her?

December 1, 2004

All right, people... you can't send me photos of your holiday fun and not expect me to figure out what's up. Yesterday Dominic told me that you were all wearing black, mourning my absence at Thanksgiving, but the photos tell a different story. I've only been able to open two so far, but even the back of Sara's head looks cheerful... and is that a white sweater I see on Mom?

I am truly shocked!

It was so great to talk to all of you yesterday at Thanksgiving. Sorry about the bad connection. It was funny to transition from everyone who I haven't talked to yet, back to Heidi, Dominic, or Dad, since they are used to the three-second delay. It made me realize that a three-second delay and Turkish pop music in the background are not normal and wasn't usual for me only two months ago.

Nonetheless, it was good to hear your voices and I look forward to chatting again at Christmas. I am here at the Internet center, since our technical session for today was cancelled and I don't have anything to get to until later in the afternoon. I'm listening to Dave Matthews on a friend's Discman, and with the addition of free Internet, I think I am in heaven. Not to mention the fact that I got to talk to all of you!

Peace,

Jen

December 13, 2004

Hey, everyone! Our Monday call came in reverse at first. At 7:00 a.m., the phone rang. It was a Russian operator, and then Jen came on the line. She was calling from the telecom center in town to tell us that her phone in her home wasn't working, so she wanted me to call a neighbor of the other Peace Corps volunteer, Kathryn; she gave me the number. (This will be a good backup number if we ever need it again.) So we agreed that I would call the neighbor's house at my normal time of 8:00 a.m., 7:00 p.m. her time. It turned out that her mother made her eat supper before going over to receive our call, so she was delayed. In fact, she was at the neighbor's front gate knocking when we called, and could hear their phone ringing. So I had to visit with the neighbor's little girl for a bit. Jen had taught me those extra phrases, so I could tell that she said, "Hold on."

A breathless Jen came to the phone, and it was wonderful to hear her voice. She first let us know that she has not yet received my Thanksgiving package that I sent on October 25th. Who knows, she may receive my Christmas package first. It is so upsetting to me, but Jen said, "Mom, let's talk about something else." I have to learn to not let my frustration become hers.

We asked how her first week at work went, and she said that basically she just studies her Russian for eight hours a day and probably will for the next month. She isn't fluent enough to do any office work yet. As she said, you can't do paperwork if it is all Greek to you. The grant that will supply them with their office needs and equipment won't be there until another month anyway, so the timing will work out.

She then said that when she went to work that morning, there was a padlock on the office's front door. In America, this would be bizarre, but Jen has learned it is no big deal. There were problems with the electricity, and the updated paperwork that allows them to be open hadn't gotten in on time. Maybe they're somewhere with my lost package. She took it all in stride and was able to do some other things. She made the half-hour walk to the Internet site; it's the closest, but is old and was not cooperating today. She was only able to read her incoming emails and not send anything out. This village is a bit more remote than her previous one, but the scenery makes up for it.

Jen told us that she recently went to Talas with her other volunteers, hoping to find some new pants that actually fit; her current ones are just about falling off. The ladies at the mercantile told her that jeans are very expensive, and cost about 400 som, which is ten U.S. dollars. There are four ladies there that sew, ages twenty-three to twenty-eight, and also two older ladies who do more of the specialized sewing. They are always busy making the big, cushy pillow mats that local people use when sitting on the floor to eat and visit. I hate to think what they use for batting material. Jen had no luck finding any jeans, but while visiting with the ladies, they told her they would take in her pants for free because of her working there! She knew that she couldn't beat that! She figured she could wear skirts while the pants are in their care. She knows that it may be longer than she would like, because, as she has learned, when you are told it will take one day, it will usually take three weeks.

Jen told me another story to make her point. Jen's director had her dad visiting, as well as another man who knew English. She thought it would be fun for Jen to talk with him; plus, the director's dad always gave the American volunteers a Kyrgyz name. Jen was torn, because she only gets one *banya* (shower) a week and it was set up for that day. She was also expecting some volunteer friends to visit from Talas. But the director said the visit with her dad and the other guest would only be for a few hours. Not wanting to insult her boss, she agreed to go. Jen's local mother had told the director that she'd need to be back by four o'clock, but they spoke in the Kyrgyz language, not Russian, and so Jen didn't understand.

The visit turned out not to last just a few hours but five, and so she got home late! Venera was upset because Jen wouldn't be able to get into the banya and her friends had already come and gone. Jen was so upset that she threw down her mittens and said, "I am not cheerful now!" Venera told her that the friends had gone into town to eat, so maybe she could catch them, and she would see about scheduling her banya for later.

Jen took a much-needed brisk walk to Ian's and then headed to the local café, but had no luck finding anyone. She ended up back at Ian's and they consoled each other; he was saddened after talking to one of the volunteers at his old village. Jen said that she should have known better, that she should have known that the visit would take longer than two hours, but when you are a guest, there is a fine line of balance of etiquette between saying yes and no.

When Jen finished her story, I told her that it was one of those life lessons that would help her down the line.

Jen has had to learn a lot of lessons, especially living in a non-English speaking country. In addition to her director/boss, Jen has been assigned to a liaison; she's what they call a "counterpart." We learned that counterparts are supposed to know English, but Jen's knows very little, which means that she doesn't get to speak English very often. Ian's and Kathryn's counterparts speak English, and they are teaching English at the school, so they have many opportunities to use their native language. I asked Jen if it was difficult for them to teach English when they don't know the Kyrgyz language that well. She said that most of Ian's kids are sixth-year students, so they all speak English very well. Kathryn has some second- and third-graders, but they are so infatuated with the language that they pay attention. And Ian and Kathryn use games and casual conversations to teach, so the lessons are not as difficult.

Frustrated with her own situation, Jen had said to them, "You guys are lucky; you have English around you and your counterpart speaks it, too." Ian and Kathryn already know her very well and said, "Jen, you would go nuts doing what we are doing." It turns out that they never know when they will have a class; everything changes from day to day. Sometimes the class never shows up when it is scheduled and all mayhem breaks out with a system that isn't organized to begin with. They are right. That would be truly frustrating for Jen.

We chatted about everyday things, like the weather and Jen's health. She let her dad and me know that, after investigating the cost of heating Jen's room, her host mother found out it would cost 9,000 som every week, or $125 U.S. dollars. So that is out. Jen said that the cold wasn't too bad now. Her Peace Corps-issued space heater seems to be doing the job and can keep up with the room. They don't have snow, and she was shocked to hear that we didn't either and that it was thirteen degrees this morning. And anyway, the three-year-old girl, Aisalkyn, hangs on Jen a lot, keeping her warm. Jen admitted that Dan's suggestion of us sending her an electric blanket was appealing but then she reminded us that it would only work when the electricity did. So she'll have to rely on her heater and little sister.

More importantly, her stomach is feeling and working much better. She will not need to get it checked out. It isn't as bad as when she first got there and she has never run a fever, so she is okay. She said it isn't too much different that when she used to deal with her gallbladder troubles. Thank God that was taken care of beforehand, even though the symptoms are still haunting her.

I let her know that we enjoyed the pictures she sent and had them copied and distributed to all of our friends. Dan told her how he took a disk of the pictures to Guardian Angels grade school to give to the first-grade class she is sponsoring. The teacher had asked Dan to say a few things to the class, so he asked them if they like being warm, watching TV, and having lights by which to eat and read. He then explained that it isn't that nice in other places around the world, and that the children should be thankful for all the wonderful things in their lives. Then he realized he was talking to first-graders and worried about being too heavy. But they had listened to him intently, and I'm sure they understood his message.

Jen loved the story, and let us know that she is compiling another disk of photos that she will send after New Year's; they celebrate that holiday and apparently it is quite the event. She told us that the second disk will have more pictures of her, as well as of local scenes. She has been getting pictures from other volunteers and downloading them onto her computer, so she can show us some areas where she hasn't even been yet.

After a half hour of talking on the phone, we got disconnected. I called back and Jen said that the electricity had gone out and zapped the phone line, but it was okay now, although they were sitting in the dark with candles and an army flashlight. To try to make her feel less frustrated, I said, "Hey, you never told me what your Kyrgyz name is." She said the closest Kyrgyz word for Jennifer would be "Jengyshgul". Then her director's father looked at her and said a Russian word that means "victorious." But he looked at her more and said, "But yet I think it should be the word that means 'sweet.'" Then he said that she needed both names. Jen said no one else has ever been given two and, filled with pride, she said, "Just call me SWEET VICTORY!" I surely hope it comes true. We set up our time to talk Christmas Eve and I wished her warmth, love, and that her package would arrive soon. Thanks for sharing our updates.

Love,

Karen

P.S. Before we hung up and as I was talking to Jen, Dan whispered, "Look out the window." There were five pairs of cardinals at our bird feeder! They are my favorite, and their presence is thought to be a sign of joy. I believe it, because when I need uplifting the most, one will inevitably appear as if to say, "Everything will be all right." We told Jen and she said, "Oh, yeah... I sent them there."

January 11, 2005

Jen's phone has been out for almost two weeks so we used the backup number again. The neighbor, Nurgul, is such a nice lady to let us call there. Even though she tolerates my Russian and she has pretty good English, we still seem to repeat ourselves and then talk louder, as if that will help us understand one another better. The exciting news is that Jen said she mailed another CD of pictures to us last week in a padded manila envelope. We pray for its safe arrival, because to us, those pictures are like gold. Luckily, she's sealed it with duct tape, a technique she's found really useful. They do not have duct tape in Kyrgyzstan, and it would be hard for them to tear it off and replace it again without being obvious. Her Christmas package from Nate and Emily Semsch (newlywed college friends) had duct tape all over it and so she took their lead.

Jen said that it has been mild but they are having snow, so her brother, Dominic, jokingly told her he would be right over! His snowmobile is twitching in the garage.

Since our package with the long johns STILL hasn't arrived, I asked how warm she'd been in her room. She said, "Well, it's cold enough that I can keep fruit cups cool on my windowsill, but it really isn't that bad." She has been using the tights we sent and knee-high socks strategically, and said she isn't concerned about having "thick ankles."

Jen told us that she had had a very busy day and, as she was eating supper, Venera had said, "Only one half hour and your parents will be calling." Jen said, "Oh, yeah; it's Monday." It makes me feel better to know that she is not sadly standing by the phone, waiting for it to ring. And the fact that her family is thinking about us—is touching.

Then Jen told us about how she had been placed with Venera's family, a story we hadn't heard before. Jen's director had told her that when she was looking for housing for Jen, she'd had two other possibilities. The first choice was a family with a teenage daughter. At first glance, it had seemed like a good fit. The director explained to the family that having Jen there would be a benefit; the girl could learn English from Jen. But the family kept asking about money. The Peace Corps pays the volunteer 4,000 som ($100 U.S. dollars) per month and they have to decide, based on how many meals a day they want, how much to pay their host families. This family thought they would be paid $250 in American money, which they then would exchange for 10,000 som. The director explained that the volunteers were only paid in som. When they heard this, they weren't interested in housing a volunteer.

The second family she checked out had a dad who was a serious drinker, but the director wasn't sure if his drinking was bad enough to be a "problem" for the family. But when she looked into things further, the fact that there were so many men coming in and out of the home for drinking and socializing forced her to realize that it wouldn't be a good situation for Jen. THANK GOD for choice number three! This was the family of Venera the doctor! Jen said she found it interesting that the director even told her this story. Jen's living situation was just one more thing she was (and we were) thankful for.

And then Jen let us in on a strange tidbit. She told us she had realized that her Russian was good, but that it got even better when she was debating or arguing with someone. She thought maybe that when emotions enter in, she gets so focused that the words just flow out. I asked what arguments she'd had, and she told us about a recent one. She had been speaking with her director about Kathryn, one of the other volunteers, and the director had said that Kathryn shouldn't help with another particular program, one led by another director. Jen tried to explain that Kathryn had extra time on her hands and didn't mind helping with both programs. The director kept repeating herself and Jen finally said, "I understand everything you are saying." Then it came out that her director didn't want this other director's program to do better than her own, which might happen if it received Kathryn's help. So Jen boldly said, "So in other words, you don't have a problem with Kathryn; you have a problem with this other director." Jen wrapped up her account by noting that she had been very careful in what she had said and how she had said it, but that it was important to stand up for oneself or others if you feel they are wrongly being judged or pushed around.

Jen put in her order for us to send her spices and we promised to send it off soon. But the best treat she asked for wasn't food. She wanted us to send her a carrot peeler! She said, "It will make my life in the kitchen so much easier." Apparently they use big butcher knives to peel carrots. She said that it would not only be so much nicer for her, but it would also be the entertainment for her family for the month.

In closing, we just want to let you know that Jen is very excited to be going to Talas this weekend to have brunch with friends and will definitely get to the good Internet site. So if anybody wants to drop her a quick email this week, she will receive it on Saturday. Thanks for listening.

Love,

Karen

P.S. Heidi, our younger daughter, moved in with a friend of ours, in order to be close to her schooling at Aveda. She stopped by to visit and decided to sleep over, so she was there for our call. When Heidi told Jen she got her ears pierced as a belated seventeenth birthday gift, I could hear Jen screaming on the phone from across the room. Oh, the joy of simple pleasures.

January 15, 2005

Surprise! I know this update comes not long after my last email, but an unexpected trip to the Internet site prompted me to take advantage of the opportunity to communicate. I hope your New Year has been happy and healthy thus far. Rumor has it that Kyrgyzstan's president announced this to be the year of Americans in Kyrgyzstan. If that rumor is true, then I couldn't have timed my service in the Peace Corps any better!

Christmas in Talas was not the bonding experience I would have hoped it to be with the other volunteers in my oblast, but it was nice nonetheless. When we arrived in Talas, we went to a volunteer's house and had a wonderful meal of fruit salad, chicken, coleslaw, soup, and fettuccine Alfredo. It was the first time I was able to see the Weckerlys, the couple that I visited in October for my Peace Corps visit. They are doing well and delighting in the fact that next year at this time they will be able to spend Christmas at home with their children. Talas has an American Corner, which I believe I mentioned after my visit, that hosts parties and cultural exchange experiences for every American holiday. The day after Christmas, we all went to the center to help run the activities, which included an ornament-making contest (I was a judge and I don't think I've ever felt as much pressure as during the judging and prize giveaway! Anything less than first place is shameful... I wonder how many students cried that night...), a song lesson, and watching *How the Grinch Stole Christmas*.

New Year's was also quite the experience. Because giving gifts is customary, I decided to get a little something for my family and the other people that I've gotten to know, including my director, my counterpart, and Ian's and Kathryn's families. I bought each family a lemon, because citrus fruit is expensive and considered a luxury here. For lunch I made my family onion rings, because it is usually what my grandma in the States makes for special events. Because everything here is fried, it wasn't hard to do, and a bottle of ketchup from the States topped it off. My family really seemed to get into the onion rings since the traditional bread for holidays is *borsok*, a fried diamond of dough, which is prepared just like onion rings. Later I helped prepare plates of fruit, salad, meats, and desserts to set the holiday table.

In Kyrgyzstan, the party starts at midnight, with neighbors going house to house "guesting" and toasting each other's homes. Before midnight it was pretty quiet, since two of my siblings were sick, so my mom and I watched the Russian and Kazak variety shows that were on and she explained what I couldn't understand. When she wanted to go to the next house to guest, I declined, because I would have been expected to toast in Russian and I think I had used all of my Russian during the other parties I had attended throughout the week. Also, after you toast you are expected to sing, and of course everyone thinks it's just amazing when the American sings, so I had done my fair share the week before New Year's. The best is when the host says, "Good toast, now sing. You can sing in English!" That's when I whip out the only Kyrgyz song I know and sing it as loud as I can. The sad thing is that most Kyrgyz don't know the words, and I end up singing alone when I thought that I would have some help. I get a lot of "Good for you!" in both Russian and Kyrgyz afterwards.

Recently I was studying Russian grammar at work, not paying attention to the conversation that my director and office manager were having when they suddenly turned to me and said, "We are telling secrets, but we think you should know, too." My director proceeded to tell me about how, before the beginning of the new year, one of the women who sews had helped her husband's friend kidnap one of the younger women who is studying sewing through my NGO. I guess everything turned out all right, because the girl's parents went to find her and brought her back home. The way this situation turned out is not normal. Often the possible husband rapes the girl immediately after the kidnapping and the family then sees her as used goods, which is a shame to the family. What blows my mind is that I am here to help start a crisis center for just this sort of thing: women who have been bride kidnapped, whose families will not take them back, or women who face domestic violence. And one of the women I work with doesn't see anything wrong with this "tradition."

My director explained that the woman who made the kidnapping possible rationalized that the man who would be the husband was a good person and that he was from a good family, so a marriage would turn out all right. Also, *she* had been kidnapped by *her* husband, and her marriage turned out fine, so she thinks that there's nothing wrong with bride kidnapping. I made my anger over the situation extremely obvious to my director and office manager, and spent the rest of the day thinking about how I could see this situation through Kyrgyz eyes, through the Kyrgyz culture, and choose to accept this woman with the knowledge of her actions.

Lately I have been conversing with my director more than studying Russian during the day. This is a very good thing, since I just flushed out her priorities for my eventual work. What I thought to be an after-work club to teach adults business English and concepts is really a full-blown American center, such as the one in Talas. And my director sees this project as the number-one priority, not the establishment and running of a crisis center. That was my number-one priority for a long time, and what I assumed was my main goal for the next two years.

There are many details that I obviously must leave out, but I struggle now with choosing one of three options in this situation: 1) Do I agree only to work on what I see as the priority and logical approach, and bully my point of view as the right way?; 2) Do I continue conversations about starting a crisis center as the first goal and the American center second, and if that does not go over well, then be satisfied with the fact that I tried?; or 3) Do I do what my director asks of me without question, because I am really just here to assist in whatever projects the community wants first? At the end of the conversation about opening these two centers, I said repeatedly that I understood what she was saying, but I did not necessarily agree and I needed time to think. In the long run, I know this situation will iron itself out, probably outside of the sphere of my control. However, in the meantime, I am evaluating my role within the organization and community.

I am the first volunteer in our village to speak Russian. For some reason, people here think that if you know English, then the second language you learn in America is Russian. It might be due to the proximity to Russia, or the fact that it has been the second language in this part of the world for a long time. Whatever the reason, I am often asked by the most random people around town (from store owners, to children, to militia) why I don't know Kyrgyz (because I obviously learned Russian in America!). I explain that as a business volunteer, it is better for me to know Russian, since many countries speak it, as compared to Kyrgyz. Then I usually follow that up with "But I'm working on my Kyrgyz, so I know a little!" (speaking the word *little* in Kyrgyz). This usually satisfies anyone.

I just received a Kyrgyz course book, by chance, from the language person at the Peace Corps headquarters. So once I feel more comfortable with Russian, I can study Kyrgyz more in-depth on my own, as I actually have the tools, and depend less on the free time and kindness of the other two volunteers in my village. At this point, the only reason that I would need to know Kyrgyz is to interact with small children. Every so often I will go to a store or kiosk where only a young child is working and they cannot speak with me in Russian. After that happened a few times, I decided to learn numbers and shopping phrases in Kyrgyz. Now I am working on phrases used for transportation so I don't look like such a tourist when the other two volunteers arrange a taxi ride and the fare.

My family continues to crack me up. They are my teachers, confidants, protectors, and friends. Recently I came home from work to find a small puppy in a box in the entryway. I asked where the puppy came from and my mom said it was a gift. They still didn't know the gender of the dog or what to name it. One of the boys was hell-bent on calling the dog Jennifer, but I pointed out that if the dog did something bad and they were scolding it, I would think they were yelling at me, which could be very confusing. For a while, the possibility of naming it Minnesota if it were a boy or Minnie if it were a girl seemed like a winner. But when we discovered the puppy was a girl, my mom suggested "Likeah." I replied that it sounded like a beautiful Kyrgyz name, and wanted to know what it meant. She said, "No, it's what you say all the time when you can't think of how to say something in Russian... 'Like... ahhh...'" I had a good laugh at that one, and so have all the other volunteers in the oblast. Another possible name was "Soooo," since I tend to say that in English in between Russian sentences. (There is a Russian equivalent, but my brain hasn't latched onto it yet.) In the end, Likeah was the winner.

Another experience with my family gives the depth of the culture exchange between locals and myself a new meaning. Randomly, my mom told me that when I was talking to my American parents on the phone for the first time after moving to Pokrovka, my little brother saw me shedding some tears and ran up to my mom and exclaimed, "Mom, she cries just like we do!" While there have been other volunteers living and working in the village before, my brother obviously never saw this aspect of them. I seem to take it for granted that I know people are people no matter where they are from, which is a luxury of knowledge due to the tossed salad of nationalities found in the States. However, since Pokrovka is not the hot-spot vacation destination for foreigners, the exposure to outsiders and cultural exchanges is limited. It puts a whole new spin on one of three objectives of the Peace Corps: to teach other people about Americans.

Seeing my little sister interacting with the Kyrgyz-speaking volunteers got me thinking about how confusing it must be for her to hear me speaking a language that she can't communicate in herself (at times I might as well speak English to her; the comprehension level is about the same). I told my mom one day that I wanted to be able to play with Aisalkyn like the other volunteers, and communicate with her in Kyrgyz so she could understand me. My mom said that it's actually a very good thing that I can only speak Russian. Before I came, my sister never spoke in Russian, although she heard it often. Now she is picking up new words every day. The last thing I expected to be doing in the Peace Corps was teaching a three-year-old Russian inadvertently, but hey, why not?!

Although I never doubt the constant presence of God in my life, I have begun playing a little game called, "Where is God today?" Keeping a positive attitude and simply maintaining a balanced outlook every day is what keeps me going through the tough days. During one of my first weeks in the village, I simply decided that I was not going to find God in all the negative aspects of my day. If I blamed God for everything and anything, I would never be able to justify staying here for two years when I know it is God who called me to a life of service. I refuse to whine to God about the cold, the drunk who stumbles after me, the multiple trips to the outhouse due to some bad meat. God is in my host mom who is obsessed with making sure I am warm. God is in the person who intercepts the drunk and gets him somewhere safe, and in the opportunity to live as the people who I am serving, bad meat and all. It's not a game that I play every day, all day, but it is a little trick that I like to use when I feel that I am getting overly negative about any situation I find annoying or challenging.

There is a saying that I have heard often lately. When an English-speaking student asked me to come to the village's disco on Saturday, I said that I did not know if I could, because I do not know what each day will hold for me. (I really just didn't want to commit to anything so early in the week.) She looked at me and said, "You are right. Only if God wills it..." She then broke down the Turkish phrase that people say; literally it means something like "If God wills something to be, then and only then will it be." In Russian it is slightly different: "If God lets or allows." It's something that I try to keep at the forefront of my daily thoughts, especially if I want to catch a taxi, if I want the Internet to work, or if I want the day to go as I have it planned in my head. Only if God wills it to be.

Caravans. There's a book of this title by James Michner that is set in Afghanistan in the 50s; it sounds like an interesting read. Right now Kathryn in my village is reading it and she says that the first chapter, on foreigners in Afghanistan, is very similar to what we are experiencing here. Some topics that Michner covers in this chapter are water sanitation, health, mountains, and the reaction to everything from a foreigner's point of view. Keeping in mind that it is set in another country, with varying cultural norms, fifty plus years ago, it might give you some insight into what life is like for me here.

I've once again sent a CD with photos, from the past two months, to my parents. If you would like to take a look, feel free to contact them. In the package I've also included recipes for Kyrgyz national dishes and spices. Who knows, my home in Chaska may become the local hot spot for Kyrgyz cuisine! You can get a hold of my folks by either calling their home number in the evening or emailing them. For those of you at St. Mary's University: pester Dominic, as he might have the photos downloaded to his computer as well.

I have just a few more items to add to my wish list. While some are available in country, they are difficult to find because of living in the boonies. Dry packets: juice mix, dip and sauce mix, Jell-O, powdered milk. Spices: nutmeg, cinnamon, vanilla, baking powder, allspice. I thank everyone who has sent holiday packages! Every day is a holiday when I walk into the post office and see a yellow delivery bag with my name on it. I can always count on people from home to be so considerate. Thanks!

Until next time,

Jenny

P.S. Uncle Paul and Aunt Patty, just wanted to update you on the status of the cappuccino mix you sent in your last package. Not only did it add flavor to our oblast Christmas cookies, but I have found a way to make turtle mochas in Kyrgyzstan. Some cocoa, cappuccino mix, and a little bit of Snickers bar mixed in, and I am in heaven. It's not the same as holding a turtle mocha from Caribou in my hand as I walk into your house to watch the boys, but it does the trick on a cold night! Love and miss you. Give the boys some hugs for me!

P.P.S. I am attempting to explain the concept of peanut butter to my new host family... it is entertaining!

January 17, 2005

We had a hard time getting through to Jen this morning. But finally, after twenty minutes, we got to hear her cheery voice. She said it had been snowing all day and that may have been the problem. She sounded so clear, but she said it sounded like I was under water. She teased me about swimming while calling her. Just as we started to talk, a pair of cardinals settled in at the feeder. We haven't seen them in about two weeks. Maybe it has been the cold, but she joked again how she was responsible for sending them over.

Jen had a good time in Talas this weekend. She said that it was fun to speak English again, although she received some bad news on Friday night. She was going to have brunch with the retired couple, the Weckerlys (who remind her of Grandma and Grandpa), but they had to go home. Mr. Weckerly has heart problems, and after not feeling very well, he found out that he has so much damage to his heart that he won't make it if he has a heart attack. He was strongly encouraged to go back to the States for the best care. They were gone within forty-eight hours.

The drive to Talas was interesting for Jen. There are no border guards to deal with because the trip does not involve going out of state. Kyrgyzstan is the country, but she lives in the oblast (state) of Talas. Only when she goes to Bishkek does she need to cross borders, due to the mountain range. They took a *marshutka* (taxi) ride, and she had a conversation in Russian with a Kyrgyz man who had definitely been drinking. Evidently he spoke both Kyrgyz and Russian and could understand her, despite the alcohol. But the real treat was having two ducks in a bag sitting next to her during the whole ride! She said it wasn't the first time that has happened. I laughed so hard when she said she has a picture of it. When I asked why they would be there, she said, so matter of fact, that they had been purchased at the bazaar and were being taken home, either to be eaten or used as income. I didn't want to ask how they would be used as income... maybe when their owners sell their eggs.

While in Talas, she got to the Internet site, a real treat, and did some shopping. She actually found a new pair of pants and got her old ones taken in by the ladies at her work. Her latest weigh-in shows a loss of fifty pounds, but at least she's healthy. She downloaded the Christmas pictures that we sent and when she got home, pulled them up on her computer, played Christmas music, and drank hot cocoa. She plans on showing them to her family tomorrow, especially the ones with the guys wearing the *kalpaks* that she had sent. A *kalpak* is a traditional wool hat worn by most Kyrgyz men. She said it is hard to receive so many pictures, because the Internet connection is so slow, so we may decide on our next gathering to put them on a CD and mail it to her.

I asked her about her job situation, because of what she told us in her last email. Would she be doing the crisis center or this new "American Corner" project? She said that when she reread that email, she realized how upset she sounded, but that she had really just been venting.

She has talked to different people and they have reassured her that it will all fall into place without too much upset on her part. So she has decided that she will be open to trying whatever they suggest, and if the grant doesn't go through, they will try her "plan B." It's just a matter of being patient in order to work the system. The Peace Corps had told us that when volunteers write home, they sometimes are in moments of frustration, but by the time you call, all concerns have passed. This was a perfect example. If nothing else, it shows there is plenty for her to do and that's what she wants.

We got together with some friends Saturday night and showed them the first CD of pictures and the gifts she sent us. When I told that to Jen, she was moved, and it meant so much to her. We will be having Nate and Emily over on Saturday to do the same and we may have the second CD by then. Maybe they will have to stay the night! It just shows how important it is to her that we haven't forgotten about her. After only four months, we sit back and marvel at how so many people have been affected by her journey and are interested in her new life. Not much else was new. I was going to suggest we call every other Monday but as we were saying good-bye, she said, "Will talk to you next Monday." It would break my heart to suggest it now, after hearing the need in her voice. So that decided that. Those calls are a lifeline for her and if they allow her to endure all she has seen and done, so be it. Talk to you soon!?

Love,

Karen

CHAPTER 5

———————•●•———————

Is There a Doctor in the House?

We are so lucky that Jen lives with a doctor. It has a comforting effect, even though I still think I am the best one to take care of her. But Venera is there and I am here. I just pray that the age-old Kyrgyzstan superstitions don't interfere with any care she needs.

January 24, 2005

Great news! The box of food and long johns I sent to Jen on October 25th just arrived! I kept asking her about it and got so frustrated at the thought that it was lost forever, especially when she needed another pair of long johns. It took three months to get to her, but that's not entirely the country's fault. It was sent to the Bishkek address about two weeks before she got her formal assignment and new address. Jen said it was the most "beat up" box she has ever seen and it's quite amazing that they finally tracked her down. I think the saving grace is the Peace Corps help. If she were on her own living there, she'd need luck on her side for this sort of thing. The news has just made my day and I'm so thankful that nothing was tampered with. My tape jobs are getting more success-ful. The plastic containers of fruit (which are lighter than canned) were a real treat, especially this time of year, as fruit is considered a delicacy. The volunteers got a kick out of the *Field & Stream* article about the hunters that got lost in the mountains while hunting. Parts actually made them laugh because they see situations like this from a totally different (unglamorized) perspective. But she finds the articles and magazines so enjoyable. I even sent our church bulletin from that week.

When I called (her home phone is now working) I heard a ruckus and a boy's voice saying, "Americanski Mama!" He was wrestling with Jen for the phone because he wanted to answer. Jen just laughed, and even from that I could tell she had a cold. I was right: sore throat, ear pain, and a raspy voice. She stayed home from work today and said she just couldn't see being at the drafty office all day. Luckily, after just resting, she was feeling so much better. But as we were talking, she made the mistake of saying, "I started feeling sick a couple of days ago." Then she stopped and quickly said, "I mean ill. I felt ill." Then "Oh, crap." I asked what was wrong. She said, "I just said a bad word in front of my mother and little sister. I will have to apologize to them later." Jen then explained that the word for "sick" in the Kyrgyz language is like our F-word in America. Of her slip, she said, "It might be okay, because most times when I am speaking English to English-speaking people, I talk so fast that they can't really catch things, so they might not have noticed." She has had to work on not saying "Ummm..." when pausing to think of the next thing to say. This is a derogatory put-down to someone and it refers to a woman's body part. So she tries to go with "Ahhh." Hence the naming of the puppy—"Likeah"— because she says that when thinking.

Speaking of the puppy, she told us that she unfortunately died. People had left her out in the cold too long. They don't seem to have the concept of the danger of putting her on the doorstep in a box in two-below weather. The good news is that the cat that ran away last summer showed up, healthy and happy. The boys thought it was unbelievable, but Jen thinks it seems awfully suspicious, because there's no way that it could have looked that clean and well-fed if it had been wandering the streets. Someone else must have taken care of it and brought it back. And as a last bit of animal news, we learned that the rooster was a bit sick. Sorry, I mean "ill," but he is doing fine, as he got some "injections" (Jen said people don't take pills such as Sudafed, sinus meds, Robitussin, etc. They seem to think that they don't work, so they get "injections," but of what she doesn't know. Many times she said she doesn't pursue getting all the details because it wouldn't make sense, at least not to an American. She just goes along with the short version.)

Jen will be having an in-service training in March and is really looking forward to it. She will be able to see all her other Peace Corps friends from other villages. The Peace Corps puts it on and the volunteers will also have a midservice training marking their one-year anniversary. What a great way to be taken care of and not just thrown out there without any nurturing or help along the way. The two other volunteers in her village finally got phones installed in their homes. These could be backups to our backup number but one line can only be dialed out and the other can only take calls. Maybe if they put the two phones together, we might get something more according to our standards.

We told Jen that Johnny Carson passed away and she said that was weird, because her friend Willie had some material wrapped about his head and she told him he looked like Johnny Carson playing Carnac. He then went into a rendition of putting the envelope to his head. She found it very funny at the time.

She was happy to hear that we received her package with her second disc of pictures. And even more special are the video clips she recorded with her digital camera. It is so neat hearing her speak Russian to people, and we're even able to see how she walks to work, boots and all. The best one is of her waiting for a taxi: cows are walking the streets past her. Many times they stop traffic! Apparently, there is a Kyrgyz word for "cow jam." In the video clip she is sitting on a stump very far away from the taxi/bus stop because she was waiting for Ian. If she were to stand at the stop alone, she would get hassled by the drivers to take her somewhere. A taxi driver won't leave until the taxi is full, so you can be waiting there for one to two hours. And her fare can go from the regular thirty-five som to 500 som if it's after dark. She was relieved when enough people showed up and seven of them packed into the backseat before the sun went down, so she saved money.

In another video clip, we saw her making Christmas cookies, and she also had filmed a "hoedown," with volunteers dancing to the music of a girl who brought her fiddle/violin. We also saw her getting her next assignment and finding out who would be with her. The Peace Corps organizers had a huge map of Kyrgyzstan drawn out on the ground and the volunteers had to go stand by their newly appointed village names.

There are so many still photos that are so interesting, and she sent a handwritten description of each photo again. The one of the "inside" of the pit toilet in her neighborhood is disturbing. I've used some bad pit toilets in my day, but this would be shut down and classified a hazardous waste site in many parts of the world. Her pits are "squat" toilets. It's a two-stall building, but there are no seats—just holes in the ground, and it looked like others who had used the toilets did not have good aim. I don't know which would be worse, having it warm in the summer and dealing with the stench or having to take down your clothes and expose your bottom to subzero temperatures. Again I say, thank God we took her camping growing up.

We so enjoyed the picture of her friends at their Thanksgiving celebration. She made them wear paper Pilgrim and Indian feather hats, just as we used to do when the kids were little. Most wrote their Russian nicknames on the front. Her coat rack–Christmas tree was complete with a hat tree topper and the picture of what her hair looks like after a week without shampooing is crazy. I find myself drawn to looking at them and lucky for me, Dan downloaded them on his laptop.

Jen will be going to the next village to try to get on the Internet this weekend. It isn't as trusty as going to Talas, but she said it is worth a try. So whoever wants to send her well wishes, she should be able to get them this weekend. I told her we sent a package with the books she asked for and that she should be sure and look inside the Valentine socks I sent. She said, "Okay... wink, wink." I have a burning desire of revenge to outsmart those corrupt customs people. When Dan took the package to the post office, they told him that the best defense is tons of tape. Then they can't open it without wrecking it and the tampering would be too obvious. (3M is our best friend.) So in summary, Jen's week went like this: she got the long-lost package, the dog died, the cat came back, and the rooster got injections. What more can you ask for in a third world country? Talk to you all soon.

Love,

Karen

January 31, 2005

Jen's call this morning was interesting. First of all, Kadim, the twin who reminds her of her cousin Jason Corby, answered the phone as usual. His excited voice makes me smile. Last Monday he wrestled the phone away from Jen to talk and I commented to Jen to just let him talk to me. So that's what they decided to do this Monday, and the rest of them sat back and enjoyed the show. He asked Jen in Russian, "Can I say, 'Hello baby?'" They all laughed. Jen told me later that she thought to herself, "Well, Mom will think it's funny, but he should never do such a thing, because all Kyrgyz have such respect for their elders." So I got the usual "Alo... alo." And then he said, "Americanski Mama?" I said, "Da," which means *yes*. He asked again, "Americanski Mama?" And I said, "Da." Then he shocked me by speaking English. He asked, "What is your name?" I freaked out and said, "Meana zavoot Karen... Americanski Mama." He then said, "(Something, something)... doma." *Doma* means "home," so I said, "Jenny knee doma?" meaning, "Jenny isn't home?" Then I heard some rustling and Jen got on the line. I asked, "Where were you?" She explained how they had decided to make my wish come true and let me try out my Russian on an eleven-year-old. She said it was really funny when he covered the mouthpiece and asked, "What is she saying?" I told her that I had been thinking the same thing! Then the little three-year-old began hitting Kadim, so Jen thought she better end the fiasco before I hung up. I told Jen to tell Kadim that he is cute. She paused and then said, "As soon as I figure out the Russian word for "cute.""

We had received an email from Jen this weekend and she said she had a sinus infection and was on amoxicillin, so that was the first real thing I wanted to talk about. She said that this was the second time she was on meds. I asked, "When were you sick before?" She answered, "During my training," and then she paused, apparently thinking. "Oops. I don't think I ever told you." But it didn't matter. I was just impressed with the fact that she had figured out how to get medical attention. She had called her Peace Corps medical director. Her voice was so gruff that she sounded like a man, and so it was obvious she was ill (don't forget; she can't say "sick"). A nurse contacted her warden who went to her home with the meds. The country may be fifty to seventy-five years behind ours, but one of the good things is house calls. It also is an example of how well the Peace Corps takes care of their volunteers.

One strange thing is that people commonly believe that if you get ill, you have done something wrong. The Kyrgyz have such a fear and superstition in regards to the cold. When Ian was sick, his mother told him it was because he had drank cold water. When Jen told me this story, I asked what Ian's host mother had meant by "cold," because their water is room temperature. Apparently cold drinks are anything other than tea. They drink everything hot or fermented, probably just to be safe. We Americans are used to having healthy drinking water when we want it, and so cannot relate to always boiling it. Jen now has to put it through a distiller, and it takes about four hours to get about two Nalgene-bottles worth. So when Jen's mom said the same thing, she calmly told her, "I have drank water ever since I have been here and I am not sick all the time." Her mother said, "Then you didn't wear your hat one day." Jen thought that as a doctor, her host mother would be above accepting such myths as truths, but they are so ingrained in them that it's hard for them to see it any other way.

The Peace Corps doctor said that it can be easy for volunteers to get sick because their diet is different. And even though they have a multivitamin issued to them, their nutrition is different. The volunteers also have the added stress of being out of their element and having to exert constant effort to understand the language. Plus, having children in the home with limited hand washing, especially a day-care child, means that there will be germs. Food is served from a communal plate and Jen has told us how hard it is at times to see dirty hands scooping up the food she also will eat.

Speaking of which, I had to talk to her about the terrible picture she sent of the squat toilet that she has to use when at work. She said she got a good laugh when I emailed and asked if someone at least cleans it once a month. She said, "We don't have a park and recreation guy that comes around cleaning toilets... we are just lucky to have a toilet." And she said that many times, people just go behind the building. I said, "If it isn't cleaned, how does it not fill up to the top?" She told us that it decomposes on its own, because they don't put any paper down the hole. I said, "WHAT?" She explained that there is a metal bucket that sits nearby. You wipe and throw the paper in the bucket. About every week, someone takes the bucket in the middle of the yard, throws a match in and burns it. No big deal. At that point, the toast and coffee that I had been enjoying didn't seem so interesting. She said, "Mom, I don't mean to be so matter-of-fact about it, but that is just how it is." The only part she finds difficult is when they use those tissues to help start a fire in their wood-burning stove to cook a meal. The smell is indescribable, but she said that they tolerate it to accomplish the end result: food.

The good news is that the pit toilet at her host family's home is very nice. It has a little raised platform, but the family still doesn't sit. She reminded me that our perception of what is clean depends on what we are exposed to. I asked, "When you come home, will you think we are too prissy?" She said, "No, because that's how it is there. But I probably will have a hard time going back to washing my hair every day. It would probably fall out! The way it is now, I don't ever need to use conditioner." Not to harp too much on the toilet thing, but Jen says there is an art to going to the bathroom and working around five layers of clothes. She says she doesn't mind going out in the cold the first thing in the morning to pee because it helps wake her up. I asked which she thought was better, winter pit toilet or summer pit toilet. There was a long pause. Then she said, "I guess the winter is better for lack of smell." I thought again that if I had a nickel for every time I was thankful she was raised doing some camping that was "roughing it," I'd be rich. If Jen were a valley girl, she wouldn't be able to hang in there in her calling to serve a third-world country.

Jen and Kathryn made "Rice Krispie" treats, but with cornflakes. A volunteer had left behind a bag of marshmallows. Jen and Kathryn do most of their fun cooking together at her house, because the kitchen is separate from where the family hangs out. Jen's kitchen, the mom's bedroom, and the TV room are all together. She also made the macaroni and cheese that was in the long-lost box, and I asked her if she had let her family try it. She said no. She has found that many things aren't as interesting to them as they are valuable to her. So she is selfish with her food from home and finds herself more open to sharing with her other American friends. I told her that, given all she was doing and how far away she was from home, it was okay to be selfish.

Jen told us about a sixteen-year-old girl that comes into the center to learn sewing. Even though she is so much younger than the other women there, the ladies really like her. She is respectful and brings her own fabric and is anxious to learn. She goes to school and Kathryn is her teacher. Soon after Jen met her, she started to cling to Jen and suggested,

"Hey, let's write some Russian sentences." Jen was open to it because her spelling needs improvement. Then one day the girl asked if Jen could help her with her homework. She said she really likes how Miss Jenny helps her because she mixes up the Russian and English as a better way for her to understand. The way this girl is taught at school is similar to how the Peace Corps volunteers are taught: total immersion and no Russian. It is similar to living in a home where they do not speak English. So the girl said, "Okay, now every Tuesday and Friday I will come and we can do extra work together." So Jen has become a teacher and a student in one swoop.

Jen is planning which video and pictures she will send next. I'd like a peek at the *banya*. It is a small sauna bathhouse. She wants to take pictures of the different trees for Grandpa, but she hasn't found a single one of the walnut trees that his Kyrgyz research said were so prevalent. And she will show us more of her family and of her speaking Russian. She is excited about the in-service training in March, but in two weeks she is going to Talas for a handicraft seminar. She looks forward to the dependable Internet connection and good food. She'll be travelling with Erich and he knows the lady in charge of the conference. She actually is the daughter of a friend of Jen's director and she speaks English. Despite being sick, Jen still sounds upbeat and happy. We continue to be proud of her and know you do the same.

Love,

Karen

February 7, 2005

The three-year-old answered the phone this time. Jen said she couldn't beat her to the receiver. She kept saying "Alo, alo?" and then in Russian, "Where? Where?" But then Jen got on and she wished me a belated birthday. We got disconnected so many times last Monday that she didn't have a chance. Her first piece of news was crazy; her local TV news that day featured the groundhog (as in Punxsutawney Phil)! Jen had asked one of the twins, "Bad weather or good weather?" He said,

"Bad." So we are stuck with winter for a while—there as well as here, I guess. I can't believe they would report on that American custom; I don't think they have it there. Must have been a slow news day.

Jen is feeling and sounding better. She said the amoxicillin did its job. She received Corby's package and when she goes to Talas this weekend, she will take the jump-drive with her to the Internet place. She thinks she will send us another CD of pictures in March after her in-service training.

Jen took a hike this weekend and took some pictures that will be included. In one of my boxes, I sent her a pedometer to clip on her belt. It showed that on her hike she took eighteen thousand steps! That is seven miles. And they weren't easy miles, because most roads weren't plowed. She said each step was deep at times or she slid backwards for every forward one. They had blizzard conditions on Tuesday and Wednesday, but they didn't plow until Sunday. She said she didn't see what type of vehicle does the plowing, but it only leaves a path that is about a car-and-a-half wide. So cars have to play chicken when they meet on the road. The snow was so bad that they were cut off from getting supplies from Kazakhstan and many stores were out of flour. Jen's home was okay, but it shows that their version of "snowed in" and our version of snowed in are two different things. It can be quite serious. Her work was closed on Friday because it was too cold.

The little three-year-old, Aisalkyn, was screaming in the background a few times while we were on the line with Jen. Jen had to tell her in Russian to be quiet, and suddenly there was no more screaming. Jen said, "Now she's just standing here looking at me." Then Jen explained, "She's bouncing off the walls because she had chocolate." That was a lot better than what Jen had for supper the other day. Her mom made a dish that is like ravioli: dough squares are filled with onion, squash, or meat. Then the edges are crimped and the little bundles are steamed. Kathryn, who was over for dinner, asked in the Kyrgyz language, "What meat? What meat?" She was pretty excited to be having meat. The mother casually answered, "Cow's heart" just as Jen was taking a bite. She said that was the end of that; Jen couldn't eat any more. It wasn't that it tasted bad; it was a mind-over-matter deal and she just couldn't get her mind to be over the matter.

Jen asked for our prayers for the family with whom Ian is living. Over the weekend, the dad (in his mid-sixties) came home with a bad headache and vomited and then it got worse fast. He passed out and had trouble breathing and was in and out of consciousness. Ian had to help get him into an ambulance and try to calm the three sisters. Understanding everyday language is hard enough, but trying to understand under stressful situations makes it even more difficult. The father is in the hospital and Ian is feeling unsure about what might happen if the dad doesn't recover or they lose him. Will he be able to stay with this family? Will he have to be reassigned someplace else? Starting all over again would be hard. I guess I've worried about the health of the volunteers and never thought about the family members. Jen went over to Ian's house today and showed him the pictures on the disc from Sue and Bill from Thanksgiving and Christmas. She thought it would be a good distraction for him.

Ian teaches English at a private boarding school but Kathryn is teaching at the public school. The conditions are so different. Kathryn's has chaos, no decent heat, and no resources. She is asking people to send books—any books—so she can assemble some sort of resource center for the kids. Jen said she is going to send out some feelers as well. Her relationship with the Guardian Angels first-grade class is growing slowly but surely. The teacher reads all Jen's emails and Jen received pictures that the kids drew and sent her.

Jen wished us all a happy Lent and proudly said, "I will have no problem giving up meat this year."

Until next Monday,

Karen

February 14, 2005

Happy Valentine's Day! Amazingly, the Kyrgyz people are aware of this holiday, although Jen says it isn't so commercialized and there isn't the link to St. Valentine. Ian tried to explain the history of St. Valentine to his class and one boy said, "Oh yeah, he is the pope." Maybe he was trying to show off his American knowledge to his class of Kyrgyz kids, but Ian quickly replied, "No, he is not the pope." (It's still unreal to find out the things they absolutely do not know about America and then the things they do.) Valentine's Day is called Vantino-den, which means the "day of love."

Jen got a package from Uncle Paul and Aunt Patty, St. Mary's, Jenna R. (the teacher of the first-grade class she is sponsoring), and a padded envelope we sent. She figures she should get Grandpa and Grandma's box this week, but I'm sure mine will take an additional six weeks because customs hates me. Jen sends a special thanks to Uncle Paul and Aunt Patty for the pudding and Jell-O and especially for the BODY WASH. Jen just had a full *banya* yesterday for the first time in two weeks and used it. She said she was soaping up and kept saying, "Oh I smell so good! Oh I smell so good!" The little touch-up cleaning in between showers just isn't the same. This *banya* isn't as nice as the one at her first family's house, and it is shared between two families. I can't imagine walking down to the neighbors' in the cold to shower and then walking back all wet. Yikes.

We got disconnected twice, even though the reception was good. In between calls Jen was playing this game with the kids where they holler each other's name and put a description in front of it. This time it ended up as "JENNY... BAD JENNY." And then Jen added (in Kyrgyz) "VERY" to the bad. They laughed so hard because she was making herself worse. Jen positioned herself at a different place at the table so she was strategically closer to the phone and would be able to head off Kadim at the pass when we called her back. She said it was fun for a bit, but then she didn't want to play that game anymore.

Jen gave me the toll-free number for the phone cards she got as going-away gifts and wants me to find out the best way to use them. This would allow her to make outgoing calls without having to walk a mile to the telecom center, where she has to figure out how long she will talk and prepay. She was holding the cards to give me the numbers and the kids asked what they were. She said something in Russian that means "phone card," but the way she said it, it sounded like "potato card." When speaking Russian, it is so critical how you inflect your voice!

There is pressure for volunteers to do well in their Russian to avoid shame. So Jen continues the struggle. She comforts herself by saying that in six months to a year, it will be so much better. One night, her mother Venera asked Jen to help her learn English. She had learned some in grade school, but hadn't retained very much. Jen was tired, but Venera wanted to practice. Jen tried to explain that her Russian isn't good enough to correlate English and Russian words, let alone explain ideas in Russian. But Venera kept on. Jen got frustrated because Venera said, "Then just speak English and do it slowly like I do my Russian to you." This further bugged Jen because she thought, "How could speaking English slowly help a woman who just learned the word *rabbit* last week?" She told Venera that she was tired and is not a teacher person and said good-bye instead of good night and went to her room. She was angry at the thought that she is expected to learn Russian in less than five months, but people who have studied English for many years still get to take their time figuring it out. In all fairness, Venera is also taking classes at the club that Kathryn teaches. I told Jen Venera's request was a reflection of her being there and that she should take it as a compliment. The moral of the story is: don't mess with Jen when she is burnt out and tired. Some things haven't changed.

Ian's Russian father died from his illness. They figure it was a stroke. That's why Venera took Jen's blood pressure when she had such a headache and vomited. What a comfort she is a doctor. But this leaves Ian looking for another home. The school where he teaches is responsible for finding something and although it will be in the same village, it will still be an adjustment nonetheless. Keep his family in your prayers. They found a burial place down south where the father's family was from. If they hadn't, it would have meant forty days of having the body in the home and people coming in and out to visit and wail and cry. Thank God for American funeral homes!

Jen finally remembered to wear her pedometer on a regular day to work. She found out she walks ten thousand steps everyday, which is four miles! She bought a nice map of Kyrgyzstan for Grandpa but realized it's all in Russian! So she will have to do some interpreting before she mails it home. I purchased new maps and a world atlas, since Mom and Dad's is thirty years old. Elevations won't change, but a lot has, and more accurate pictures make me feel closer to her. She found out the meaning of her village name, Po-krov-ka. *Krov* means "shelter" and any time they put a *ka* on the end, it means "little." But she also has seen *krov* used to mean "blood" and was very unsettled to think her village means "little blood." At least it isn't "lots-a-blood." The state of Talas is one of the poorest of all the states in Kyrgyzstan. Obviously that's why she's there.

Her mercantile seminar in Talas was good. Reliable Internet was the fun part. Listening to the presentation in Kyrgyz, instead of Russian, wasn't. Almajon (the teacher) speaks English, so she would randomly holler to Jen (who was sitting in the back), "I just told them..." Lovely. In conversation, she asked Jen where she was from. Jen said, "Minnesota." She asked what nationality is most prevalent there and Jen said "Scandinavian, with blond hair and blue eyes." Almajon said, "But you aren't." She then asked what nationality Jen was, with her curly hair (she hadn't straightened or worked with it) and freckles. Jen replied that her freckles are so prominent because even though it's winter and she's pale, walking everywhere and getting sun (not like in Minnesota) makes them (the freckles!) show up. She told the woman that her ancestry is German and Welsh-Irish. Almajon said, "I knew you had some Irish in there." Must have been the curls.

Jen is interested in getting a DVD of a Catholic Mass as I had suggested, but I can only get it on VHS. If anybody out there has the knowledge of how to transfer it, let me know. Erich from a neighboring village is also Catholic and he said the idea of Jen watching this tape all by herself makes her seem like an eighty-year-old homebound woman, so he said he would watch it with her. She said, "Then you can be the priest." She suggested they could partake in *borsok* (fried bread) and a fruit drink for wine, if that isn't too sacrilegious. Just being able to hear the words of the Mass will probably seem like sweet music to her ears.

We got a list of more things that Jen needs. I am sending her a cloth bag like people use at a grocery store, because they have to buy the kind of plastic bags that we get for free at the supermarket (I have a hundred stored in my closet). That way she can carry things, and if it's empty, she'll put it in her backpack. Wish I could go in her backpack. There are days I want to mail myself to her.

Thanks, everyone, for your support.

Love,

Karen

CHAPTER 6

What Did You Say?

Although Jen learned Russian by total immersion, somehow I thought a teaching tape from the library would do the trick for me. I wanted to be fluent, just in case we got the chance to visit her. That was fruitless. All I needed to learn was what Jen taught me, which were the basic phrases we used when trying to call her. I felt proud when I would speak those words and understand in return. It helped me feel closer to her.

February 21, 2005

We submitted an article in our local newspaper to help raise awareness for the Peace Corps on their forty-fourth anniversary, and it did! So now I've had to add more people to the list of Monday emails. When I told her, Jen said, "You realize, Mom, that your distribution list is going to get as big as mine." That's the price of popularity. Jen's good news was that she received packages this week: one from Grandma and Grandpa (Jen was tickled by the Scotch tape dispensers), one from Megan (her best friend since kindergarten), and a letter from Jessy, a college friend. The letter took a month to get there, maybe because it came from France. But she did receive our package. This was the package for which I had a mission to fool the customs guards. Jen said, "Mom, the valentine socks were very good to me." The twenty-dollar bill (800 som) arrived safely. I won't send cash again. I just had to get revenge. Who says vengeance isn't sweet?

Venera was late coming home from the clinic, so supper was late. When we called, Jen said, "We're just having supper"—I was eating a morning donut—"but go ahead and I'll eat my ramen noodles while we talk." I started in with some questions and then stopped, asking if her mother would get upset if we talked while Jen was eating or whether it would be considered rude. She said, "Don't worry about it; it's okay." You never know. Since everyone was sitting so close, Venera said hello in the background. I asked Jen to thank her for taking care of her. Jen thought about how to do that, spoke to Venera, and then I heard a giggle. Jen said, "I must have said something wrong, but she got the message."

I tried out my "*dobrae utra*" on Jen, which means *hello and good morning*. She corrected me. There is a long A at the end of *dobrae* and a long u at the beginning of *utra*. I told her that I had learned it from my new tape; it's entitled "Fast and Easy Russian." She said, "Oh, that's crap... throw it out!" We laughed. I knew she would get a kick out of it. Then she decided to put the little girl on the line to tell me how to say it correctly. It took some coaxing because she speaks Kyrgyz but is learning Russian by Jen and Venera speaking it. So the girl's soft, cute voice tells me "hello and good morning" in Russian. How I wanted to hug her! It would be like holding Jen. I repeated it back to her. She walked away from the phone and Jen asked if I had said it correctly. The girl turned and said, "NYET!" (no). So, I guess I have to keep trying if a three-year-old is better at a new language than I am.

We found out that the phone cards Jen received at her going-away party will not work in Kyrgyzstan. They will only allow cards bought there to work when calling out. So Jen said she will mail them back to us. We could use them, or we could give them back to those who gave them to her so they can call to say hello. When we told Kathy Rasmussen (a close family friend) about that idea, she said, "Oh, I just got the goose bumps." I relayed that to Jennifer and with her wit, she said, "I have that effect on people."

The situation with Ian is in limbo. He is living with the same family, although the mother is still in Issyk Kul doing the forty days of mourning, so he is there with the three sisters. It's a bit awkward, but they chose to finish their school year before moving to where they will be. So he can be there until May and has two other possibilities pending. He is taking it in stride and will adjust to a new family, but Jen said he has shed his share of tears. Another hardship was that one of the volunteers, who was working east of Talas, has gone home. Alisha was from Minnesota, and was all alone in her village. Jen said she had volunteered before, teaching English in China, which is why she was placed alone. The school where she worked really didn't want a volunteer (not sure how they got one in the first place) and things were far from ideal at home. She was depressed, gained weight, and got a terrible short haircut. The Peace Corps stepped in and is sending her not home to Minneapolis but to Israel, where her family is volunteering. Then she will go to China to teach English again. I guess it's the first time a volunteer from Jen's state (Talas Oblast) has left, but Kyrgyzstan isn't for everyone. You might wonder how she could possibly gain weight. It seems a truism for volunteers that the woman who are thin, gain. Those who are heavier, lose—and men generally always lose due to lack of protein in the diet.

One of Jen's questions (because she has trouble understanding Russian news) was whether a dam broke in New York. We were confused, but figured out she had seen images of a highway collapsing due to the heavy rains in California. She also asked, "How is the pope?" We told her that he's out of the hospital. She said, "You wouldn't believe what actually is televised." She then said, "And Michael Jackson was in the hospital with the flu?" This is what she hears about? PLEASE! We talked about the contrasts, and then she explained the word for flu is greep. They joke, "Hey, you got the *greep*? It's the dreaded greep!" Guess it's comparable to our "creeping crud."

I asked Jen if she gets mail delivered to her house. I think she was trying not to laugh as she explained that they don't even have mailboxes. They have to go to the post office and ask for their mail. The neat thing is that if one of the volunteers goes and sees a package for the other, he or she can take it. They keep the American Peace Corps mail separate, and the volunteers have learned that if they see packages, they need to take them; otherwise they usually disappear for another five days before they resurface. Where they go, nobody knows.

Jen informed us they had a slight tragedy last week. She was sounding silly, so I didn't get too concerned. But then she told us that the modem at the Internet place in the next village died. Unfortunately, there isn't money to have it fixed at this time. So now the nearest Internet site is two hours away instead of a quick taxi ride. Her emails will probably only be once-a-month things, so our Monday calls will be like gold. Trying to make light of the situation, Ian joked that he felt bad about the modem dying because he used to give "Modey" so much trash talk when it didn't work right. Kathryn said, "It's a sad day. Poor Modey." Jen comforted them and said, "Let's just try to look at it like... he's in a much better place." Crazy kids.

One of the possible homes for Ian would be right next door to Jen, but she has mixed feelings about it. If all three of them were on the same street, it would be too much English in one spot. Plus, he would be using the pit toilet right next to hers. As it is, when she goes to the bathroom late at night, she runs into girls next door who have learned some English and they whisper in a singsong voices to her, "Hello, Miss Jennifer... and good night." She said, "Having so many people knowing my every bowel movement is not my idea of fun."

I finished up talking with Jen, and Dan was next on the phone—I had to get ready for work. We had a few tense words about why he was hooking up an earpiece to the phone and how HE wanted to be the one to tell her about the snow, etc. Then he said, "Ola" to her. I gave him a look and he said, "What? What did I say?" I told him he just said hello to her in Spanish and informed him he's supposed to say "Alo." Guess Dan figures, what's the big deal? It's all the same letters (more or less)! Funny thing is, all this snipping was probably music to her ears. I said good-bye and the usual "I love you" more than once and ended with "Life is good." She said, "Yes, it is!" So thankful she feels that way, too.

Love,

Karen

February 28, 2005

Dobrae utra! Our connection this morning had such a long lag time, more than normal. It went like this: say a sentence—wait for a response—say a sentence—and then wait for the answer. Since I am such a patient person (not really!), it was no problem for me. It doesn't matter how long I have to wait... I will hear her voice.

She didn't get any packages this week but she talked about last week's packages. I forgot I had sent her three potato peelers in our last box. I asked how they were working because, as I mentioned before, she usually has to use a huge butcher knife to peel carrots or potatoes. She said she hasn't used them yet. Thought that was odd, but then she explained that it's International Women's Day next week and she is planning on giving them as gifts. When she gives one to her mother, she will demonstrate how to use it; that will surely be the entertainment of the month. She also talked about Grandma and Grandpa's box and how she will also give some Scotch tape as a gift. But more importantly, she gave two each to Kathryn and Ian, since they are teachers, and it was like gold for them. Jokingly she said, "Sharing certain items can be compared to bartering for cigarettes in prison."

The good news of the week is that they actually got a new modem up and running in Kirovka and Jen is thinking of trying to go there on Wednesday. But this new one has a problem: if you're idle too long, it will disconnect you and you might not be able to get back online again. So it's hard to read all her emails as she sits there, and her jump drive doesn't work at this site (only at Talas) so she can't download the emails and take them home, something she prefers to do. She gets very emotional when she tries to read emails at the café. If she can read them at home, it's easier. She plans on trying to get to Talas the weekend of March 11th.

Jen is sending a CD of pictures this week. We can't wait to see the picture of her in the taxi with the two live ducks sitting next to her. She wasn't going to mail it yet, but needs to send us some Peace Corps tax information as well. She gets an automatic two-month extension for being out of the country.

We got disconnected and in the time it took for me to call back, Aisalkyn had been hilarious, or so Jen told us. They were finishing their dinner of carrot and potato stew but the little three-year-old wanted to just drink tea. Her mother said, "No, no; you need to eat your soup first... then you can be big like Jennifer." Aisalkyn looked at Jen, then lunged at her bowl and took a big spoonful. Jen wasn't sure if being called big was okay, but it was so cute how much Aisalkyn wants to be like this American girl living in their house.

Then as we were talking, Jen started giggling and I heard some commotion in the background. I asked what was going on and Jen said, "Now Aisalkyn is getting on Kadim's case and shaking her finger at him." Shaking a finger at someone is seen as an insult and very degrading and should only be done by adults. But what made it so comical to Jen is that she had a belt from a robe wrapped around her head. Jen said, "So as I talk to you, I have a 'ninja' three-year-old handing out disgrace to her brother." Never a dull moment with her.

Jen's mother asked Jen if they could have some copies of the pictures she took of them. It is a luxury to have photos. I told Jen I had sent the article we put in the paper, so they should really get excited about their picture in print. They might be considered celebrities in their village!

There is a big school English-language competition in Kirovka and many classes from nearby schools participate. Teachers bring students to compete in speaking English, singing in English, and putting on plays. Since Jen is not a teacher, she has been asked to be one of the judges. There are even critiques for correct grammar and punctuation. That should be fun for her. The people talk about volunteers who had been there years ago. Ian found out that one lady they kept referring to was the Peace Corps recruiter at his college, though he was recruited from his home in Colorado after college. The info got around and the recruiter ended up emailing him. Small world.

But the big news about Ian around town is that he shaved off his mustache and beard and even got a haircut when in Talas. His search for a new home continues and he decided that he better find something before the last week in March when they go to the in-service training in Bishkek. His fear is that they won't understand why he's gone and when he would come back, his things might be on the curb. When he tried to explain and ask the sisters about when his host mother would be coming back, they were offended. I suppose one shouldn't say, "How long will your mom be mourning your dad?" He's kind of between a rock and a hard spot, planning out how to move.

Jen had a bout of sore throat and nose congestion again after finishing her antibiotics and called the medical contact. She didn't want to give her any more antibiotics, since Jen wasn't running a temperature or getting worse. So it has gotten better, but her Russian mother keeps telling her that her sickness is from drinking cold water. The normal amount of tea that people drink in a day there is around ten cups!

The problem for Jen is that Kyrgyz tea tastes terrible and has a lot of caffeine. She doesn't have that in her diet anymore, since she doesn't have chocolate or Mountain Dew, so if she drinks even a few cups, she gets the shakes and a headache. I asked if she wanted us to send her different tea from home, but she said she isn't really a tea drinker, so we shouldn't send any. It's just the way they can drink the water safely. It's hard for them to understand how much Americans drink water.

I told Jen I'd better get going to work because my public awaits my email with all the news. She groaned, "Oh boy." Then she asked, "Do you have the mayor of Chaska on that distribution list, too?" But I know deep down she doesn't mind and it only makes her feel more loved.

Take care.

Love,

Karen

March 7, 2005

After many rings, a breathless Jen answered the phone. Of course there is no answering machine, so I almost hung up to try again when she picked up. She was down the street "guesting" at the cousin's house. They had said they would have food ready on time but didn't, so she was left gulping down two *mantis*, a kind of dumpling with mutton, animal fat, and onion on the inside. They did send her home with a piece of cake, so it made up for the mantis. But she stubbed her toe rushing into the house because it was dark. It was odd for me not to hear the background noise of the family, but we could say the word *sick* all we wanted, without any worries. (Jen has become so accustomed to avoiding the word that she cringed when reading an email from Heidi that referred to being sick before realizing, hey... it's ok to read it!) I asked why she had been out guesting, since people usually only visit homes for special occasions. She figured it was because of International Women's Day tomorrow. They make a big deal out of it and Jen actually will have the day off from work. She explained that in a third-world country recognizing women is very important, because it is International Men's Day the rest of the year! Sad but true.

Ian is now living in the home of one of his students. It was a possibility from the beginning, so hopefully it will be a good fit. He had lunch with the family yesterday and the mother seemed odd, but is involved in the teacher–parent organization and his student is top notch. And Jen said, "It will be easier for him because he's a guy. Ian could poop on the floor in the corner and they would all fight over who gets to clean it up." Since he's a man, he is revered no matter what. It's just another confirmation of Jen's International Men's Day theory.

To celebrate International Women's Day, Jen is trying to figure out the gifts she will give out to the special women in her life. She may just bring candy to her work for all the ladies to enjoy and then give Venera the potato peeler or some perfume that Grandma and Grandpa sent in their package. It also is Venera's birthday in a couple of weeks, so Jen needs to plan out her gift giving. She is going to give her the Russian/English dictionary that the Peace Corps gave her, since the one I mailed from Barnes & Noble is better. Venera only has old grammar books and because she is so willing to learn English, Jen thinks she will really appreciate the dictionary.

We talked about some trivia I heard on TV; the question was, "What country does NOT have an *American Idol* program: Kazakhstan, Italy, or Australia?" Of course, I thought it would be Kazakhstan but Jen blurted out "Italy!" She was right. She said they actually had a program like that two years ago in Kazakhstan, but it was called *SuperStar KZ*. Can you imagine having to sing to the goofy fast-playing music that is typical there? Jen also reprimanded me about our last box. Kathryn picked it up at the post office for Jen and begged her to open it at her house, because she figured there had to be some Valentine's chocolate in there. So she did and I had put an old pair of Jen's underwear on top. She was slightly embarrassed because she had forgotten about Father Larry's advice to put your unmentionables on top in your suitcase or package, because custom agents won't touch them and therefore won't pillage through your things. She said it reminded her of her college days when I mailed her the bras and underwear she had left at home because she was going on a mission trip, and she opened it by her mailbox at school. Not good.

Jen will be going to Talas this Saturday where there is reliable Internet. Although she found out that old "Modey" in the village next to theirs was resurrected for a couple of days (you know how they rally at the end), she's sure that it's most definitely dead for good. Jen had sent an email with the addresses of Kathryn's (New Hampshire) and Ian's (Colorado) parents and encouraged us to connect with each other. So last week, I emailed both families and got a response right away. We've been getting to know each other. Interesting tidbit: all three kids are eldest children. Trailblazers! I told Jen this morning and she was so excited. I think it makes the Kyrgyzstan crew feel more loved and supported. Reminds me of the *M.A.S.H.* episode when the gang arranged a reunion for their families back home and Radar's family hit it off with Charles Winchester's. Go figure.

Jen will be traveling to Bishkek on March 19th and then returning March 27th for her in-service training. She plans on trying to find a Catholic church and the timing would be great, being that it is Holy Week. They don't start training until Tuesday because it is a holiday on Monday the 21st. Everything is shut down and it would cost triple if she traveled that day. So we won't have our Monday call, but it is the Kyrgyz New Year called "Nooruz." They celebrate the same New Year we do, but this is more a spring solstice revolving around the harvesting cycle, not a countdown like the January celebration.

They have been having warmer weather there, so she did laundry outside. It really is a treat at her current home to have an electric machine that swirls the clothes. Then she takes out the laundry, dips it in buckets of cold water, and wrings it out by hand and hangs it up. So much for fluffy clothes. Her mother told her to take the machine into the front yard because it's warmer there than in the backyard, which is shady, and she will get sick if it's cold. But Jen said she was sweating from all the hard work and thinks Venera wanted all the neighbors to see her machine. It's about a sense of pride. That's why Jen washes her undergarments in a bucket in her room. The neighbors can be spared.

Jen says so many shirts get stretched out because of squeezing the water out. When clothes freeze on the line, some of the water evaporates, which is rather efficient. Then they bring the laundry inside, where it thaws and finishes drying. She uses her room heater and her mother uses their cook oven. She says there's a picture of Kathryn holding frozen laundry and her clothes looks like flags. Jen is planning on including a video on the next CD of her scrubbing laundry.

She mailed a padded envelope last Wednesday with the next set of pictures. But they only charged her nineteen som. When she mentioned this to Ian, he said they had done that to him and it had taken a month for his family to get the package. So I hope that isn't true for Jen's. She gets so frustrated with the post office people who have no tolerance for her broken Russian. She also complained about the phone system and lack of a sanitation system. The warm weather has brought the flies around the outhouse. I hated to suggest to her how it will be when it's eighty-five degrees this summer.

Dan shared with Jen that he will be a best man this summer, so we will be traveling to New York to be at Uncle Doug's wedding. That means that if we can swing going to visit her, it would have to be next spring or early summer. The timing should work out with having her here this Christmas. If we go there in the summer, it will give us more time to save up money. And then she will be home in 2006 for Christmas. Just the idea of being able to touch her, hug her, and feed her keeps me going.

Until next week.

Love,

Karen

CHAPTER 7

Political Unrest

Oh, Mr. Peace Corps... no, no, no. This was not a part of the plan. I
realize unrest can happen at any time, but couldn't you arrange it to be
AFTER my daughter left your care? I'd like to think that a mother's
hug lasts long after she lets go. But now she may be in danger and a hug
can't fix it.

March 14, 2005

Talk about a bad connection. It sounded like Jen was under water. She
answered and I began to speak in my simple Russian and she said, "Mom,
it's me." I told her it didn't sound like her. She said, "That's because I answered the phone like a Russian." She said that she didn't want to do the
American high-pitched "Hi!" in case it wasn't me. I didn't want to say
that her "Alo" sounded like one of the boys'. We hung up and tried again,
but that time she couldn't hear me. So the third time we just offered up
thanks for being able to hear each other at all and went with it.

Jen's frustration was due to the fact that she wasn't able to get online
this weekend as planned. She had been ready to leave when Kathryn
knocked at her window at 7:30 a.m. It scared the bejeezus (as she says)

out of her, but once she realized it wasn't a wandering drunk man, she let her in the house. She told Jen that the Peace Corps warden had informed Erich from Kirovka that they were not allowed to travel to Talas due to the election situation. The letdown of not being able to read emails from family after four weeks was bad enough, but the frustration of being informed by "email" about the travel restriction was even stronger. It was pretty ironic, since they needed to travel to get their email, yet the email was saying not to travel.

Jen and her friends will reiterate that, in the future, they need a phone call warning. She will be able to retrieve and send emails this Sunday, as she will be traveling to Kant and then Bishkek for the in-service training. She asked me to go into her account and delete any unnecessary emails, e.g., St. Mary's sports updates, alumni gatherings she can't attend, etc. It helps with her jump drive retrieval. She can't wait to see the other fifty-eight volunteers again. The redo of the elections should happen this weekend and their travel should be okay after that.

Some sweet news was that she had a very nice International Women's Day. In the morning, the boys gave her a handkerchief and pen. It comes as a prepackaged set. Cute. Jen gave Venera the potato peeler and enjoys the bonus of using it herself. Since she didn't have work, she went to Kathryn's house, where Kathryn was making pancakes for the women of the house. Jen went over to Ian's, too, and brought the sisters some candy and hot cocoa. He gave her and Kathryn Pez dispensers that he actually found there. Jen's was a shark–skeleton figure (too scary for kids there) and he also got her a poster of "Tarkan," a Turkish pop singer popular in Russia she likes and about whom he likes to tease her.

Later they went to a "disco," as they call it. The local people usually hold a dance in the community for any holiday, usually in an old warehouse type building. This time, Jen talked to the DJ guy, whom she said was very nice. He also is a taxi driver. He is Kyrgyz but speaks Russian. He praised Jen for the three of them coming there so often, because the volunteer before them only came twice in her two years there. Jen has waved to him when she sees him driving and he had been calling her "Miss Kat" by mistake. Jen hasn't wanted to correct him, but Kathryn finally did because her students were saying, "That's not Miss Kat?" So now the DJ calls her Jennifer. No "Miss," since she is not a teacher, but many other people do use "Miss," because both Ian and Kathryn are teachers, and you know, all Americans are the same. It's funny how the local people think of Jen and her friends as a group, but then again, they are the only tall white people on the dance floor.

Some students dedicated a song to Ian for him to dance to with his American girls. They also dedicated a song to Kathryn in order for her to find a husband. No dedication for Jen (not being a teacher), but a Russian woman came up to her and gave her a real carnation. It was very touching, because flowers are so rare there, especially this time of year. Guess they put more effort into planting food than beauty. (As a treat for her family for the spring, Jen requested that we send her flower seeds and Grandma and Grandpa just sent some. Just hoping they will get there before the growing season is over.)

Jen received our padded envelope that had a copy of the *Chaska Herald* article about her. It was a hit! The boys kept staring at their picture in the paper and Venera actually asked to read it. Jen didn't know how successful that would be, but when she was finished, she said, "You are going home for Christmas?" Jen had to reassure her that it would only be a temporary visit and that friends of ours have a travel agency and can get a good deal on tickets. Then the shock set in that Venera could understand English well enough to ask the question. That dictionary Jen gave her is better than she thought.

Venera has lots of trust in Jen; she left for the weekend to go to a seminar in Talas from Thursday to Saturday and put Jen in charge. Actually, it is not so much trust as it is common for kids to be left at home with little supervision. She made sure she had cooked a big meal for supper on Thursday so that they would be able to eat leftovers for breakfast, have bread for lunch, and eat leftovers again for supper. Not the American way of "What should we have for supper tonight, dear?" Then she made a big batch of soup that lasted the rest of the time.

Jen had been having stomach trouble for a couple of days, but attributed it to some meat that hadn't looked the best. When Venera came back, she told her, "I will be making a delicious dinner tonight" but Jen had to decline. Jen has learned that the best way to make her stomach better is to give it a rest from food. Without thinking, I said, "Yeah, I had a stomachache this morning from the pizza we had last night." She said, "Please don't say that, Mom." I got so mad at myself. I forget that for her, every day is like Lent, since she "gives up" so many things.

We are still waiting for her padded envelope that has her third disc in it. I told her how we met with (our family friends) Guillemettes and Rasmussens to show them the first disc and that I am busy scheduling other get-togethers. I might need a pie chart to keep up with things! "Oh, Mom," and a giggle were Jen's responses when I told her. I schedule the entertainment part of her travels, but Jen asked Dan to be her news connection. She wants him to pass on information from CNN so she can feel up-to-date about what's going on. Since he is not trying to learn Russian, it gives him a way to support her.

The wooden pole supporting our mailbox rotted and fell over, so we have been going to the post office every other day to get our mail. I told Jen that we wanted to be just like her. She laughed (scoffed, actually) and said, "Unless the post office is trying to give you mail for Peter Freeman who's on the U.S. military base in Bishkek... you aren't like me." Apparently, the last time she went there, they tried to give her this guy's mail and she refused to take it, saying, "I don't know him." A couple days later, Kathryn said she was at the post office and although there wasn't anything for Jen, the people kept trying to convince her to take mail for Peter Freeman! They had a good laugh, wondering when it would be Ian's turn. Kathryn finally told them to send it to the base in Bishkek and that she and Jen had no connection with him. Just another example of the assumption that all Americans know each other and are the same. We're just glad that Jen is Jen.

Love,

Karen

March 21, 2005

We weren't scheduled to call Jen today, as it was supposed to be a travel day for her in-service training in Bishkek, but all travel is still on hold due to the unrest with the elections. Jen said, "The beauty of being in the most remote area is that there's no protesting or violence around us." But the roads that lead from Talas or Osh to Bishkek have been closed or have heavy roadblocks. The volunteers will probably only get to travel directly to Bishkek, without visiting their old home sites on the way. They want to keep everybody as together as possible.

Jen asked me to go into her email account and delete all the junk mail, seeing she hasn't picked up her mail in five weeks. I deleted fifty-eight of the 168 emails! I also saw that they had cancelled the training for a second time. It seemed so odd and wrong in a way that I knew about her schedule changes before she did. Jen told me that later the same day that the officials sent the email, the volunteers got a call from the wardens giving the info from the email. It appears they have learned that the three stationed way out in Pokrovka need a call.

"Modey" the modem was fixed in Kirovka, so Jen asked Erich (who lives there) to send us an email letting us know that her training was cancelled and please would we call on the 21st as usual. She didn't know that I had figured that out from her email account. We take our communication here so much for granted.

Jen received a padded envelope from Uncle Bill and Aunt Sue and Grandma and Grandpa. She says thanks for the great family pictures. She also got an Easter box from Katie O. and Dixon's package with the freeze-dried, vacuum-packed food! She was even more excited to find out that we received her padded envelope containing her third CD of pictures. She also sent the phone cards that don't work calling out from Kyrgyzstan. She wants us to give them back to the people who gave them to her and would love to hear their voices. Maybe she can answer the question so many have asked: Why are all the homes, fences, sheds, etc. painted aqua blue? Jen said that she thinks it's the same reason barns were always painted red back in 1930s. It was cheaper.

Jen said that the weather was so nice and she was lucky: she had the day off from work, since it is the Kyrgyz/Muslim New Year. People were outside and she said she even got some sun on her cheeks. Because people were outside, the celebration turned out to be like a block party instead of guesting from house to house, and she said it was fun, with music in the streets. *Borsok* was the food of choice and was had by all. But we don't think Jen is eating enough of it, since her latest pictures show an even thinner girl. When she had to punch another hole in her belt, she weighed herself and found out she is down twelve more pounds. So that's a total of sixty. She said, "Hey, I had it to lose and I feel healthy." As a mom, I think it just doesn't seem right. And it doesn't seem right that I have to be okay with it all. I'm still working on that.

We talked about her new pictures and videos. I asked her about the picture that Ian took. Her eyes were so pretty and those cute dimples were still there, just as they were when she was born. It was such a close-up, I felt as if I could touch her. I asked if she was growing out her hair, because she had pinned it back with hair clips that Grandma sent. She said, "Oh, that's just the third day of not washing hair, so it's my I've-got-to-get-it-out-of-my-face look."

Some of our favorites are the pictures of her in a crowded taxi with two ducks in a bag sitting next to her. Apparently, they laid their beaks on her thigh, but when the taxi turned quickly and the wings started flapping, she feared pecking would be next. Kathryn got the moment with a picture, and then reassured her it could be worse—she could be sitting up front by the dead carcass of a chicken.

There's a video of Jen talking to the camera in her room and speaking Russian. I had asked her to do that because I still find it so amazing to hear her talking that fluently. There also is a video of the boys playing a game called *Altchik* in the house. Jen told us that whenever a sheep is killed, all the parts are used, even down to the bones in the spine, which kids use as marbles. This game was like a shuffleboard–craps game, where they lined up bones and then rolled one into the wall so it would shoot back and hit another bone.

In the video, Jen asks them if Mom likes them doing this in the house (in a no-no-no tone) while Aisalkyn pulls on Jen to see herself on camera. She carries around a small box and pretends she is taking pictures of everyone just as Jen does. Kadim, the boy who always wants to answer the phone when we call, waved at us in the video as if it is so normal for an American to film him in his home. Guess everyone is adjusting.

Grandpa wanted to know about Jen's work. She had a meeting with a new program director and her site director that was very frustrating. They were checking on Jen's progress, but it was difficult because they didn't let her get a word in edgewise and would switch from Kyrgyz to Russian. She could keep up, but it was difficult for Jen to break into the conversation or ask questions. There hasn't been as much progress as there could be, but Jen said it's not a reflection on her as much as on her director. The first thing Jen's director did was apologize to the country director for not having the desk, chair, phone, and fax that she was supposed to have set up before even getting a volunteer. Jen doesn't know how they have functioned and done business this long with no phone! Everything has been by word of mouth.

Other people have reassured her that the only thing a volunteer has to do in the first three months of a permanent assignment is learn the language, not change the world. So she's going to write a letter to the country director, letting her know her frustrations of not being able to express herself in the meeting and giving her a clearer picture of what she's been doing. She has decided she has to be more aggressive without being offensive to get things done. She is asking a K-11 (a volunteer who has a small time left to serve) from Kirovka to come and help get things organized. He speaks Kyrgyz and can help Jen get them to start a mission statement and establish a business plan before she takes on the task of asking for grant money. He is a man and drinks lots of tea, so the women will love him.

Jen says she doesn't mind this program being so behind others in the country. Most of those places have English-speaking counterparts who work with the volunteers on well-established projects, unlike her site where the program has been operating for only two years. But she says she likes it this way; it is more of a challenge and fits her education better. Brave girl. Before we said good-bye, she said, "Happy belated Palm Sunday!" I didn't know if she would remember. Easter is her favorite holiday of the year, so it will be hard without her here. Pray for the resolution of the elections in Kyrgyzstan.

Love,

Karen

March 25, 2005

Please see the email below from Jen. We saw it coming, but are confident that the Peace Corps will take care of them, and Jen says they all feel the same. Her family had a hard time seeing her go because there wasn't any rioting in their village, but it's a matter of having volunteers all together in case of a need to evacuate again. She told them she is not leaving for good and not saying good-bye, just "I will see you later." We are still going to try to make our Easter call to her, but she may not be where she is now. But the warden speaks English, so it will be easy to get information—if we can get through. They may be able to go back to their village, stay where they are, or be further evacuated to the American embassy in Kazakhstan. If anyone wants accurate information, Jen said to go to the BBC online.

Will keep you posted.

Love,

Karen

WE ARE SAFE! We have been consolidated to our warden's house in Kirovka for the time being. Our warden, John, has a cell phone and the number is 011.996.502.70.20.15. This is how you can contact us, but please *parents only*. No need to worry; we haven't seen any protesting, and we wouldn't even know there was something going on if not for TV and radio. Mom, please make sure this email gets forwarded to Ian's folks or give them a call. Hulick, Lawrence, Ruge, and Heckel parents, please call if you feel the need. Know that we will contact you again when we can, if anything changes. The next step from consolidation is to either return to our villages or further consolidate and evacuate. We all hope the latter doesn't happen.

Happy Easter and Happy Revolution!

Jenny, Kathryn, Ian, and Erich

Easter Sunday,

March 27, 2005

We had quite the stressful Holy Week, but our Easter was a blessing. It was so nice to have access to Jen's emails from the Peace Corps, but before she was even aware, we were seeing that tensions were building and becoming unstable. On Thursday, the Kyrgyz government was overthrown with riots in Bishkek. Within hours, the volunteers were given warning that they needed to pack a bag (only one) and be ready to evacuate to a safer location. They call it consolidation. Jennifer had to pack her bag knowing it would contain the only things she would take if her path took her to the embassy and then to the United States. She took her teddy bear.

There hasn't been a consolidation–evacuation in the last eleven years, but learning that really wasn't a comfort. The time difference between us made it difficult to know what was going on and at what time. On Friday morning we received the quick "We Are Safe" email, letting us know that Jen was in a different village with three other volunteers at the warden's residence, waiting for further instructions. Trying to call her that morning was not too successful, but we finally got through. Even though it was a terrible signal, it was so good to hear her voice. She assured us that there was no violence in the streets where they were, but that they had to be together to make further travel easier. Roads were closed, but their next move would have been north to the embassy in Kazakhstan. The volunteers in the Bishkek area were in the most danger and were held at the hotel next door to the embassy. Jen said she felt confident that the Peace Corps was on top of things. I wanted to say, "Hey, this wasn't part of the agreement," but we just kept saying we loved each other. How I wanted to be able to hold her like I did when she was little, and sing the song, "Jesus Loves Me—This I Know." It was the first song I ever learned, and I passed it on to my children as one of comfort and truth. We decided to think positively and use this same number for our planned Easter call. For days, I kept singing that song in my head.

We made that call to the warden after Easter Sunday Mass and were happy to hear that after four days, the volunteers had been allowed back to their villages. They still are under "standfast" rules, which mean no travel allowed. It's kind of like a tornado "watch" instead of "warning." But we didn't care. We excitedly called her home, and Venera answered.

As I started with my usual Russian introduction routine, she blurted out, "How are you?" in English! That was so touching, and then she went to get Jen, who was resting in her room. They had been allowed to go back home at 3:30 that afternoon. They hadn't had much of an Easter dinner, since they couldn't go shopping or plan anything like they did for Thanksgiving and Christmas. They weren't allowed in the streets, but she sounded thankful to be back at her home, and Aisalkyn was thankful that she had returned. She thought that Jen had to go off to fight in the war. And since she thinks she is "little" Jennifer, she said she wanted to go fight, too. I think the TV broadcasts they were seeing were scary and hard to understand. And the boys feared she would have to go back to the United States.

As we chatted, Grandma and Grandpa got to say hello, which means as much to Jen as to them. We told her that we had seen her third CD of pictures the night before with family and had been praying nonstop. It will be interesting to see how things go from here, especially with new elections coming up again June 26th. Don't know when they will be able to have their in-service training that was planned for the last weeks in Bishkek. Sure glad they didn't travel there when all this happened, but all fifty-nine would have been together in the same spot. We are very happy with how the Peace Corps was so protective and took all precautions for safety. And knowing that there is a U.S. military base in Bishkek is comforting, too.

Through it all, this doesn't seem to have changed Jen's decision to take this path and she got back to her normal habit of asking us for a few things that she would like us to send. She wishes she could get to the Internet site again, since she hasn't been there for seven weeks, but that will come soon. So true to form, Easter brought hope and we continue to pray for peace here at home and halfway around the world. Love,

Dan and Karen

April 2, 2005

I AM SAFE! Just to get that out of the way, since it sounds like Kyrgyzstan has been at the top of the news for a couple of weeks in the States. I'll give you a brief rundown on what has happened here that's made it extremely difficult to keep in touch with you all via email. Literally, the morning that I was going to Talas, about three weeks ago, to have access to the Internet, we were told that we were not allowed to travel due to some protests happening as a result of corrupt parliamentary elections. While there was some protesting (including people assembling yurts outside of the government building) in Talas, the worst was in the south, in Osh and Jalal-Abad oblasts. If it weren't for the traveling restrictions, no one in our part of the oblast would have known anything was happening.

On Tuesday morning, the 22nd, we were upgraded to stand-fast status in the Emergency Action Plan system, which means we are not allowed to travel at all outside of our village without special permission. Then, on Wednesday, we were notified that we were at a heightened state of alert (which we nicknamed "stand fast-er!") because both of the southern oblasts that I mentioned had moved to the consolidation phase, when the volunteers live in small groups with their respective wardens. Roads were blocked by the opposition forces between the southern oblasts, as well as between our oblast and Bishkek (once again, taking advantage of the size of yurts to do the trick!). Things were peaceful until Thursday evening, when we were notified that the opposition force had taken over the government building in Bishkek, the president had fled, and there were mobs in the capitol. At that point we were consolidated, which meant finding transportation to our warden's village thirty minutes away, packing one bag of essentials and our passports, as well as taking an inventory of our rooms. We were consolidated for three days before getting the word on Sunday afternoon that we could return to our villages, while remaining on standfast. Consolidation wasn't all that bad, but it was difficult not knowing whether we would be returning to the States or returning to our villages in a few days, as well as having to say good-bye to our families in that same frame of mind. To pass the time, we played baseball (there are six of us in this warden group) and Frisbee, watched plenty of movies, listened to the BBC every hour, caught some of the footage on local TV, and talked about the possibility of going home only three months into our service.

Upon returning to our village, the Russian television station reported that Kyrgyzstan would split along the north and south line, the north seceding to Kazakhstan and the south to Uzbekistan. Also, they have predicted a civil war, because there are two opposition party leaders at the present time. We are still waiting to see what develops up until the time of the presidential elections, now scheduled for late June.

Peace,

Jenny

CHAPTER 8

Back to the Grindstone

A government is overthrown, but then nothing changes. It doesn't make sense. I guess all Jen can do is get back to normal. Whatever that is.

April 2, 2005, written during standfast

The week of February 14th, my NGO hosted a handicraft seminar. It was organized and run by an NGO out of Bishkek, Kyrgyz Heritage, which focuses on teaching sewing techniques to women who do traditional sewing. Almajan, the director of Kyrgyz Heritage, has run a seminar in Talas before and I was able to spend a lot of time speaking to her about Kyrgyz handicrafts. It was interesting to hear the meanings behind certain patterns, the differences between handicrafts from the north and south, and the importance of zymology in Kyrgyz art.

The first day of the weeklong seminar focused on color theory, patterns, and designs, as well as stitching. The following four days had projects for the women to work on, partly as inspiration and an awakening to different styles and techniques that the women could use, and partly so they could experiment with trainers present to assist with problems or questions. On the final day of the seminar, local administration, press, and NGO leaders were invited to see the women's products during a reception and certificate ceremony. I along with two other volunteers participated, and was surprised to see the national news show up. There are some great photos of Kyrgyz grandmothers, wearing the traditional garb, being interviewed with a TV camera six inches from their faces. Almajan is a wonderful NGO leader who I intend to keep in touch with over the next two years, and visit in her Bishkek studio whenever I am in town. I even got a handbag out of the deal, since I took pictures all week long and then put together a CD of the photos for Almajan. That was definitely the most interesting and enjoyable week of work thus far.

In February, I participated in a hike with Kathryn, Nicole (Kirovka), Ian, and his students from the neighboring village of Bala Saru. Over 18,000 steps and seven miles later (Thank you, trusty pedometer! I found out I also walk about four miles on an average day), we had walked from our village to Bala Saru, joking with the students we had started out with, and picking up more along the way. We visited a sacred water spring (you drink from the water, tie a piece of paper to the nearest tree, and make a wish), and eventually took some pictures of the dam in the mountain pass and the Lenin Head that is carved in the dam. It was a great day, with a bean burrito dinner, some *SuperStar KZ* (think *American Idol*), and quality American time to finish it off in the evening. I look forward to this hike again in the late spring when I don't have to trudge through snow up to my knees in certain spots along the journey.

Kyrgyzstan celebrates Men's Day on February 23rd. It's traditional to give gifts to the men in your family, or male coworkers and friends. I limited my gift-giving to Madim and Kadim, giving them each a pack of gum and a sucker. Kathryn and I made macaroni and cheese, hot dogs, and cornflake "crispies" for dinner for Ian, our favorite man in the village. Both on Men's Day and International Women's day, businesses are closed so people can rest and celebrate. Although I work with an office of all women, we were closed for both holidays. While Women's Day is international, it is much more celebrated in developing countries than in the United

States. As I told my mom over the phone this week, "Every day in a third-world country is men's day; that's why this holiday is such a big deal for women." My counterpart came into the office a little tipsy after a party with the teachers at her school and kept saying, "Just one day a year, I can have fun one day a year." That may be a little exaggerated, because I know for a fact that Rosa has fun almost every day, since she is such a jovial person, but I get the sense that many women feel that this is their one day a year to celebrate who they are. There was much more buzz around town the days preceding March 8th (Women's Day) than there was for Men's Day, and much more consumerism around the village.

The weather was a hot topic this holiday. We had just had a stretch of really warm, sunny weather and the cloudy, cold day put a damper on some of the celebrations. I heard many theories about the reason for the lack of sun. My two favorites stem from passing conversations, one with a local NGO resource director who said that the sun was also a woman who decided to rest (the word for *sun* in Russian is a feminine noun, which caused me to have a good laugh). The second was from Kathryn's counterpart's husband, who said the sun was honoring women by being temperamental, just like the honorees of this holiday. Overall, it was a crazy day for both Kathryn and me as we went to various houses visiting women we know, giving them small gifts like tea or candy from the States.

After a dinner of *plov* at my house, which Kathryn and I helped prepare, we headed to the disco with Ian and his host sisters. The disco is always the highlight of a holiday here for the high school kids. The DJ, a taxi driver in town, always points out the three Americans over the microphone when we arrive. Throughout the course of the evening, a random Russian girl gave me a carnation; the DJ dedicated a song to Kathryn ("Miss Cat") while wishing her luck finding a boyfriend, and then a slow song to Ian ("Mr. Yawn") so he could dance with his two American girls. I can't wait for the next Kyrgyz holiday in May!

On March 21st we celebrated the Muslim Kyrgyz New Year of Nooruz. The weather leading up to the holiday had been warm and sunny and luckily stayed the same for the big day. Kathryn

and I decided to join some of her best students on a hike to Jilegone, a village thirty minutes from Pokrovka. Jilegone proved to
be a scene from an American Fourth of July, or Kyrgyz equivalent, with a stage and sound system, music, traditional games,
picnic-style eating, and plenty of food for sale. We stayed to watch
some of the traditions and then headed back to our street to catch
the block party of sorts that had been organized. The street that
we live on is really a great community with some of the most prominent people in town living there, not to mention two Americans!
We got back just in time for a dance party (where we both won a
bar of chocolate for our dancing skills), some Frisbee playing, and
then the feast. In place of the traditional American BBQ was *besh
bar mak,* the sheep dish where everything is cooked and served,
plenty of treats, and bread. Later on for dinner, we had *plov* and
some fireworks to close the party. It was really a great day and I
look forward to the next Nooruz in Kyrgyzstan.

This isn't a loaded paragraph on the intricacies of surviving in a
Kyrgyz office of only women. It's actually a lesson on hospitality in
Kyrgyzstan and how that applies to me and the day I sat close to the
door during the lunch break. In Kyrgyzstan, hospitality is a matter of
pride and there are dos and don'ts when it comes to being a good
host and a good guest, as there are anywhere. Being a good guest
means eating food and drinking tea; lots of it. As a good host, you sit
your guests at the appropriate places of honor. What we would consider the "head of the table" is the seat farthest from or opposite to the
door. Traditionally, in yurts that is the warmest spot and given either
to the eldest or the most honored guest. As a good host, you remind
your guest to eat and drink, even if they are putting a fork or cup to
their lips at that exact moment, as a sign that you are concerned with
their comfort and happiness.

Now, let's apply these concepts to my daily lunch break at
work. My little corner of the sewing table is already the farthest
spot from the door, so all day every day I sit at what would be
considered the place of honor, and that carries over to lunch. Even
when there are women three times my age eating with us, I still get
the honored spot, which at times makes me very uncomfortable.
Not only do I worry that I look like the impudent who thinks she

deserves respect that she does not in this society (I'm an unmarried woman in her twenties, which means I am still a silly child, and the lowest person on the totem pole...), but it also puts me in a position to be constantly reminded, "Eat bread!" "Drink tea!" "Eat, Jennifer; drink!" by every woman at the table.

This week I volunteered to buy bread and butter for lunch, since the woman who was going to bring in lunch was "ill." (I later found out that her husband had beaten her so badly that both of her eyes had swollen shut.) Due to some hot bread (Russian *lepios-ki* or Kyrgyz *non*, which is the circular bread with a design in the middle) and a package of butter in the same bag, I had a mess on my hands once I got back to the office, and in the shuffle of trying to clean up, I ended up sitting in a chair close to the door. Although this chair was the correct spot for me to be sitting in (given my age), one spot away from the student who was pouring the tea, it was not proper in the eyes of my office manager. Elmira panicked when she saw me sitting at such a lowly spot for an American "guest," and insisted I move. I stuck to my guns and settled in for what would be an interesting change in point of view.

I couldn't have guessed just how different my lunch would be by simply moving six spots around the table. I did not exist to the rest of the table and not once did people tell me to drink or watch what and how much I was eating. I was not even alive to the women as they passed their teacups to me without making any eye contact or breaking stride in their conversation. It was definitely a relaxing meal where I felt for the first time that I blended in with the group, but it was shockingly despairing at the same time. So many women, even older than I, live every day in this invisible role of unmarried daughter or daughter-in-law and go about their business unseen and unheard. I can only imagine what it must feel like to be invisible every day for a good portion of your life.

Since I was getting emails with the same basic sentiment, namely "I would write more but you have other emails to read and I don't want to keep you too long..." I thought I would let you in on my usual Internet routine. If I am at the Internet café in Talas, with USB ports, I bring my jump drive with pre-composed emails to copy, paste, and send (like this one!). I clean up my inbox, then copy and paste all of my new emails into a Word document, and save it to my jump drive. I can then enjoy reading each email thoroughly in the comfort of my room instead of in the craziness of an Internet café. If I go to the telecom center in Kirovka for Internet access, I bring a floppy disk and do the same thing: send letters I composed and bring back letters to enjoy at home. I usually go to Talas once every three to four weeks, and Kirovka possibly once in between. So feel free to make those emails as long as you want. The juicier, the better! In the past month, the modem at the telecom center in Kirovka ("Modey" is his name) has died and been resurrected twice. Even with Modey working occasionally, I really consider the only dependable Internet source to be two hours away in Talas. Hmmm... that two-hour ride sure sounds worth it when you want to communicate with friends and family!

Kathryn from my village writes a monthly article for her hometown paper in New Boston, New Hampshire (pop. 5,000). Her article for the January addition really impressed me and I think it gives great insight into what life is like as a volunteer in Kyrgyzstan and our village. I included most of it below:

On Saturday December 4th, I arrived in Pokrovka, a small town in the most northwestern corner of Kyrgyzstan, about twenty minutes from the Kazakh border. As I emptied my bags onto the floor of my new room, I finally realized that this is it: the beginning of my service as a volunteer. Just two weeks ago I was crammed into a taxi with one other trainee and four Kyrgyz people. It was the last taxi going to Sovetskaya, my tiny village by the mountains, so we all piled in and I wound up sitting half on my friend Andy's lap, and half on this old Kyrgyz grandmother.

At first, they asked the usual questions: How old are you? Where are you from? Do you like Kyrgyzstan? Are you married? They soon exhausted this line of questioning, and actually asked me, "How many kilograms of meat do you eat in a month?" Now, many of us, me included, have never had the chance to fully ponder this question. Does "meat" include sheep fat? How about eyeballs? And what about meat-flavored croutons? [Side note from Jenny: Flavored croutons are the closest thing to chips that we have out here. A Coke and bag of pizza croutons have become my junk food fix!] Although this question made that taxi ride memorable, the more important questions I am always asked are: Why are you in Kyrgyzstan? When do you leave? What are you doing here? It is easy to answer that I am here to teach English, but sometimes I wonder if this is really the reason. Last Saturday, I was sworn in as a Peace Corps volunteer. Until then, I had been in training. Well, now I'm here at the beginning of my life for the next two years. The setting is Pokrovka, population 5,000. Two schools, some stores, a bank, a post office, one small hospital. So why am I here?

The Peace Corps has three goals: to provide aid to developing countries, to promote a better understanding of Americans in other countries, and to bring home to America a better understanding of the rest of the world. As an English teacher, I am fulfilling the first goal. My students in Pokrovka are excited about learning English. Knowing this language opens up a world of opportunity for them in government, tourism, commerce, technology, and many other areas. But I am more than just a teacher; I am an anomaly. A real, live American. They should tell you at some point that joining the Peace Corps is like volunteering to be a minor celebrity for two years! Everyone always wants to know everything about me, even how much meat I eat in a month. This kind of attention can be overwhelming, but I realize now that this is what I'm really here to do: to share myself with these people, at the same time as they share their culture with me... I am thankful for the opportunity to share my traditions with my new families here on the other side of the world. We have a lot to teach each other: language is just the beginning. Where this adventure will lead, I cannot say.

My mom recently wrote an article in honor of the Peace Corps' forty-fourth anniversary for the *Chaska Herald*. You can check it out online at www.ChaskaHerald.com. Also, Kathryn submits articles to the *New Boston Bulletin* almost monthly, and there are a few articles about Ian (Ruge) in the Greeley, Colorado paper. Search for them on the Web if you've got time! Also, the third CD of photos is on its way to Chaska, and features the hike to Bala Saru, the seminar at my office, and everyday sights around my home and village. Once again, contact my folks if you are interested.

Peace and love to you all!

Jenny

April 4, 2005

As I was dialing Jen this morning at 8:00 a.m., I realized we had daylight savings on Saturday and maybe this would throw everything off. Would it only be 6:00 p.m. there? Would she not be expecting the call and be next door or eating supper? So it was a relief to hear her answer the phone. I think she thought I was strange for asking right away if it was 6:00 or 7:00 p.m. there. She told me it was 7:00 p.m. and then I explained why I was concerned. She said they had daylight savings last week while they were in consolidation. She had forgotten about it, so when we called at Easter, it was 11:00 p.m. for her but she said, "Hey, don't worry about it Mom. I'd take the call at 3:00 a.m."

They are still at standfast status until May 1st, and she really shouldn't have gone to Talas to the Internet café this weekend, but the warden went with Jen and Ian and he carries the cell phone with him. Kathryn stayed at her home in case there would be a call there as well. They plan on having the in-service training that has been postponed twice in Bishkek in May. Maybe they're trying to get it in before the elections in June.

Jennifer didn't know about the pope, which was surprising, because she had heard on the news that he was ill about a month ago. Maybe the coverage on TV has been about the strife instead of the Vatican. She wanted to know what would happen next. She should get the info from her upcoming *Newsweek* from the Peace Corps. Jen got a padded envelope from Megan with pictures, and three boxes today from the

Guillemettes, Rasmussens, and Uncle Paul and Aunt Patty. We thank all of you, because it helps with the expense of sending her everything we'd like to. Would like to suggest good times for those we gave Jen's phone cards to, to call her, but her phone has been so terrible. She says it seems like every time they try to repair it, it gets worse. We could hear her, but for me it was holler... wait for answer... holler... wait again. Dan said it sounded like I was talking to my Grandma Vacek (she is the wonderful, hard-of-hearing, ninety-six-year-old in my life!)

Before Dan got on, Jen went down the street to Kathryn's house and had us call there. Heidi also talked to her and told her she has moved back home. She planned to in August, but her older roommate seemed anxious to be on her own now since the divorce. Jen said, "Heidi, is that okay?" (Gee... thanks Jen) She told her, "Sure... there's more food here, it's warm in my room, no stinky dogs, and I can be with Dominic when he comes home from college in May and enjoy the pool this summer." A win-win situation for all.

The weather in Pokrovka has been crazy. Saturday it was in the high sixties and then that night they got a windstorm, followed by rain and hail, and then it snowed today! I could swear she is in Minnesota. That may be the reason they have been out of electricity for two days. She had to take a *banya* by lamplight. I asked if food is going bad, but Jen said that the small fridge is not the best, so thankfully, since it got cold, some foods can sit on the step and stay somewhat fresh. They don't worry so much about food going bad. Hmmmmmmm.

Jen's work situation has been better for her. She is working on advertisements for the mercantile in both Kyrgyz and Russian. Don't know how she speaks it so well, but writing it is even more difficult, as they have a different script and alphabet. So she is busy and just doesn't just work from 8:00 a.m. to 5:00 p.m. She sometimes leaves to seek out people that can correct her grammar or calls the Peace Corps through the telecom center to get advice on how things should be worded.

Ian moved into his new home over the weekend. The family left, even though the school year isn't over. He was concerned that they would leave while he was consolidated and find his stuff on the step outside when he returned. But it worked out okay. His new home is large, but it is hard to get used to everything all over again. And when Kathryn and Jen come over, they are still seen as "guests" and have to be offered food and the best places to sit. It's not a big deal when they go over to Jen's house or Kathryn's house. They like it that way better. It will be that way at Ian's soon.

Despite some of the hardships she shared in her emails (they were dated February and early March), they have all been resolved, seven weeks later. The Peace Corps had warned us about that [the time difference]. But we wanted to make sure that all was well and she does sound her normal, happy self. Guess she sees civil unrest and evacuating as just a bump in the road.

Oh, that girl. Let's pray for what she is there for: bettering a society but more importantly, peace.

Love,

Karen

April 11, 2005

We called Jen at Kathryn's house because Jen's phone hasn't been working very well. The problem is that when appliances act up, Kyrgyz people think they are all electricians and try to fix it themselves. This usually only makes things worse and ends up costing more for a professional to repair. Jen said, "But it's not only the phone. Today I plugged in the TV and got slightly electrocuted." I was upset and said, "How? Was it bad?" Giggling, Jen said, "Well, I didn't die, but my tongue sure did tingle." Seems Kadim didn't like the reception and took it upon himself to try to fix it. But Jen just takes it in stride because that is her "normal."

Some good news: they got a call from their warden that it's okay for them to go to Talas for Internet access, and they are going to take advantage of that this weekend. So anyone wanting to get a note to her in a reasonable amount of time, you can send one this week. Then we played the game "Did you get?" It can be a frustrating game, but sometimes a happy one. She hasn't got our Easter box yet, which has some summer clothes. It has been spring there and nice, but then they did get snow last Monday. It has melted, but she said it was the principle of the thing. Maybe it will help her to be patient for the summer clothes arrival.

She asked how I was and I went on about how we were rearranging the living room for the second time and had brought out the patio furniture and she interrupted, "No; I mean, how are YOU, Mom?" Don't know if she has ever asked me that with such intensity before. I realized that I tend to be more interested in how she is doing than in telling her about everything going on here. But I guess it's just as important to talk to her about me. Lesson learned.

It was Kathryn's birthday last week, and when they were together celebrating, they talked about her family, and Ian's, coming to visit. Unfortunately, they already have purchased their tickets for the week of June 26th—election time. Maybe the airlines would understand if they were not allowed in. But Kathryn called the Peace Corps and asked if it would be okay and they reassured her that it should be, because of where she is located, though anyone entering the country would need a formal invite. So she's going to arrange with her school to write a paper requesting their visit. I guess I shouldn't be surprised that you would need permission to come to a third-world country experiencing civil unrest.

Ian will be meeting his family in Turkey for a week and then they will come to his village for a week. I asked Jen where we would stay if we visited. She said, "At my house, of course. It would be shameful if you didn't." Not that I thought there would be a nearby Sheraton: I just wouldn't want to infringe. Her room would be big enough for us to sleep there, but I would worry about their food supply. Maybe I should just worry about the food. We will cross that bridge if it happens, but will pray for the safety of Kathryn's and Ian's families.

Jen wanted to inform those that have phone cards to read the fine print. To call internationally, you are charged six minutes for every one minute you are trying to connect, and then it goes to about four minutes per our one minute. Katie O. found out after trying to get through twice, then when she did, she ended up with only twelve minutes to talk out of the 120 that was on the card. Kind of the pits, but when you think you are talking halfway around the world, I guess it makes sense to not get a deal!

The excitement of the conversation was about the pope. She got a *Newsweek* that had a large story all about John Paul II and when I told her that the funeral was on Friday and Grandpa taped it, she hollered, "Kathryn! Kathryn! They have a tape of the funeral! I told you someone in my family would tape it!" Then she said to me, "I hope you won't mind when I get home that I say, 'So good to see you again... now where is that tape?'" Guess when you don't get to practice your Catholic faith, this kind of news is important to you.

We saw in Jen's emails for the Peace Corps that there was fighting in Naryn and then they were told they couldn't stay at the Issyk Kul motel where they usually stay in Bishkek. They are encouraged to stay outside the city. The new government isn't too established yet, so groups are trying to claim land. And the road going into the city is also the road toward the embassy, which is one of the areas they are fighting over. This can all change, so it seemed like no big deal to her.

Not too many requests from Jen this time. Most things are already en route. But she did send us off with a story about when they took the field trip to the mountain pass and dam in Kirovka. That was the trip she figured she had walked 18,000 steps (seven miles) in knee-deep snow, but the sights were breathtaking. She and Nicole had headed back early to start supper and the others went ahead to the top of a dam.

As they headed back, Ian found a treasure. When he walked in the door at the home where they were eating, he pulled out something from his pocket for Jen. It was a button from her backpack that she didn't even know she had lost on her walk back. He said he saw something shiny and picked it up. What are the odds of them coming across that little thing? When one of her Yaktrax on her boots came off—it is big and bright orange—they spent twenty minutes digging through snow to find it. She said she was so glad it wasn't her "I Love Chaska" button. I asked which one it was. She giggled and said, "It's the one that says, 'If you think education is expensive, try ignorance.'"

Praying for more knowledge and awareness to keep the peace in Kyrgyzstan.

Love,

Karen

CHAPTER 9

A Family Member Dies

We didn't tell her about the loss of our nephew LeBron in Michigan. He was twenty-six years old and died in his sleep. The autopsy is pending, and so we thought we would wait for more information and a better time to tell her. I don't know when a better time will be and it is going against her orders that nobody will get married, have a baby, or die while she is gone. It will be difficult for her being so far away, but life goes on and things happen. Honestly, that statement doesn't make any sense to me, but I am hoping it will to Jennifer.

April 18, 2005

We called Jen at Kathryn's house and got good news that her family has a new phone that works great, so next week we will call there. Actually, we had to call Jen on Saturday. She had a scheduled call with our neighbors, Jim and Lori Dixon. Afterwards, Lori let us know that Jen wanted us to call her because she was confused about some emails. We were perplexed, but called her right away.

Her voice was shaky as she said, "Brother Bob from St. Mary's emailed me and offered his condolences for the loss of my twenty-six-year-old cousin. What's going on?!" Unfortunately, Brother Bob hadn't known that we hadn't told her yet. So we did. She was hoping he got her mixed up with someone else, and if not, it would be even more upsetting because she has two twenty-six-year-old cousins. Which one was it?

We told her that LeBron had died in his sleep and that the autopsy results weren't in yet, so we had decided to wait to tell her. Plus, all this happened when she was being consolidated during Holy Week. She understood and then asked how all of us were doing. I assured her that if something like this happened again, we would call right away. It was just a shocking loss and at a hectic time. I told her, "I guess this goes against your wishes that nobody get married, have a baby, or die while you're gone." She replied, "Well, I said that, but I know it wasn't too practical." And now there are a few weddings she will miss as well. That leaves a pregnancy. Anyone?

Even though they're having warm spring weather there, Jen's workplace is so cold. She calls it the concrete bunker. Those who have seen the pictures know what she is talking about. So she still wears sweaters and tights to work. One day walking to Ian's school after work, she thought she would have a meltdown. She asked him, "What will I do in the summer?" I told her that it might not be as bad as she thinks because of her weight loss. And her work will feel like it is air conditioned! However, she is going to check with the Peace Corps about getting a fan for her home during summer.

Jen didn't get any packages, including our Easter box that has shorts, T-shirts, flip-flops, and cargo pants. Hopefully she will get her chocolate bunny before the Fourth of July. They have been told that they will probably be automatically consolidated during the week of elections in June. They won't have a wait and see policy. Jen told us that it won't be so bad, because where they would be going has a reservoir and hopefully it would be okay for them to go swimming to pass the time. Way to think positive. Unfortunately, that's when Ian's and Kathryn's folks are visiting, so it should be interesting how it will turn out. Maybe they would be able to be with them in consolidation?

At this point, their training is set for May 23th to 27th in Bishkek. I think they are trying to sneak it in there before the election protests. The medical officer is really pushing that it be done, because these volunteers need a break and need to be together to gain strength from each other, comparing notes, speaking English, and relaxing and learning about how they have done so far and what to expect from here. There have been seven volunteers total that have gone home. They've left for different reasons, but the main one is not being happy with the assignment or country to the point of depression. One girl left her village, and the other guy there decided he couldn't go it alone and requested to be sent home, too. One had a family emergency (a loved one with cancer). I would think that the unrest has left an impact on all of them. Jen went through a struggle as well. She told us she was frustrated with her work (things are better now due to her being more forceful and aggressive), and then they were consolidated with the knowledge that they may have to go home. So her mind wandered and thoughts of eating Caesar salad and just walking around in our house were looking pretty good. She started to accept the fact that she may not be there the entire two years.

Then they were told they could go back to their villages. Her family was so glad she could come back, but it was mentally hard on Jen to get back to the focus of staying strong and accepting staying in this different lifestyle again. After tears and support from Kathryn during a walk, she said that she realized this was an okay thing to go through. Usually on her walk to work she asks herself, "Why am I here?" and "What do I hope to accomplish?" She said that she has many different answers, but it is a good check and balance and keeps her on her toes.

I asked her today how she was feeling and she said, "Good, and back on track." Her strength leaves me in awe. I asked Jen if she wanted to talk to Heidi and she said, "That's great, Mom, but it's like talking to a bear." I laughed so hard. She's right. Heidi is low-voiced and groggy in the morning, but I still handed the phone to Heidi. Jen told her that she decided she better start doing things with Flat Stanley. He is a life size paper cut-out from the first-grade class she sponsors. Her job is to bring him to different locations and take pictures to show all the places he has been. They've had lots of other correspondence, including pictures and keepsakes, but Stanley has been lying low. So she had a picture taken of her helping him pet Kathryn's host family's cow. She thought it would be funnier if he got pooped on, but worried it would be too traumatizing for the kids! So Heidi had a good laugh, too. Guess you get your fun where you can find it.

Love,

Karen

April 25, 2005

Dan talked with Jen first and she asked about his birthday. She had told Venera that it was her dad's birthday and Venera started to giggle. She said, "It also is Lenin's birthday. Is he like him at times?" Jen said, "He can be, he can be." Then they laughed again. Dan didn't laugh as much. When I told Jen that we got him a new Hawaiian shirt, she said, "Oh, Mom; you are just feeding the addiction!" She wants to know the trivial stuff, so Dan told her that he was looking out over his half-mowed lawn. The mower gave out, he told her, but he would give it a try again. She commented that he should just get sheep to take care of the grass, and that way, when she comes home, she'll be around what she's become used to. Then they joked back and forth about how the manure would be good, wool in winter... crazy talk. Was good to hear both of them being silly while halfway around the world from each other, but I had to give Dan the "wind it up" sign.

She knew about our new pope, but didn't know that the elections in Kyrgyzstan have been pushed back from June 26th to July 10th. I found it out on the BBC.com site and learned that Donald Rumsfeld (United States Secretary of Defense) had visited there with the interim president. She said, "Really!" Kind of bugs me that I know things before she does, but that is the difference in our access to technology.

I reassured her that pushing it back will keep it safer for them to travel to Bishkek in May for their training. Things won't be getting heated up for June. She agreed and then said, "Hey... what the heck; we'll just have our Fourth of July American party at the reservoir!" I laughed so hard, thinking, "Yeah, don't we all usually go to the lake for our holiday? But we aren't getting to swim because we're being evacuated." It seems like the consolidation will be an easier thing to do this time, being they know it will probably happen and have done it before.

Jen had sent Grandpa a Russian atlas she picked up at a bazaar. She thought she could translate some of the main parts before sending it, but she didn't have time. What she didn't expect was that he would go to the library and check out a Russian–English dictionary and go through it line by line. I told her he is only on page two, but is having a great time. She said, "I can't believe he's doing that!" I told her, "It is just another way he can feel closer to you."

It was Aisalkyn's fourth birthday and Venera went to Taraz to get her a present. It was a plastic backpack with a doll inside. The doll had blond hair and blue eyes, which is completely opposite of those around her. She quickly said she would name the doll Jennifer because it looks just like her. Jen said, "What the heck; it looks nothing like me," but this reiterates how so many view Americans. She proudly showed her doll around and kept telling everyone, "I have a big sister named Jennifer and a doll named Jennifer." One day, Jen took her to day care and the teacher asked Aisalkyn, "Who is this that is bringing you?" She answered kind of irritated, "That is my big sister." Like, duh... can't you see the resemblance?

Jen has requested new tennis shoes. Walking everywhere takes a toll. But she told us that there's no hurry, because the duct tape is holding together the place where her current shoes split. WHAT? We said we'd order her favorite New Balance shoes and told her that we could send them right away; being a smaller box than usual, it would go through faster. Hence the reason she received a package we sent in April and not the Easter package we sent on March 15th. She reassured me it will come, and used the examples of letter from Grandma and Grandpa that can come fast or take forever. I get frustrated, but actually, it sounds like it can be a fun game for her to check out the postmarks.

Jen is planning to go to Talas this Saturday for Internet access. They haven't gotten official notification about going to Taraz, which is over the border in Kazakhstan and closer, so instead of waiting and missing out on sending emails where it is reliable, they're going. They are really excited to have a new place to explore when they get the permission to travel there.

April 29, 2005

Spring is finally here! The flowers are blooming, bugs of all kinds have returned, and the temperature has at times been in the eighties. It's great! I'm nervous, though, that winter will return. We had a week with warm weather about a month ago, and then suddenly a windstorm turned to a rainstorm and then into a two-day snowfall. I've put my winter boots under my bed, but my heater is still out because I feel like I'll jinx the warm weather if I put it back in the box. Not to mention that's what I had done the day before that last snowfall.

Well, here's what's happening in my corner of Kyrgyzstan. Kathryn's twenty-third birthday was the latest birthday in our group in the beginning of April. On the actual day, Ian and I cooked dinner for her, gave her our gift (a bedside lamp), and indulged in some Scrabble. That weekend the rest of our K-12 group in the oblast came out and we once again made American dishes and played some cards. The most surprising aspect of Kathryn's birthday, which may or may not be replicated for Ian's and my birthdays, is the fact that everyone in the village seemed to magically know that it was her birthday. Of course, when we first arrived, everyone asked how old we were and what was the date of our birthdays. But we never thought they would remember. However, Kathryn's students—who never remember to do their homework—somehow remembered the words to the birthday song in English and to make cards for her. People were coming out of the woodwork, giving her gifts ranging from flowers to juice (pretty expensive here) to homemade wine to handicrafts. The well wishing from people she barely knows, let alone people expected to know it was her birthday, was overwhelming. Celebrity status truly is an aspect of Peace Corps life that none of us were prepared for.

Peace and love,

Jenny

CHAPTER 10

The Secret Club

"If two groups of girls in one village cannot be friends, then how will Kyrgyzstan be one good country after the revolution?"

— ALBINA. A GIRL FROM JEN'S VILLAGE

April 29, 2005

After returning from consolidation, I decided that I wanted to do something in the community not directly related to my job. Through some Peace Corps resources, I decided to begin a "girl's club." It would be a leadership and empowerment support for girls. However, there was no way that I would be able to pull off a leadership club for girls without parents thinking I was a liberal American who was trying to steal their household servants away from them. So I have presented it as an acceptable way for their girls to better their English from someone other than their teacher. Students from Ian's school and Kathryn's school decided to join.

The first meeting was somewhat challenging. I had twenty-two kids at the first meeting and we met at the government center. But I quickly realized that it wouldn't work well when they only have ten chairs there. So I arranged to meet at a classroom at Aisalkyn's day care. It is quite a long walk, but all the girls said that they didn't care. But then a bigger issue erupted. The girls from the public school didn't want to share this club with the girls from the private school. It boiled down to their insecurities over their English-speaking skills. Just when I thought I had a full-out mutiny on my hands after the first meeting, one of the better English speakers from the public school said, "If two groups of girls in one village cannot be friends, then how will Kyrgyzstan be one good country after the revolution?" I don't think I could have stated it better myself!

After a few more meetings, during which I forced the two groups to interact through team-building games, it seems as if we have a more united front. I am not blind, however, to the fact that the circle of chairs where we have the club is split in half: public school girls on one side, private school girls on the other. The chalkboard and I maintain the neutral zone in the middle. So far our activities have been brainstorming things to do and talk about. This includes everything from making American food and playing Frisbee to talking about the revolution, love, and bride kidnapping. We've talked about the history of Earth Day, choosing a name for our club, and having a discussion about the difference between being a student at either school. And like any teenagers, they are very interested in what American girls are like and what they do.

The name of our club was a highly debated topic that ended in a group vote. The possibilities were "GirlsKG," "Girl-ship" (as in friendship), "Evrika" (Russian for coming out of a difficult situation), "Club Edelweiss," and "JenGirls" (as in Jennifer's girls). Of course, the only one I didn't want won by one vote: JenGirls. I've already talked to the girls about switching the spelling to "GenGirls," which translates in Russian to a formation of girls, and when I explained the meaning of the term generation in English, they seemed to get it. So GenGirls it is, a name that I can stomach a little more than one partly dedicated to me.

A funny moment happened when we were trying to schedule a picnic. Trying to work around the schedules of two schools is difficult and ended up in a free-for-all in Kyrgyz and Russian as I stood and watched the girls talking chaotically across the room to each other. I realized that I needed to jump in to mediate, so I held up my hands in a T, which in my head indicated a "time-out" for the conversations. One of the girls saw me and yelled, "Tea-ha!" to the others, which means "quiet" in Russian. I started laughing as my symbol crossed cultures, but not in the way that I anticipated.

The Russian greeting is "How's work?" and the reply is, "It goes." After coming back from consolidation, I offered to make some advertisements for my organization. We hadn't any before, because it costs money to make signs and/or put ads in the paper, and people don't plaster the village with ads like people in America do. Even for a garage sale. It took about two weeks to mock up an ad in my pathetic Russian, and then have a friend correct it and write up a Kyrgyz version as well. Then I had to have about four more people help with the grammar and wording before I was able to make copies. In the States, I have a feeling this would take three to five days, even with the translation. Here it took two weeks. That's the pace of life! But now the village is sufficiently plastered with signs in both Russian and Kyrgyz advertising our alteration, custom-clothing orders, and handicraft sales. There have been an increased number of customers coming into the office with their own material wanting a shirt, dress, or suit made. And plenty of people want something made but don't have the material at this time. So I think it was a step in the right direction.

Currently I am working on a Peace Corps Partnership grant for funding to repair and renovate an already-owned apartment across from our current location. The apartment will be a secure area to set up an office since we finally got our computer, phone, fax, etc... hooray! And it will provide adequate space for business and handicraft seminars, as well as courses for girls who want to learn sewing basics.

Now, this isn't the crisis center or Internet center that I was frustrated about opening a few months ago; instead, a multipurpose consultation center is more fitting for the organization at this time. After reviewing the Small Project Assistance grant through local headquarters that started the organization as it is, I realized that my director had many goals when she began work as an official NGO. They have not happened due to a need for more space. Right now, I am pretty close to completing the application, but it has to go through headquarters here before being sent to headquarters in Washington to be posted on the Web and distributed to other sources. Since our in-service training has been rescheduled for the end of May, pending another revolution, I am going to hopefully have everything approved at that time so it can be posted a few weeks after. You can check out current Partnership Projects, and have a better idea of what I am doing, at www.peacecorps.gov. Look for the Partnership Program link.

During the past week, I have been spending time translating for consultants from the EBRD (European Bank for Reconstruction and Development). I specifically have been working with a Greek consultant, who is here to teach cheese-and-sausage making methods. Through my broken Russian and his excellent English, I learned that he is teaching people how to take what they have and use it to their advantage. For example, we tried to make cheese this week in a *kazaan* (a huge cast iron Kyrgyz wok) that was propped up on a gas stove by rocks... you use what you have; that's the basic lesson.

The EBRD travels to countries that have undergone a major economic and social collapse, like those affected by the fall of the Soviet Union. Consultants visit interested towns and villages in countries that meet certain criteria and try to survey the resources the community already has available that they can work with, produce, and market, and through which they can create income. In Pokrovka, they are focusing on mutton sausage, cheese, and teaching organic gardening methods for increased volume in produce. I have really enjoyed this experience, not only because the consultant I am working with is amazing, but also because it gives me the opportunity to really flex my Russian muscle. Two realizations during the second day of translating were somewhat alarming, in different ways. The first being was that I could follow the conversation throughout the day fairly well. The second was that my speaking skills cannot convey all that I can recognize and understand in Russian.

I'm pretty sure that I've mentioned before that my village is a thirty-minute taxi ride to the nearest big city in Kazakhstan, Jambuhl (now known as Taraz). Jambuhl has all the amenities of Talas City, but is closer. We are not allowed to go there, though, because we would technically be leaving the country and need to do so with permission from the country director. We were told by the old country director that he must also notify the Kazakh country director. Well, with several four-hour one-day trips to Talas under our belts, the pros and cons of us traveling to Jambuhl versus Talas, and a new country director, the three of us in Pokrovka decided to take up our case with the Volunteer Advisory Committee. We wrote a letter to the new country director, which our oblast representative presented at the last VAC meeting. It seems that our request has been approved for two trips a month to Jambuhl, although we are still waiting for official permission. The stipulations that come with this privilege are that only the three of us can travel, we must submit our paperwork by noon on the day prior to travel, and we cannot stay overnight (unless there is an emergency or weather conditions make it impossible to travel). So we are all excited to visit the city that students and adults claim to be so much nicer than Talas.

Through all of the consolidation stuff, with the state of the government in Kyrgyzstan, and then the following standfast (when we were not able to leave our village), my dad commented that it seemed unfair that I was restricted from email simply because my village doesn't have Internet. Meanwhile, there are volunteers still obeying standfast with the ability to communicate with friends and family back in the States without violating Peace Corps policy. We had a nice conversation about it, and I told him that it would be great if I could casually check email once a week. I wouldn't have to travel four hours round trip just to send and copy emails without being able to reply to anything until the next trip. But I told him that at the same time, I like being in a village. These are my reasons. First, it's flipping awesome knowing that I am living a life that I wouldn't live in America. Instead of checking email every five minutes like I used to, I have to be very purposeful about the emails I write and the time I spend checking them. In the city, the temptation to go to an Internet site every day would be present and I am kind of glad that I don't have to fight that luxury every day.

Second, there are extra pressures that come with living in a village, like the increased number of drunken male teens and adults without jobs who consequently drink their days away because they have nothing better to do. So obviously dealing with their slurred catcalls and their just plain getting in the way when they stumble through the street can get annoying—when I let it. But pressures such as this test my strength and character, and in the long run I see that as a good thing.

Third, in the cities, volunteers spend more money than do those in villages. Sure, I blow about 200 som alone on the transportation into Talas. Not to mention the cost of Internet, meals, and anything that I buy because it's not available in Pokrovka. But on a daily basis, there is really nothing to buy. I might spend money on phone calls to a Peace Corps office or to other volunteers or postage for the occasional letter home. Maybe I'll buy some crackers or juice, but that's usually it. In the city, it's easier to spend your allowance simply because there are things to spend it on.

Fourth, in a city, I would be at an NGO that has its act somewhat together, and that may have national or international ties. In a village, I am assigned to an NGO that can really benefit from the advice that I offer and since their problems are not so complicated, I can really help with my level of education. I can actually be of service because this NGO definitely needs it.

Fifth, although the attitudes and gender roles are traditional, sometimes disgustingly so, I appreciate the fact that I am living with people who take pride in their roots, who celebrate their heritage. I do see the occasional cell phone out here, but I see or hear much more hospitality, traditional colors and designs, dances, songs, and the like.

And lastly, the fact that everyone knows my name, the language I speak, the family I live with, the people I work with, my favorite Kyrgyz food, the schedule of my bowel movements (no exaggeration on that last one!), is important to me. There is nothing conspicuous about living here! Therefore my actions and words have a gravity that they wouldn't in the States. I am truly an ambassador and an oddity for those who have never spoken with an American. In the city, you run into less of that, just because there are more English-speaking foreigners or foreigners in general.

Until next time,

Jenny

———— •◦• ————

CHAPTER 11

Only in My Dreams

On Mother's Day, I dreamt that Jen came home to visit and I hugged her and she hugged me so hard that she lifted me off the ground. That's the second time I've dreamt that she has come home since she has been gone these eight months. With how intense I feel about her being away, shouldn't it be more than twice? I crave sleep. Then I think of all the other dreams I have had that are not about the Peace Corps days and I feel better.

Mother's Day, May 8, 2005

We made our call from Dominic's dorm room at 9:30 a.m. Sunday morning (8:30 p.m. Jen's time). We went down to college to move out Dominic's big things; he will fit the rest in his car and come home when he completes finals on Tuesday. It was a perfect Mother's Day to hear her voice and for us all to be together.

Jen got the box of dehydrated food from the Dixons and also a small package from us with odds and ends and mascara. Not that she uses it often, since what you put on has to be washed off. And when you use leftover water inside a teapot to clean up, you shy away from the hassle.

But since her curling iron broke, using a little mascara helps her to feel pretty when she dresses up. We are sending her a new curling iron and hopefully it won't be misconstrued as a weapon. No sign of our Easter (soon to be Fourth of July) package.

I know she hates to hear me harping on it, but I said that her bunny will likely be stale. She said, "Mom, any chocolate is better than in-country chocolate." I told her, "No, I mean it was a real live bunny. That's why I am so concerned!" She laughed so hard and then it turned into a little-girl giggle that was better than any Mother's Day present or card. We have figured out that bigger boxes are not the best way to go. They take too long and bounce around the country, so we are sending two smaller packages rather than one big one from now on.

Her weather there has been very similar to ours: seventy to eighty degrees and then rain all day. Her laundry was on the line and got wet all over again for the second time, but she said it was okay because she didn't think she got all the soap out in the first place. She is sending us a padded envelope with some paperwork and then another CD of Kyrgyz music. She already sent one, but it didn't burn correctly and was blank, so she wants to try again to give us a taste of the music she listens to. It will be interesting. We will be sending her some pictures that we just took of a vivid rainbow that looked like the one that showed up on her graduation day and also pictures of the crabapple trees in full bloom where we always took prom pictures. But the picture from home she will enjoy the most is the one we took of two wood ducks that were perched on the edge of the pool and then jumped in for a swim! (With the cool weather, we haven't gotten the pool squared away and at this point it must look like a pond. Since she had to sit next to the ducks in the taxi, I'm sure she will appreciate our backyard adventure.)

Jen's enthusiasm has seemed to soar ever since the consolidation. It proved to be a time of reevaluation and she is really digging in to her call to be there. She has been busy and answered alumni requests to tell her story as a student update for both her high school, Academy of Holy Angels, and her college, St. Mary's University. She gushes over her girls group and said just this last week she told them the history of Mother's Day and all it stands for. They have the Women's Day celebration that is very similar to ours. She said that even though the group only meets once a week, she spends lots of time preparing and planning for their gatherings. I said, "Hey, Jen; it's just like being a college RA all over again!" And she agreed. "Yeah, I guess you're right." Guess you can take the girl out of the college, but you can't take the college out of the girl. And thank goodness. That just brings more gifts to those she serves.

They got an email and a call from the warden (for those who don't have easy access to the Internet) that cautioned them about the dangers that still linger with the revolution. Their in-service training is still scheduled for three weeks from now, but I think she accepts that the schedule could change at any minute, and that is the best way to look at it. She will be able to travel to the Internet café this weekend, so anyone wishing to send info that you know she will receive in a timely manner, enjoy. Thank you to everyone who continues to support her through email, packages, and prayer.

Love,

Karen

May 16, 2005

As it looks, Jen will be in Bishkek from next Monday, the 23rd, until the 29th. They joke that they think this "training" is doomed and may get canceled with all that is going on in Uzbekistan, but the fighting is more southwest of her and their capital city. Guess Uzbekistan decided that if it were good enough for Kyrgyzstan, they would try to have a revolution, too. But there has been more violence and even deaths there. So we pray for a peaceful resolution and that things will stay at the status quo for Jen. She's not sure how much Internet access she will have, but I'm sure there will be some. The volunteers who serve in that area will know where and how to access it. She looks forward to the Bishkek motel again, with its running water, and possibly pizza and Coca-Cola. Watch out, tummy. She said a cucumber upset her stomach the other day. She figured it was from too much cow manure in the dirt that didn't get washed off well enough. It's hard to boil a cucumber; plus, she was hungry.

Jen said she got an excellent article on our new pope in the international *Newsweek* that the Peace Corps sends them. That was the highlight of her week. No packages. My Easter bunny continues to travel over the ocean somewhere.

There is a new volunteer in Talas Oblast. She is Korean–American and was serving near Osh. She was troubled by the unrest, but mostly because she was hassled about being a native Kyrgyz woman. Because of her looks and then because she had been trained to speak Kyrgyz and not Russian, it was hard for her to convince the community that she was an American. She got so frustrated and was afraid of the violence, so she asked to be sent home. That was the last Jen heard. Then when she was in Talas to use Internet this Saturday, they were hanging out at her friend Willie's house and in she walked! Jen said it was such a nice surprise. The Peace Corps had suggested that, if she were willing, she could try to serve in the northern part of the country, where there wouldn't be so much pressure about ethnic labels. She is ten miles outside of Talas and hopefully things will go well for her. If not, the Peace Corps will give her ET (early termination).

As we were talking, Jen started to giggle and said, "Okay, great; there are some little boys peeking at me through the window ledge." I asked if they were neighbor boys. "Yeah, they just want to watch me and how I can talk to America. Oh... that one should wipe his nose." That was a good laugh. She was hoping they wouldn't step all over the peonies blooming around the house. Venera asked Jen to come and smell them. She did, but apprehensively, and had to explain to Venera that she associates peonies with big black ants! But it is not so in this third-world country. Small favors. She has her flowers growing on her windowsill, and the ones in the Spam can are doing the best. Thanks, Uncle Paul and Aunt Patty for the turkey Spam. Recycle/reuse!

Kadim and Madim were a bit upset with Jen because she didn't have to work in the vegetable garden. She wanted to remind them that when she wasn't there, they had to work in the garden by themselves and that she is doing other work in her room. Guess no eleven-year-old boys like pulling weeds, no matter where they live.

Jen used our phone call to pass on a message to Kathryn's parents. I emailed them to call Kathryn on Tuesday or Wednesday about their visa. Carol emailed me back within the hour, thanking us for passing on the information. If only it could work that fast over there. We talked about Heidi and me having gone to the Peace Corps open house on Thursday.

There were eight kids about to leave to serve, their families, past volunteers, and then families like us that had someone presently serving. It was so interesting, and one of the staff members saw on our nametags that Jen was in Kyrgyzstan and said, "Oh, they were having some problems over there, weren't they?" We explained everything, and praised the Peace Corps for how they handled it. He said that was good to hear.

Mike introduced himself as the leader for the evening; he was dressed in traditional garb from Slovakia, where he had served. He looked at some pictures I brought and was mesmerized by a shot of Jen with all her sewing ladies around her, taken at the seminar they attended. He asked if he could use it. Mike is putting together a gallery of Peace Corps pictures that depict the relationships that are built between cultures, not so much the chores that are done. Bringing two cultures together is where the peace happens. Hence, the organization is called Peace Corps and not Work Corps! The pictures will be blown up to eleven-by-seventeen prints and hung at a gallery at the University of Minnesota, and then will travel to many other colleges in celebration of the upcoming forty-fifth anniversary. Jen needs to send a paragraph about the picture. So we swapped emails and information. You can't underestimate the power of a picture.

We talked to one mom of a returned volunteer—he had been assigned to neighboring Uzbekistan—so our stories about traditions, food, and struggles were so much the same. She also gave us ideas about how to ship books more efficiently and about a GLOW camp opportunity for girls in the summer. It could fit right in with Jen's GenGirls, as glow stands for "Girls Leading Our World." I have to download the handbook for Jen and email it to her. Good information all the way around. At the end of the evening, Heidi asked, "Mom, why do we always have to be the last ones to leave these kinds of things?" but it was so enjoyable talking to everyone. Jen's recruiter, Andy, wasn't there, and it would have been nice to meet him. Don't know if I would have hugged him or hit him. I guess it would depend on the day and my mood.

Jen said a friend of hers was feeling down about being there, so Jen told her to do something for herself. She went to the bazaar and actually found a coffee cup... WITH a handle! All teacups there are small and round, with no handles, which burns your fingers. Then this gal got some coffee and sugar. So each day, she heats up water in her room and enjoys a cup of coffee the

American way before she joins her family. It was all she needed to get back on track. Jen says that small things can make such a big difference and I encouraged her to continue to do that for herself, too.

She sounded in a good mood, and when we got cut off one time, I called back and she answered, "Harry's Fried Chicken!" I laughed so hard and then she said, "Oh, sorry, I should have said "**%@$#$%%^^," which was the same phrase in Russian. The only word I recognized was *plov*, which is a fried rice dish. Didn't ask about the rest. It took awhile to say good-bye, but we plan to call on Memorial Day and hope she is able to travel, as she looks so forward to seeing other volunteers, especially the people in her language group whom she hasn't seen since December. It puts a whole new spin on having a "sleepover."

Keep praying for peace.

Love,

Karen

Memorial Day, May 29, 2005

Thank you to all of our vets! As soon as Jen said hello, I wished her a happy Memorial Day. She immediately got upset and said, "Ah, I was going to be the first to say it." I think it is important to her for us to know that, even though she is far away, she is still in touch with our holidays. Good news: she got our Easter package! It took nine weeks. It was a big one because it had summer clothes and flip-flops, but we won't send big packages like that anymore. She also got a padded envelope with her St. Mary's University yearbook in it that we just sent two weeks ago. Got to love those padded envelopes. She hasn't eaten her Easter bunny yet, but had a few of the Reese's Easter eggs. She gave one to Ian because he helped her carry the package back from the post office. Her room is a shambles because she hasn't totally unpacked from her seven-hour trip back from the training in Bishkek. She traveled all day Sunday on a route through the mountains, which ironically is quicker but bumpy and curvy, so she got carsick, despite having taken Dramamine. Her training was very good and she remarked how nice it was to see everyone again.

She got to connect with Ian number one from her language group and he is doing well with his assignment. She didn't anticipate the attention she'd get for how different she looked. First of all, her weight loss. And second, her longer hair.

They had language lessons one day and she was shocked by how easy they were. Malika, her favorite teacher, wasn't there, but another Russian teacher was impressed at how much Kyrgyz she knew, in addition to Russian. As a matter of fact, while we were talking, we got interrupted by Aisalkyn. She had asked Jen where Venera was. I listened to Jen speak to her and could tell she was repeating herself and then switched. She told her where her mom was in Russian, and then asked in Kyrgyz, "Do you understand?" and apparently Aisalkyn gave her the why-of-course look. Her day care teacher says she is the only Kyrgyz girl who can play with both Russian and Kyrgyz kids because she can speak with both.

The night before Jen left for training, Aisalkyn had had a bad toothache and was up half the night. Venera tried to put some gel on it for pain relief, but that only lasted a half hour for her to sleep. So at 3:00 a.m., Venera decided to go to Jen for help. She went to the hall and hollered, "Jennifer, Jennifer." Jen answered her back by saying "Oh," which means "Yeah" in Russian. Venera said her name again, and Jen answered, "Sto," which means "What" in Russian. Venera said, "Do you have any medicine for teeth?" No answer. She said her name again. Nothing. Venera thought it was weird that Jen didn't come out of her room and just gave up.

Two weeks later, she told Jen the story. They laughed so hard because Jen didn't remember a thing. But what's bizarre is that Jen realized she had been "sleep talking" in Russian. They say when you dream in Russian, you have pretty much mastered the language.

Her favorite part of the training sessions was when they shared their experiences with each other, including the nitty-gritty of struggles. Most often, people share how great things are going or all they are busy doing. She found more strength in hearing how very hard it can be. She learned that most everyone was struggling with arranged housing, a job site that had to be up, and running with a plan. Since these things happened to a majority of the other volunteers, Jen did not to feel so bad for the slow going at her work. But now her site finally has a phone and computer, so she is thankful.

She also was excited about a session in which they were asked to suggest how the initial training could be improved. Jen appreciated how open the Peace Corps was to listening to their input. So she and the other volunteers offered ideas based on what they found they needed most once they started in the field, and she was excited and felt confident some of their improvements would be implemented for the next group of volunteers. One idea was to have an American person visit the possible work sites to see if they would be a good fit, instead of having a program director from that culture decide. Jen loves the challenge of making improvements.

The weather is pretty hot there. It's supposed to be ninety degrees tomorrow. I told her that we should be having that kind of warm weather here, too, but we've had three weeks of rain and cold. Regardless, it was a beautiful morning as we called her, so we sat outside on the patio as we talked. There was a Memorial Day ceremony in the graveyard right next to us and she was able to hear when they shot their guns in the air in salute and played "Taps." Maybe it made her feel like she was right there on the patio with us, experiencing it all, including the wood tick that fell into Dan's coffee!

She paid one of the sewing ladies to take in her skirts, but after eating in Bishkek, she may need to rethink that. While in training, she got to partake in some modern food. She didn't mention pizza this time; she seemed to go toward the meat. She had chicken twice, as well as meatballs, a ground hamburger, and peppers wrapped in a pancake. But her total ecstasy came from a cheeseburger and Coke. As she told us about it, she made a moaning sound and you could just picture her taking every bite. She even had a Caesar salad.

Her friend Melissa had gone home to the United States for her brother's graduation and came back on the second day of their seminar. She said she didn't get sick from eating the rich American food, but was surprised that she didn't have the appetite she thought she would. She spent the first three days crying about how she didn't want to leave, but in the end, leaving wasn't as bad as she thought. It sounds like when we went on a vacation to Hawaii and didn't want to leave, but then went back to Minnesota, and were actually glad to be home. It got me thinking that maybe a shorter visit is better and I wondered how it will be for

Jen to be here for three and a half weeks in December and then have to go back. Will cross that bridge when we get there.

Another plus from being at the motel for training was having flush toilets. But she still had a little container (with lid) by the toilet for the paper, since their plumbing system is so poor. Jen said that it was weird to be able to sit down to go to the bathroom and flush, but still use the paper container. Kind of a combination of both worlds.

Jen's next adventure will be at the end of June when she is going to help with a girl's camp in Karakol. It is quite a ways beyond Bishkek and the longest travel she will have done. It will be classified as program travel, but she sees it as fun travel. She hopes to observe how they run the camp, and determine if she can bring a similar program to their village. She already has the GenGirls as willing participants. She will be back on the Fourth of July and hopefully it will not be too close to the planned July 10th elections, when they will be consolidated again. Kathryn's and Ian's families will be visiting during this time, so it will be interesting to see how it goes.

Kathryn met a girl in Bishkek, the daughter of a man who runs the tourist center, who told her that she was interested in becoming a foreign exchange student. She said she would check into it and was totally shocked when her parents said, "We will take her!" She will arrive in August and stay the school year. Talk about sharing cultures—both ways!

We got Jen her new tennis shoes and will be sending them off with a new curling iron, since she has duct tape on both. She will be able to go to Internet café on June 11th and this time it will probably be in Taraz, which is only a half hour away. They got final approval and are excited to scout out the city. Dan and I will be in New York for his brother's wedding at that time, so Grandma and Grandpa will handle the Monday call.

We discussed the progress on the article for the *Chaska Herald* for the book drive, her alumni articles for St. Mary's and Holy Angels, and the pictures about the Peace Corps for the University of Minnesota gallery. It gives me parent homework, but it is easier and quicker for me to be a middleman than to have to wait on her.

As we talked, a beautiful cardinal hopped around on the grass nearby. These birds have always been something special to me, so I asked if she sent him to me. Jen said, "Sure." When the cardinal moved over and sat by our Virgin Mary statue, I knew she truly had.

Love,

Karen

June 6, 2005

Some Peace Corps volunteers from Talas came to visit Jen this weekend and they decided to swim in the river. It went well until their legs turned numb from the cold. So the weather there is not too different from our weather. Jennifer got powdered milk from Uncle Paul and Aunt Patty, and on special occasions she has been using her distilled water and mixing it up for breakfast. Since she had guests from Talas, and we had sent her cereal in the late-arriving Easter box, she got some milk ready in a Sprite bottle and left it in the kitchen for when she needed it, only to find in the morning that Venera was boiling it to make fried dough. That changed their menu. One of the volunteers, Sadie, said she didn't care, since she had a stomachache and wasn't hungry. It wasn't until the next day that Jen asked Venera, "How was the American milk?" Venera felt bad because she said she hadn't been sure where it came from. Jen thought to herself, "Hellllooooooo; it's in a Sprite bottle!" But they had a laugh together, anyway.

Jen had planned to borrow Ian's DVD of the Russian version of *Spider-Man* to show her GenGirls. She had made arrangements to use a facility that had better seating, but as they came in, there was a tribunal situation going on. A young girl Jen knew was up in front of a panel of adults, and they were telling her in many ways how bad she was. Jen wasn't sure of the circumstances, but felt bad for the girl. It puts a whole new twist on kids thinking their parents are "on their case." But Jen plans on using the *Spider-Man* movie to prep for next week's GenGirls meeting, when they will discuss the question "Who is your hero... and why?"

This week Jen received a package of drawings from the first-graders at Guardian Angels. And she told us that she has been wearing the dress

Sara (Dominic's wonderful girlfriend) sent. She has had many compliments, but the ladies refer to it as a "mini" dress. It goes a bit past her knee, which isn't a mini by American standards, but all her other skirts are ankle length. I asked her if this was a problem and she quickly said no; other women have shorter skirts, too, and I think she likes being a bit of a rebel.

After being disconnected five times, we asked Jen what the deal was. She explained that the wires where the phone goes into the wall are exposed and twisted. So if you bump them, you lose your connection. She said she should take a picture in order for us to understand the insanity of it all, but would keep an "evil eye" on the cords for the rest of our conversation. We had a good laugh, but remain thankful for the connection. Jen asked, "Wasn't Father Larry supposed to be on this call?" We had planned on that, but had to tell her that things had changed; he had forgotten that he had to be with the eighth-graders on their Valley Fair field trip. Amusement parks aren't his thing, but we want him to know that she missed him and I can see how she takes pride in keeping track of what is supposed to happen, even when she is far from home.

Last week they had a visit from the Peace Corps medical doctor to have an emotional evaluation. Jen has spoken to her many times over the phone, given her sinus infection troubles, but when she opened the door, the doctor was shocked at her weight change. Jen says she forgets about the difference and is surprised by others' reactions. She got a clean bill of health but was more interested in the doctor's journey. Jen's area was one of the last on the list of sites to check, and then she was going back to America (she is Russian but married an American), to Missouri. Ah... the United States of America. Those words sound so good to Jen's ears.

Jen found out that there will be replacement Peace Corps volunteers coming into her area. That is a good reflection on the work being done there. We talked about how wonderful it is that they now have a phone at the office, as well as a fax machine and a computer. Jen said, "Well, the fax would be great if we had paper"—it is an older fax machine that takes rolls of paper—"but the computer is pretty modern." She is working on taking pictures of all the different handicrafts to create a catalog that people can look through when ordering. It would be too expensive to have samples of everything displayed. So she is making a made-to-order catalog. Hello, Sears!

The good news about the influx of volunteers is that the side of the building that was being considered for a women's shelter is now being formed as a "business consultation center." This would allow them to have sewing seminars and a teaching facility, and take in outside organizations to rent the space. Jen is working on the grant writing as we speak. This plan will probably go further for women than just trying to create a shelter.

Jen says the garden they have in their backyard is going very well. Potatoes are the main crop. Unfortunately, the prominent pest is the Colorado potato beetle. Ian gets teased for being from Colorado, as though he is somehow responsible. They were eliminated in the sixties in America, but have thrived in the third-world countries. For all the damage they do, they actually are very colorful and Jen said she will take a picture of one.

When we called, they were eating outside, since the kitchen gets moved out there in warm weather. As the phone rang, everybody jumped. Jen came inside, Venera was behind her with the chair, and Kadim turned down the TV volume. Jen said, "I guess it was a family affair just to get the call." Venera said to say hello to us. So I asked Jen if Venera is allowed to date or socialize. Jen said, "She really only goes to others' houses when there is a birthday party or other celebration, but in this country, if you are divorced or widowed, you really don't date. You just decide, hey I like you and you like me; let's get married. People marry mainly to get out of hardship and to gain a better life."

Later as we were talking, Jen got interrupted twice: once by Madim asking where his mom was. I understood Jen when she told him "*Knee doma*" which means, "She is not home." Then a guy came to the door, knocking, but Jen didn't get up to answer because she was on the phone. But they do this thing of nodding their heads to one another to acknowledge each other without having to say anything. So he head bobbed her and she bobbed him. About ten minutes later, Venera walked by the window, bobbed her head to Jen, Jen nodded back, and then Venera winked. Jen thought it was strange, but then she noticed three men walking behind Venera (who was wearing her fancy, flowered capri pants). We laughed so hard, because I had just asked Jen about her dating, but Jen figured out that she was just getting their help with some heavy work in the garden. Hey, whether halfway around the world or in America, a girl has to do what a girl has to do.

We won't be talking to Jen next Monday, since we will be in New York for Dan's brother's wedding, but Grandma and Grandpa are going to enjoy touching base with her. Funny thing is that Grandma told us that she dreamt that Jen came home. And Grandpa dreamt about her the next night; in his dream she was home, but the dream didn't have anything to do with the Peace Corps. I told this to Jen and she freaked out, because she had had a dream about them and we figured out that with our night being her day, they pretty much had the dream at the same time.

Jen's dream was about going to the post office. The workers aren't the friendliest people, but they were kind in her dream and kept asking her why she didn't pick up her letter from her grandma. So Jen had to travel back to the post office to get this missing letter and as she walked in, it ended up that she was at the farm and Grandpa was behind a counter. He was the postmaster who was going to give her the letter! Then the dream ended. Even though we have been apart for almost nine months, it is so nice to know that love can bring us together in our dreams.

As we were finishing our conversation Jen said, "Hey, we should have planned to meet in New York!" But I told her, "It wouldn't have been good, because then we would have cared less about Uncle Doug and would have talked with you through the whole wedding and kept hugging in a corner during the reception. So the most polite thing to do is wait until Christmas when you come home." We laughed, but I don't think I believed the statement that it would be better to wait any more than she did.

Love,

Karen

CHAPTER 12

The Power of a Girl

In one email, Jen wrote, "At the end of lunch I asked one of the girls to say the *banta* or blessing that precedes the sign of the omen. You hold your hands out, palms up, and then make a circle in front of your face resulting in your palms wiping down your face. One girl volunteered to do it only if I would follow her with a prayer in English. It was great to pray with these girls even though we were praying to God under two different names." That in itself was a blessing.

June 17, 2005

Hello, friends. If you are reading this email that means... I AM IN TARAZ, KAZAKHSTAN! We are finally here, making our first visit. I have to admit the big city is a little overwhelming. As we walked past a large grocery store, similar to something you would see in America, I commented to Ian and Kathryn, "I feel like I'm in Bishkek again... I don't know if I like that." We had to exchange our som into Kazakh tenge (a one-to-three exchange rate) and noticed Pringles and Lipton ice tea in a shop window on the way to the telecom office. Kathryn said, "I think we might be broke after a couple of visits! Maybe this wasn't such a good idea." Time will tell. On to the meat and potatoes of the past month!

During May, there's a string of three consecutive holidays: Labor Day (the 3rd), Constitution Day (the 5th), and Victory Day (the 9th). Labor Day and Constitution Day were pretty lackluster holidays. Victory Day took the cake, because we have been preparing for it since we got to our site. We were wondering why every fence, wall, and sign had something about "Talas Oblast—60 Years!" In anticipation of the big day, our WWII monument in town was repainted and the students practiced their military formations and marching. It was a pretty big day, with everyone coming to the square to watch a ceremony that involved local WWII veterans, students singing songs, and people laying flowers next to the monument and eternal flame. The most interesting part of the day was the fact that the entire Kurdish population came from the fringes of the village to participate. There were so many Kurdish people present that I truly wondered if it was their holiday. Since the Kurdish community lives so far from the center, they hardly ever venture in—and they never see the three glowing white Americans doing their daily business. Several times while going about my business, I was surrounded by Kurdish kids just staring at me in disbelief. It really made me appreciate the people who are, for the most part, a part of my daily routine. For them, my novelty is wearing off, but for the Kurdish community it has only just begun.

The GenGirls decided that they wanted to go on a picnic on Constitution Day. After a passionate debate, a vote settled that we would go to my next-door neighbor's "cabin," located in a spot where there are three lakes. En route to our destination, I got to see a predominately Kurdish part of our village, the mysterious third school that everyone talks about, and large compounds that I had never seen before. When we finally got to the cabin (forty-five minutes later), Kathryn opened the first Kyrgyz chapter of the Polar Bear Club by taking a dip in one of the lakes while a group of astonished girls looked on. Then everyone started marching single file, with Kathryn and me in the back wondering where the heck we were going and why we couldn't just eat by the lakes. The head of the procession was the twenty-liter *kazaan* (Kyrgyz wok) that the girls took turns carrying, two by two. When we reached a stream, some of the girls crossed gingerly over the rocks, while two others and I took our shoes off and went through a deeper, muddier section in order to pass the *kazaan* across without falling. Then there were the brave four who convinced two horseback shepherds, who were watching their sheep and cows graze, to ferry them across. I got my camera out to video this, and I now have the evidence of what are to be chronic back problems later in life, as one of the girls and shepherd fell off a horse. Luckily, they weren't in the stream or moving quickly, although the girl was moving slowly the rest of the day.

When we got to the "forest," an area that had trees barely taller than me, we began preparing lunch, since we had been walking for a total of nearly two hours. The girls unsuccessfully tried to convince me that I shouldn't cut the carrots. I think they meant to make me think that they were doing this out of respect, that the older person or guest should not work. But I think the girls were more motivated by the fact that they assumed that an American doesn't know how to do such a challenging task as cutting carrots. I have learned from experience that it has to be done in the "right" way but when they saw what I produced, after many evenings in my kitchen helping with *plov*, they oohed and aahed. I proved them wrong while they were busy starting a fire, preparing the *kazaan* and washing dishes in the river. I don't think I would have the confidence or the knowledge to do the same thing when I was their age. These girls handled everything like old pros, which they are; they've been preparing meals with their mothers since they had both strength and coordination enough to carry a dish full of *plov*.

When we were dishing up fried potatoes for dinner, I realized that two girls were missing. I asked Chinara, my cousin and the potato chef, who was gone. She yelled, "Aigerim! Jongul!" into the forest and two girls came walking out from where they had been talking. I stared at Jongul, because at that moment I remembered something that Kathryn told me earlier in the week. She was going through her grade book when she said, "I have a student named Jongul, and I looked up her name the other day since I had never heard it before. It means mistake." There are always new girls coming to my club, so the fact that I didn't catch this girl's name before the craziness of the hike began was nothing new. I am constantly asking the names of new girls under my breath to the regulars. I don't think I'll have a problem remembering Jongul, since for whatever reason she was named after what her relatives thought she was. Maybe she was supposed to be a boy after a long line of girls; maybe she was a surprise or an unexpected arrival too soon after the wedding. I can imagine a million scenarios as to why she was named that way, but all that it comes down to for me is imagining growing up with a name that conveys the negative thoughts your father's family had for you when you were born (the matriarch on the husband's side of the family does the naming of new children). For whatever reason, I have a beautiful girl in my club whose name is Mistake.

The weekend of May 13th to 15th, our oblast group gathered in Talas to celebrate the birthday of one of our fellow volunteers. Kathryn, Ian, and I went in to the city in the morning to visit the Internet café, and then went to the apartment of the couple who were hosting all of the village volunteers. As we were sitting and talking with a few other volunteers, wondering if Kirovka village would ever show up, they did... accompanied by a guest. All of a sudden, a short Kyrgyz-looking girl walked into the apartment and as soon as she smiled I realized it was Sadie, a TEFL volunteer from the south who was one of the first people I befriended during our staging event in Philadelphia. The last we had heard was that Sadie, as well as quite a few people volunteering in the south, was returning to America. Through the grapevine, we heard that it was due to the fact that she didn't actually have a teaching job; that she organized several clubs and after battling low attendance, decided it was best to stop wasting her time and return to the States. Well, Sadie was standing in front of us and informed our shocked group that when she began to do the paperwork for early termination, the Peace Corps doctor convinced her to try a site change before making the decision to go back to America.

Later in the evening, Sadie confided that, due to Uzbek and Kyrgyz tensions in the south, she was constantly being confused as a Kyrgyz girl and harassed by Uzbek boys (she is Korean-American). I later got a small inkling of her daily frustration of being an Asian volunteer in Kyrgyzstan when we were dancing at a café and I had to tell some Kyrgyz men several times that she was an

American and that people of many different races call themselves "American." On a lighter note, before finding this café to dance at, our group almost crashed a private KGB party at our favorite café. After about thirty minutes of smooth talking in Russian and Kyrgyz from our guys, a marriage proposal from a KGB officer to one of our girls (sadly, this is not the first time that any of us girls have gotten a half-serious, half-joking marriage proposal), and watching a member of the KGB vomit over the café's second-floor railing while another officer taught us the Russian verb meaning "to vomit," we decided to find another place to dance!

In letters and emails since the revolution, the same question has opened each correspondence: "How is the government?" Honestly, as far as I'm concerned, the political situation is the same as it was before the revolution. I am so far removed from any area of political significance in this country that I only hear what Peace Corps officials feel necessary to tell us, which at this point is only news that affects our travel or safety. Most people in my oblast have not talked about the revolution often since it happened, and the country has gone back to a relatively normal, daily routine. The students speak of the revolution the most, since it is the event that marks their adolescent years (just as 9/11 marked my college years).

After a recent GenGirls meeting, two girls, Marriam and Nurzat, walked me home and asked me what I thought about the revolution, and what other countries thought of Kyrgyzstan post revolution. Nurzat sadly stated, "Many countries are probably thinking we are silly, stupid Kyrgyz people. They probably think, 'Why would they steal from each other and loot stores?'" I tried to convince both girls that while some people may think badly about Kyrgyz people based on what they saw or heard in the media, most intelligent people would realize that a president's running away does not mean that the entire people is cowardly. Just because some people steal, not all people are thieves, and because a government is corrupt does not mean that all people are bad. It took a long time to convey such an idea, coming from someone raised in an individualistic society, to two teenagers raised in a collectivist society. Finally, I resorted to the example, "Nurzat, if Marriam ran over to that grandmother and hit her, would that mean that I could not be friends with you because of what Marriam did?

If Miss Kathryn stole from that store over there, would that mean you would think that, because I am an American, I steal also?" I wasn't trying to show them that collectivist thinking is wrong, just that many other educated people realize that the actions of one person or group of people does not reflect on the behavior of an entire country. I sure hope my words were true.

The week of May 23rd to 29th, we finally had our in-service training that was postponed by the revolution. Our conference was held in a hotel in Bishkek. It was the first time that I had been back to the capital city since the swearing-in ceremony in December. As we entered the city, I got the immediate gut feeling, "Well, this is nice, but this is not the place for me!" After spending a week binging on American, Indian, and Turkish cuisine (I had my first bacon cheeseburger in eight months!) and overindulging in consumerism at all the available stores and shops, I was ready to head back to my sleepy village. It was wonderful to see all of the volunteers, although the group seemed a little off, since a handful of people from our group had terminated their service early. Ian and I were able to have dinner with his host sister, Aigul, from his first host family (they moved to Bishkek after his host father died). It was great to see Aigul again, and speaking Russian and Kyrgyz throughout the meal to communicate with her was a nice way to end the week of speaking English and ease back into village life. She's one of those special people who never makes you self-conscious about your language skills, or lack thereof, which actually makes communicating a lot easier.

Our midservice training is only six months away and I look forward to seeing everyone again. I will be spending a week with a fairly large group of volunteers at the end of June when I am a counselor for a girl's camp near Lake Issyk Kul. More on that experience to come! That's all from my neck of the woods, or crevice of the mountains.

Take care!

Jenny

Peace Corps volunteers building a yurt during
Culture Day at pre-service training.

Jennifer and the Russian language group
with their culture facilitator and teacher, Malika.

Jennifer's Turkish host family in Krasnaya Rechka, Kyrgyzstan.

The home of Jennifer's Turkish host family.

Jennifer and the other Pokrovka village volunteers, Kathryn and Ian.

Jennifer's Kyrgyz host family in Pokrovka—
Madim, Kadim, Aisalkyn, and Venera (left to right).

This picture was featured at the "Peace & Friendship" exhibition that toured local colleges in Minnesota, sharing the stories and photos of Minnesotan Peace Corps volunteers.

Kathryn's host father, Jakov, gets ready to add two feet to the fence to protect her from being bride kidnapped.

A sunset in rural Talas, Kyrgyzstan.

A kumuz (fermented mare's milk) stop in the mountain pass
between Bishkek and Talas.

A woman selling fresh and smoked fish at a Tokmok bazaar.

A family selling carrot salad at a Tokmok bazaar.

It's Kyrgyz tradition for people to provide their own birthday lunches, so in 2008 Jennifer brought plov (a local dish of rice and vegetables), watermelon, tomato salad, eggplant, rolls, and cookies.

A woman selling tandoor naan (bread) in a Tokmok bazaar.

The public well that was conveniently located across the street from Jennifer's first home in Pokrovka.

A typical pit toilet in Pokrovka.

CHAPTER 13

Parents Galore

Jen seemed down this conversation and even admitted it by saying, "I've been good for a long time. So I can feel sorry for myself a bit right now."

June 20, 2005

We have returned to the land of Minnesota from a wonderful vacation out east. The wedding in New York was so special and the monuments in Washington were breathtaking. Thank you to Mom and Dad for being our "substitute callers" while we were away. Jen's big news was her trip to Taraz, which will be their new Internet site. No more two hours to Talas. It is only thirty minutes away and is as plentiful as Bishkek. They have real grocery stores and she was amazed that they stocked American brands. She also bought a fan, which has made her room more comfortable. I asked which she liked better, summer or winter. It wasn't an easy question for her to answer, given that each one has such hardships. But after some thought, she said that she thought summer is better. Her office building is a cement bunker, so it stays cool, and there is more freedom to be out and about in summer; the brutal cold of winter keeps people hibernating. I didn't want to bring up the hot weather and outhouse combination, which might sway her vote.

The new country director came to visit her site last Tuesday and he also met with Kathryn and Ian. He was pleased with all that has been happening and all that is planned. He looked over Jen's office and was the first to order some stitchery out of the catalog that Jen has created on the computer.

Jen got our package of tennis shoes and a curling iron that we sent June 4th! But she hasn't gotten the package from Uncle Bill and Aunt Sue that was sent in April! Jen was upset that we haven't received her disc of pictures and music; hearing how frustrated she got, I realized that our roles have switched. I have accepted that there is no sense to how things are mailed, and that packages will eventually get to where they should be, but she was ready to go postal on someone.

Jen will be leaving this Thursday for the camp in Karakol. It will be the first time she will travel to Bishkek on her own. Once there, she will meet up with three other volunteers to go the rest of the way. The elections are set for July 10th (they always have them on Sundays) and they still aren't sure about their consolidation plans. There was some slight protesting in Bishkek this last week because one of the candidates was disqualified due to the fact that he was from Kazakhstan. It was not a big deal, but people are still touchy. Jen will get back on the Fourth of July and then will see what the plans are. If they are consolidated during elections, Ian's family will be with them.

Venera is asking Jen if there is any miracle drug in America for women's skin, especially for the liver spots that most women get after childbirth. Apparently other women worry about this too. Jen said she saw a lady rubbing smashed cherries on her skin. Guess that was supposed to help. I told her I would check, but Jen doesn't want us to send something so great that the village women will line up and ask for shipments from America. And what would happen when Jen leaves? Who would be their supplier? I still think I would like to send something to Venera to try. I asked Jen about her complexion and she said it was very good. She used the acne meds the Dixons sent because her skin was breaking out from washing her face in well water; complete with plenty of bacteria. She doesn't use it as much anymore and thinks that getting tan from being in the sun has helped, too.

I asked how the kids were and she said fine, except that Aisalkyn has turned into a "klepto." She wants to be like Jen so much so she plays with her stuff. Also, the house is open now in the warm weather, and so there's no need to close off rooms to stay warm. And that means Aisalkyn wanders into Jen's space. She took her keys, ate her yogurt, and was playing with the bottle of milk Jen mixed up. Jen said she may say something to her, but has to remember she is only four. If she were fourteen, that would be different. As we ended our call, Jen said, "Hey, Mom; I've been over here for nine months!" I told her, "I could have had another baby daughter in that time." We had a good laugh, but then I realized... there is no way Jen could ever be replaced.

I know you all feel the same. It would be great if you could help us celebrate Jen's birthday abroad by sending her a card!

Love,

Karen

July 6, 2005

We tried to call Jen on our planned Fourth of July, but she wasn't home yet from her travels to Karakol. I was proud of my Russian when I spoke with Kadim; he was the one to let me know that she was still in Talas. Our concern was that she was consolidated (there was a planned standfast for travel starting July 5th), so I called Kathryn's counterpart who can speak English. She gave us the number of the place where Jen was staying; that was sheer luck, since she had just gotten the number from her husband, who doesn't speak English, who got it from Kadim minutes earlier. So luckily we got through to Jen and she explained that she was not consolidated, but had to stay in Talas because her travel there took too long and it was too late to try to get a taxi to her village before dark. They were in the mountains and their taxi kept overheating, not to mention that the drivers kept stopping to get fermented mares' milk every time it was being sold alongside the road. I asked if the milk could make you drunk, since it was "fermented." She said not really. So I said, "Oh, then it would be like us stopping at a gas station to get a pop?" She answered, "If you call drinking something that tastes like a baby's poopie diaper drinking pop, then yeah." She plans on trying it before she leaves but doesn't want to try it now and have the taste haunt her the whole time she is there. (There is a drink called *bozo* that is made from fermented wheat and has the taste of beer but the consistency of a milkshake. Some volunteers have said they've gotten drunk on *bozo* and they probably acted like ones, too.)

Jen had her physical while in Bishkek and found out she lost seven more pounds, even though she had stabilized for a few months. She is blaming it on the heat and on sweating all the time. But her new fan in her bedroom keeps it more comfortable. Her experience at camp was a good one. They spoke Russian (better for Jen than Kyrgyz). They had university students there volunteering and when they spoke English, they also interpreted, because not all girls spoke English. Jen even helped and she said it was a very good language lesson for her Russian as well. One of the volunteers offered a quick lesson in yoga one morning before breakfast for ten minutes, and the girls loved it so much they asked to have it every day and did it for forty minutes. They also did the normal American camp things like scavenger hunts, skits, etc., but also had a culture day, a thank-you ceremony at the end, and lessons on AIDS and an info session about bride kidnapping. Not something that is ever discussed at the YMCA camps I know.

Jen was explaining to Dan about the troubles related to the upcoming election on the tenth. Due to the poverty, it is a common practice for the bad guys to buy the right to vote off of farmers so as to get more votes for their guy. The farmer takes the money and runs, not realizing how he may be contributing to the problem. She keeps saying that there shouldn't be too much of an uprising, but time will tell.

Kathryn's parents have been there for a week and will be leaving tomorrow. Jen enjoyed time with them and could see the likeness of Kathryn in her parents. I didn't ask how she felt having Kathryn's family there because I didn't want to make Jen feel sad. Ian's family comes in a few days as well. They (Jen and Kathryn included) think they may go to this resort-type place near the reservoir. It can be allowed during the standfast because it is near the warden's home and he plans to go with them and would be available for any call from the Peace Corps.

When Dan was speaking to Jen yesterday, their connection was broken into. A lady started speaking Kyrgyz and Jen knew enough to tell her, "I am speaking, why are you talking?" She sounded surprised and kept on talking to her party, so Jen said again, "I am talking to my family." She seemed to understand and then kept talking. Finally, Jen said, "Helloooo! You need to stop. I am talking to MY family." That made the lady hang up. Go figure. They have party lines in a third-world country. Dan found this entertaining, as he was still connected and laughed. Then they felt leery as they tried to figure out how that had happened.

Jen may go to a Internet café the weekend of the 17th, but with Ian and Kathryn traveling and getting to bigger cities, they may not be interested, so she would travel alone. She will decide on that later. I told her how we are enjoying the new pictures she sent, but Grandpa gets frustrated at the conditions of buildings and says he could do wonders with his hammer and nails. He wonders how Jen can have a phone but the outhouse is in shambles. Jen explained that in a Muslim culture, families can never have a bathroom in their homes. It is offensive. I said, "Fine, but get a platform and toilet seat, for God's sake." She had a good laugh.

During our talk, Jen said Aisalkyn was sitting quietly, playing with her dolls. It didn't seem right to Jen, so she asked her if she was okay. Jen has learned you should never trust a quiet four-year-old. Then we talked about the cream I got for Venera for hormonal blotches. Jen said that at night she puts crushed berries on her face, and another morning, as she was smearing cucumbers over her cheeks, she asked if Jen wanted some for breakfast. Jen stopped in her tracks and was thinking (but didn't say), "Would they be the ones on your face, or could I have fresh ones?" So we will see how this cream works. Jen didn't want me to get trapped into being the supplier, but I told her it might not work and I can empathize, one woman to another. And it is the least I can do, from Jen's American mother to her Kyrgyz mother.

Love,

Karen

July 12, 2005

Hello (preev-yet)! We had to call Jen on Tuesday instead of Monday. Over the weekend while we were at Uncle Paul and Aunt Patty's cabin, Kathryn's dad called and said not to call her Monday, because she wouldn't be home. Our thoughts immediately went to the election that was on Sunday, wondering if they had been consolidated, but as it turned out, she was with Ian's parents and they went to the reservoir and swam. Even though they are on stand fast, it is very near the warden's residence and he was aware of their location. Dan called Jen a "rebel." But I guess they figured that since the election went off without any violence, and family was visiting from the States, they'd make concessions.

Jen seemed a little down this conversation and even admitted it, saying, "I've been good for a long time, so I can feel sorry for myself a bit." Maybe it was because Ian's and Kathryn's parents were visiting and we weren't. Maybe it was because she hasn't had a decent *banya* in a long time, which is terrible when it is so hot (the people just go for dips in the river and consider themselves clean, but Jen says you can come out of there feeling worse: silt in your hair and scum on your skin). She has been doing her regular bucket-bathing and washing her hair in the backyard, but was feeling down, because if her family doesn't use the *banya*, she can't. Or maybe it was because she had to do her laundry for ninety minutes in the one-hundred-degree heat. She said, "Dad, can you just see me in my bathing suit crouching over the buckets?"

She said she is going to send us a list of all the things she wants to do when she comes home for Christmas and here are two of them: take a shower every three hours and do her laundry every day. Mainly she said she's getting sick of being a celebrity, always being watched, asked the same questions, and scrutinized. Dan told her to wear those glasses that have a plastic nose and mustache, and also to put on a sombrero. She laughed, and said, "Funny you should say that, because I did see a place where they were selling those hats." She is tan enough to be Kyrgyz but speaks Russian, so they ask if she is from Russia. She has to say, "No, I am American." I told her that when we have foreign exchange students, we tend to do the same. But she said, "Not to this degree."

It's also the fairness that isn't the same. Venera can just take off and not say where she is going and Jen can wonder, worry, and not know what to expect, but if Jen did that, she would be reprimanded and thought to have been bride kidnapped. And for any argument she makes, there always is a comeback from the Kyrgyz standpoint. There is not the give and take of being able to discuss your standpoint when you are a visitor and that gets difficult for her to swallow at times. Once when Venera was reprimanding the boys in the garden, she could see Venera was riled up, and when Kadim spilled tea, she ranted on and on and then asked Jen, "How do I say I am going to give you a spanking in English?" Jen wanted to say, "I don't think you need to spank him for such a small thing," but she wouldn't be allowed to, so she said, "I don't know." It was better to pretend not to know a word than to lose her head and offend by saying what she really thought. Jen has accepted that, but it's really bugging her. I told her that it's not wrong to feel frustrated and down. Most people couldn't handle half of what she has to endure for even a week.

Our air conditioning broke at my office and I wanted to find the maintenance guy right away. Then I decided I would offer this up as a suffering, for Jen's sake, in hopes she could find coolness in her day. But as I told her in our phone conversation, I was ready to give up my sacrifice five times and just march into the boss's office to see if he was doing anything. She laughed. In America we get to do what we want and when we want. So it must be difficult to play by their rules to keep peace.

Jen hasn't gotten any of the magazines free for Peace Corps volunteers that I requested, but she did get a padded envelope from us with the Washington, D.C. shirt that we bought for her while visiting New York. Funny thing was, it was in a yellow bag. Usually letters and envelopes come as they are, but boxes or large packages are sorted with a yellow bag. She loves yellow bags, even though she has to prove identification and sign for it. It was no big deal, but a lesson learned about big manila envelopes.

We talked about the election, and even though the voter turnout was poor, it was enough to be considered a viable election. But the president is talking about having a democracy, and in the same breath saying there is no need to have a U.S. air base in Kyrgyzstan and Uzbekistan. Jen's feeling is that if these bases close, all other American organizations will pull out as well. The Peace Corps wouldn't have the backup or stability to serve there. But that will be down the line and probably after Jen's stay.

The GenGirls are pretty much on hold right now over the summer, since most girls have to work in the fields with their families. I think that is a letdown for Jen, too, but Kathryn is going a little stir-crazy from not teaching, so she's going to have an art camp for the next two weeks. Jen plans on helping on some afternoons. There's also a trafficking/gender development seminar being held in Bulgaria and a lady from the Peace Corps headquarters called Jen to invite her to apply for the chance to attend. It is in August and the Peace Corps staff member (Tahmina) is allowed to take one volunteer, so anyone interested has to apply and say why they feel they can help. Since Jen has no access to the Internet before the 15th, the lady told her she could fax her application. I asked how far away that would be and she said, "I don't know. I will have to look at my map. Grandpa, can you do that?"

Then I got an idea: since we can't email all the time, we could send her a fax of a little letter. I asked if I could do that and she said, "I don't know; we've never received one." I laughed so hard I cried! I said, "You mean your office has this fax machine but nothing is ever sent to you?" Apparently, they mainly use it as their phone and charge people who want to fax/call in order to create income. I told Jen, "Tell your director that we will try this as a test to see if it even works and that it should be at no charge." Don't know if Jen was too hip on giving it a go, but it was a comical moment, anyway. So send those birthday cards and well wishes before Aug 2nd. Imagine how she can answer when asked, "Where were you on your twenty-third birthday?" Good-bye (pock-ah)!

Love,

Karen

July 15, 2005

The month, so far, in review... let's take it from the top! The week of June 27th to July 1st, I was in Karakol for a girl's camp, organized by Peace Corps volunteers from Issyk Kul Oblast. The camp was extremely well organized and the two volunteers in charge were really on the ball. When we got a schedule for the week, my first thought was, "Am I still in Kyrgyzstan?!" What a refreshing return to American organization! The camp was for girls in the Karakol area, and local Kyrgyz and Russian university students volunteered as translators and seminar facilitators. The girls came every day at 8:00 a.m. and started off with some yoga and a light breakfast. Before lunch, they had two seminars on topics such as bride kidnapping, effective communication, AIDS awareness, etc. After lunch, they had two hours of sports, cooking, or arts and crafts. The girls wrapped up each day with reflection and journaling. My part in the camp was as a counselor. I co-led a group of girls along with a Kyrgyz-speaking volunteer from the south. As a counselor, I mainly had to herd them to various activities, make sure everyone was accounted for, and be an overall cheerleader.

When the girls were in their seminars, all the volunteers were able to go into the city to run errands, or we would help the leaders of the afternoon activities, or set up tea breaks. It was a great week of fun activities with the girls and quality time with other volunteers, not to mention a great first visit to Issyk Kul Oblast. It truly is beautiful there and I look forward to more trips in the future. A few volunteers and I were able to get to a beach of Lake Issyk Kul outside of Karakol the day before we left and it was really enjoyable. I never thought I would be lying on a beach in Kyrgyzstan when I agreed to this placement. I never cease to be surprised here!

Although a group of volunteers went to Cholpon-Ata (a tourist town on the north side of the lake) after the camp, I, along with two other volunteers traveling to Bishkek before the 4th, decided to stay in Karakol. What we didn't realize was that arriving in Bishkek on the 3rd would allow us to attend the U.S. embassy's Fourth of July barbeque. At first I didn't want to go; I needed to shower, I didn't have anything to wear, etc., but I was glad I went. I was able to enjoy good food, live music, and a firework display, not to mention the company of Peace Corps staff and random volunteers who were in the capital. It was the first holiday that actually felt like an American holiday since my arrival in this country. However, being surrounded by so many red-white-and-blue-wielding Americans caused a bit of culture shock as I and the oblast-mate with whom I was traveling just couldn't stop staring.

The funny thing is we also realized a little too late in the evening that we really needed to censor ourselves. Unlike when riding in a taxi, we couldn't say anything that popped into our heads... everyone could understand us. That took a little adjusting to, as did watching parents chase after their kids, not allowing them to play with pinwheels that were "just too sharp!" After spending nine months in a country where bones are the favorite toy of the local boys, the idea of taking a pinwheel away from a child seemed so strange. Since I had fine-tuned the internal censoring of my thoughts, a mother telling her child not to throw things at other kids made me scream inside, "What are you doing? You're going to let the kids go soft! How will they fend for themselves in the real world?" I quickly realized that the real world that all of these Foreign Service and missionary families are training their kids to be in is nowhere to be found in Kyrgyzstan.

When I returned from Karakol, both Kathryn's and Ian's parents were in the village visiting. First came Kathryn's, after a flight into Almaty, Kazakhstan, and a tour around Issyk Kul, which included horse trekking and guesting. They brought with them two extra suitcases of stuff just for Kathryn, ranging from paint and art supplies to two four-pound containers of peanut butter. I'll be benefiting from their visit for a long time to come! They spent two days in Pokrovka, which included taking a tour of the village, sitting in on one of Kathryn's clubs, visiting my office, and checking out what we do here. It also included taking a dip in both the Talas River on the edge of town and the Black Water River on the edge of Jilegone village with some students. It was a brief but busy stop in Pokrovka.

Then Ian's parents and brother came to the village after spending a little over a week together with Ian in Turkey. Both of his parents are former Peace Corps volunteers and have spent time volunteering in other countries, including Turkey, where his mother was a teacher for a few years. After arriving in the village, the Ruge family enjoyed going to the local Edelweiss resort on the reservoir with students and oblast volunteers, visiting the Manas Ordo (the museum) outside of Talas, and being the reason behind Ian's host family's slaughtering of a sleep. Kathryn and I were both there for the *besh bar mak* feast (the meal in which you give the sheep's head to the most honored guest, this time Ian's father, who did eat part of the face) and the visit to Edelweiss. It was great to hear stories about both of Ian's parent's experiences in Peace Corps and how I am serving in a much different organization than the one they remember.

Although it was wonderful for both sets of parents to see where their children call home, it was somewhat confusing for the village. I had several people come up to me and ask, "And your parents came, too?" They must think American parents travel in clusters. The question both annoyed and saddened me. I started down the road of being upset that Kathryn and Ian got to be with family. Why do they get to have their parents with them and I don't? I soon realized that was not a good road to take emotionally, so I put it out of my mind so as to stay strong.

Well, thankfully things here went smoothly up to the elections and as I write this email the week after, things continue to be quiet in my neck of the woods. We were put on standfast as a precaution from July 5th until July 13th, which meant no traveling away from our sites unless for international travel or for an emergency. Bakiyev, the acting president after Akayev ran away, is the new president, which everyone anticipated. The day after the polls closed, I asked Ian's host mom if they knew who the president was yet. She said that they would know accurately the next day. I said, "Well, how's Bakiyev? What percent does he have?" She responded, "Ninety percent, but we won't know until tomorrow who the president is." Right. Good little Kyrgyz girl... I have noticed lately that I am really starting to take on cultural norms of conversation and behavior. It's been unconscious until now, when Kathryn pointed out a question that I asked in conversation that I would never ask in English. While there is a mile-long list of all the things I do here that I never did in America (like take off my shoes when I enter a house, never let bread sit upside down, never sit at the corner of a table, bathe in the river, etc.), there is a growing list of things that have begun to appear in my speech or actions.

For instance, taking off my sunglasses when I speak to people. Normally in the States, it may seem slightly rude to talk to someone when they can't see your eyes, but Americans tend to worry less about offense and more about comfort and eye health. Here, after Ian was chastised for talking to one of my neighbors with his prescription sunglasses on, I have begun the practice of lowering or taking mine off completely when someone stops me to talk or when I am walking down my street greeting neighbors. I did so when I talked with Ian's American family and was obviously uncomfortable while squinting into the sun to the point that his dad asked why I had taken them off and told me to put them back on.

On the way to my director's house, Kathryn and I ran into a group of students. In English, Kathryn asked them, "Where are you going?" immediately after she greeted them. Once we arrived at my director's house, I greeted her and she told me she was ill. My immediate response was to ask why. Once we left her house and continued our walk, Kathryn teased me for becoming Kyrgyz and asking why my director was ill. That is the first response here, which drives us volunteers crazy, instead of asking what was wrong like I would have in the States. I came back with, "Well if you're so American then why did you immediately ask where those girls where going, like a Kyrgyz person?" We both laughed at how these questions that normally irritate us had somehow slipped into our vocabulary.

While hiking in Karakol, our group came across several natural mountain springs that started higher up on the mountainside and then crossed the path we were following. Everyone went straight through the flow of water except for me. I stopped dead in my tracks at the edge of one of the small streams until another volunteer came up behind me and coaxed me to cross. In Talas Oblast, the idea of water sources being sacred has been drilled into my head a lot. Once when I went on a hike with students, we stopped at a spring and each student tied a piece of string to a tree near the water and then said a prayer before taking a sip. It was a quiet and very reverent process for these students, and trees with strings have been popping up all over the place since the winter thaw. In Karakol there were no strings tied to trees, but the thought of walking through the runoff of a spring seemed as offensive as washing my hair in a baptismal font full of holy water.

During the *besh bar mak* feast at Ian's house in honor of his American family, his Kyrgyz family brought out three platters of sheep meat on oily noodles. The name of the meal is literally Kyrgyz for "with five fingers," because that's how you eat it, by hand. That's how all three of us have grown accustomed to eating this dish—with hands, from a communal platter—but to accommodate the new Americans, the meal was served on individual plates. Kathryn, Ian, and I stared at the empty, individual serving-size plates and took a long time deciding if we would indeed use them. When we were explaining to Ian's family how to eat the meal, I said, "Okay, there are these plates here; I don't know why they are here. This seems really Westernized—" (Ian and Kathryn chimed in a unified "Uh huh") "—but we usually just eat with our hands from the same platter. I actually really don't know what to do with these plates."

Until next time, keep your eyes uncovered, know where you are going, why you are ill, don't offend any sacred springs, and keep your plates clean!

Peace,

Jenny

CHAPTER 14

Moving Out

One of the hardest things for me to accept about Jennifer serving in an area with such limited resources is the fact that so many times, she goes hungry and I can't feed her. That is the main reason why I joined the Loaves and Fishes program at our church. If I can't take care of her, at least I can serve food to someone else who is in dire need of it. Her continued weight loss has forced a change, and the focus is now on how to make that change without shaming her family. However, as a mother, my thought is, "I don't care. My daughter is suffering."

July 18, 2005

We got an email from Jen saying that she probably won't get the opportunity to go to Bulgaria because she hasn't heard anything. She had to send her application twice because the fax wasn't sending all of it. But then she got a call today that she was selected! She flies August 14th, through Turkey, and the seminar is on the 15th and 16th. The Peace Corps staff member will fly through Moscow, as she has other business to do as well. So it will be quite an adventure for Jen to see another country and another area, and to have another experience. It is just the boost she needed.

Right now we have more important news. Jennifer is going to move and the process is going a lot better than she expected. With all the frustrations she has been having with Venera, the medical director is most concerned about her weight; the tensions in the home have caused some of that. Other reasons include a lack of food made available to Jen, depending on the mood in the home. She will live in the village and have the same job, but will be on her own. Many volunteers do this, but she wants to do it in the best way possible, where no feelings will be hurt. She doesn't want the shame of offending anyone, but yet has to put herself first. This is a balancing act she has danced many times before.

She could live in what is called a compound situation, meaning a separate house from a big house. What we call the "guest house," they call a compound. I raised the safety issue of being on her own, but she shared with me that in the house she lives now, they keep both doors open at night in order to get some breeze, so anyone could walk in and cause harm. And she said the Peace Corps is more involved if a volunteer is on his or her own, like making sure there are bars on windows if the volunteer is living in a complex on the first or second floor. She will have a family nearby, but wants to be independent, especially when it comes to cooking.

Her director at work is playing a major part in the search. When Jen explained she had to leave due to health reasons, Gulnara questioned why and Jen said, "It's just my weight," not wanting to say more. Gulnara nodded, understandingly, maybe because the week before, the ladies were teasing Jen about her weight and making faces by sucking in their cheeks. Jen said, "They used to tease me about having such a round face; now they don't like me being thinner." But they are going to sew her a linen suit to wear at her seminar in Bulgaria so she can look presentable and have something that fits well.

The plan is to find her a place to move to by August 1st. Jen worried about Venera's reaction to her needing to move out, but she was surprisingly understanding about it and seems okay because, as she told Jen, Jen will be in the same village and she wants Jen to stop by there and they will visit her. But in her next breath, Venera said, "People will think you are losing weight and have to leave because I am a bad mother." Jen wanted to partly agree, but assured her that people will talk no matter what the reason. Jen then said, "All we have to worry about is that the people we love and who love us know the truth." So it seems to be going smoother and as she wants it: on friendly terms.

Jen got emotional when she talked about missing her street. On her walk home every night, people call out to her and say hello and Aisalkyn runs to greet her. Jen always asks the same questions: "How are you? What is new? What did you do today?" and the answer is always the same. "I played." What more does a four-year-old do? But I told Jen that whenever she visits them, she will get the same greeting and that helped her tears. Any change brings both good and bad.

Jen has been helping Kathryn with her art camp, which has been fun. And there is another kids' camp the first part of August in Talas that she would like to be involved in, but that will depend on her move. She says she misses her GenGirls, but with all that is going on right now, it is best they aren't meeting. She will see them when she helps with the three-week art classes. Her friend Erich likes to tease Jen whenever she refers to the club, and he says in a silly voice, "Would that possibly be... the GenGirls?" And then breaks into the *Batman* theme song. Jen says, "I think he sees us as crime fighters for the village and suggests we should wear big GG letters on our shirts!" They will pick up their meetings again when school starts.

Speaking of Kathryn, the cat that lives at her house keeps coming over to Jen's place (five houses down). While on the phone, the twins said, "Look at our cat." She told the boys in Russian, "That is Kathryn's cat." She said it three times. They looked at her and said, "No, it is ours. We are sure of it." Apparently the poor cat is just wandering, and unknowingly, he is part of the game of finders keepers.

No packages this week and that brought up a question of sending them to a new address. Jen said that it doesn't matter which address we use at this point, because the main delivery goes off of the village and sits at the post office. So her packages don't really need a street address. But we will get the new address as soon as we know it.

Then we got cut off and couldn't get the connection back. Hate to end that way, but we had discussed the most important issues. We need to trust that this is the right decision for Jen. Dealing with a third-world country is hard enough without having health issues or dealing with personalities. So pray for her big step to be a good one and a part of the plan God has for her.

Love,

Karen

July 25, 2005

We were very anxious to hear from Jen this week how finding a new place is going. Her director at work has been very helpful and there are two possibilities. One is a one-room apartment right next door to her work. Another is a three-room apartment right next to Ian's school. Here is the comparison: the one-room place is cheaper and already has bars on the windows (a Peace Corps rule) but loses electricity frequently. The three-room apartment is more expensive and in an affluent neighborhood, with more people around. The utilities are much more reliable, but the window doesn't have bars. Jen will have to pay upfront to put them in, though the Peace Corps will eventually pay her back. No one knows how to contact the landlord, so if Jen and her director want to look at it, they'll have to break into the place, and as Gulnara says, "That would pretty much mean you would agree to take it." There also is the issue of them thinking they will be paid in American money, but she would be paying in som. She may also have to purchase some appliances. Don't know where she would get them, and why someone already living there wouldn't have had them, unless they took them with them. So the search continues and her move won't be by the first of the month, as they had hoped.

In the meantime, Venera has changed her tune and become upset with the whole deal and even called Jen's director twice to complain. Basically, she worries about what are people going to think of her. Jen says she can understand, because she has to live and work in this village, whereas Jen will be leaving in a year. Venera is worried that people will think she was cruel to Jen and refused to feed her the whole time she was there. She is worried people will think she has gone crazy because she doesn't have a husband. Even though this is the first volunteer she has had, people might judge her because she didn't have her for the whole time.

The frustrating part for Jen is that staying with Venera and the children can be so wonderful at times. There have been many good and close times between her and Venera, but now they avoid each other. Venera has never mentioned the lack of money that Jen's moving out will entail, but Jen says sometimes people portray themselves as a lot poorer than they really are. As a matter of fact, Jen said that they tore down an old shed and are adding on to their summer kitchen and Jen heard Venera talking to someone about building a *banya*. Jen said, "Sure, when I'm leaving."

Jen told us that Venera doesn't know how lucky she has had it with the type of volunteer Jen is. She could have been stuck with a partier, or a drinker who had people over all the time. The village is full of notorious gossipers (a hobby) and they obviously have more clout than an American. Some of the rumors even have Ian and Jen as secretly married. But regardless, Jen sounds upbeat and has a good attitude. She says, in the bigger picture when all the dust settles and she comes back to visit and everyone is happy, the truth will be known, but it sure is crazy in the meantime. She told Kathryn that this hasn't affected her wanting to stay and finish the work she started. She has a plan for her life and just wants to make the last half of her time there better. And she will.

Some great news is that Jen received both boxes that Grandma and Grandpa sent two months ago! Surprisingly, they came together on the same day. She said she hadn't had the kind of snack foods they included in a long time, so she's almost eaten half the food. She really appreciated the marshmallows and Hershey bars on her birthday. Ian and Kathryn are going to take her by the river and they're going to have a bonfire and make s'mores! We have planned to call her Tuesday morning instead of Monday in order to talk to her on her big day, and will sing "Happy Birthday" to her like Grandma usually does.

The last part of our conversation was spent on the specifics of her trip home at Christmas. Our friends that run a travel agency are anxious to start planning the tickets, so it was fun to exchange ideas back and forth with her. She plans on taking thirty days off, but about five days will be spent traveling: two days to America and three days to get back. She wants to get home before St. Mary's University is out for the holidays, so she can visit staff, so we are thinking December 15th to January 15th. The conversation truly felt like "Christmas in July!"

As serious as our conversation was about her move, I got her to laugh when I told her that Grandma and Grandpa brought us veggies from the garden and had fun in the pool yesterday. She really laughed when I said, "I gave Grandpa a haircut and Heidi gave Dad a haircut at the same time, but they refused to face each other in the kitchen, so they were sitting in a line, like a choo-choo train." But the loudest laugh came when I told her that Grandma gave us all a surprise by modeling her old bathing suit and swim cap, because Dan said he wouldn't let her in the pool unless she wore the suit with the little skirt. It's the same suit she had when they came out to California to see us twenty-seven years ago!

Jen and I shared the shock that not only did it still FIT her, she actually still HAD it! We called her Esther Williams all day.

Jen enjoys these kinds of stories, even the boring ones, but the neat thing is that I can tell her giggles are a reaction to really being able to picture everything in her mind. I guess that's the next best thing to being there. She told us that on one of her bad days, with the stress of all this change, she read a book about a missionary who was in Afghanistan and he said, "If God calls and leads you somewhere, he will provide for you to be there." So that has been the focus in her prayers and she said she believes it will be true. I told her that I hadn't thought or prayed so much for her since she left as I did this last week. She said, "Thanks, Mom. The housing will fall into place; just pray for me to deal with all of the other stuff." I know we all will.

Love,

Karen

August 2, 2005

We were all perched, ready to sing "Happy Birthday," but couldn't get through to Jen. I thought, "No, Kyrgyzstan... not on this day," so we called Kathryn's house in desperation. I was pleasantly surprised when Kathryn answered! I told her my trouble and she said, "I'll run down there and you call back here in five minutes." So we did. We sang, laughed, and I could hear her smile over the phone. I asked how her day went and she said, "Great!" Kathryn had come over early, singing to her, then took her to her place, and made her a pancake breakfast. The ladies at her work gave her a tea set and Kathryn hand-stitched a pillow that Jen said was amazing. She also loved getting a package from the Dixons with all the wonderful freeze-dried food and a birthday card from Chad and Lee Ann and Father Larry. Then she got a call saying she needs to go to Bishkek tomorrow in preparation for her Bulgaria trip and to talk more about moving at Peace Corps headquarters. Just after hanging up, she said, "Happy Birthday to ME!" So she will be able to get to the Internet café and maybe get more progress on her move.

There was a possibility of her renting a house from people who were trying to sell it but couldn't, but that fell through. Turns out the lady selling it is a bit weird anyway, so maybe it's okay. They are down to the one-room unit by Ian's school, but she is worried that the Peace Corps wouldn't pay for all the safety precautions in a timely manner. Dan said to tell them to ship him over and he will have bars welded on in a hurry. She saw this apartment and it isn't in the best condition. The oven has been pulled out of the wall. The pipes are there, but no unit. So it doesn't have a real kitchen, but could be fixed up.

The limbo of still living with Venera's family is difficult for Jen. The kids seem fine, but Venera called Jen's director and said she understands everything now, but yet doesn't really talk to Jen. She did make a birthday dinner for her on Sunday. Jen was having stomach problems, so she told her that she wouldn't be able to eat much and Venera said, "But I am making this, this, and this." Jen thought, "As if that would make my diarrhea go away!" So they ate and then Venera offered Jen a beer. Jen said, "No, I don't drink." Venera said, "I would like to have a beer with you." Jen told her no again and got angry, because she figured this was all for show so she could say how she made the dinner and shared a drink, therefore she is a good host mother. But Jen said to herself, "I'm not playing the game."

They are almost done building a *banya* in their backyard, in addition to adding on to the summer kitchen. Jen said, "Sure, just when I have been bucket bathing for eight months and am leaving." I think things are basically okay, but Jen knows it will be best for her to be on her own. I did ask if she wanted me to send the pictures that she'd asked me to copy off her disc for Venera. She thought a bit and then said, "Yeah, go ahead." Maybe she will use it as a going-away gift.

Jen was excited to tell us that her Partnership Program was approved and is online. She will email specifics on where to go on the Peace Corps website for information about the multipurpose business center she is creating.

As I got ready to hand over the phone, Jen said that it had been a cloudy day but just got sunny, so she was looking forward to her trip to the river with Ian and Kathryn for their bonfire party. She got to hear all of our voices this time and as I left for work, Dominic was talking; hearing them congratulate each other on their birthdays and comparing their days made me smile all the way to work. They might be two worlds apart, but their special days will always be two days apart.

Continue the prayers for her move. Thanks.

Love,

Karen

August 3, 2005

Hello. Just writing during a trip to Bishkek to let you know that the partnership grant I wrote with my director has been approved and is currently on the Web. I am asking for your help in raising the funds to renovate a previously bought apartment so my host organization, History Sources, can use it for education and business purposes. Having an adequate facility to teach girls how to sew and women how to dye wool naturally and then create traditional handicrafts will be a great asset to the productivity of History Sources. It will also be a great asset to the women in the village, many of whom do not have any education or skills that would help introduce them into the workforce.

If you would like to donate, the site walks you through the process. There are also mailing addresses, email contacts, and a phone number for you to get more information about my project specifically or about the process in general. Only with your help can this goal be actualized. If you cannot donate at this time but know of others who can, please pass this information on. I greatly appreciate your help and the women of History Sources excitedly anticipate your response.

Peace,

Jenny

August 8, 2005

It was good to hear Jen's voice, since we won't be able to call next Monday because of her travel to Bulgaria. It seemed we talked an extra long time to make up for it, but really, it was to help her sort out her moving situation. It's still in limbo, and even though Jen knows things don't progress too quickly, she finds it frustrating. She keeps to herself, and her room is her refuge. But that isn't the way to go, either. When things were getting tense, Jen tried to talk to Venera, but she ended up being offensive and said some mean things. That is what prompted Jen to pursue moving.

Jen's Peace Corps program manager (not her director/boss at work) called her. She wasn't as empathetic as the medical Peace Corps person had been. She seemed more interested in creating peace between cultures than the health struggles Jen has had. She did talk to Venera and told her she needs to apologize to Jennifer and then go on from there. Well, Venera was only willing to "go on from there." That isn't going over so well with Jen, and she admits she is being stubborn, but wonders why she has to be the adult. She wants an apology, because she doesn't want to just pretend everything is okay. But we told her that's how it is in America, not there, and reminded her that she's a visitor. I told her, "The bottom line is that you need to feel less tense in the home until you move. So maybe you can budge a bit—for YOUR sake. Let Venera know that you were hurt by her comments" [we never asked Jen what they were; we figured she would tell us if she wanted to] "and wish things could be better, like they had been."

I don't want to diminish what she's going through, but I told her that she needs to take care of herself and if that means bending a bit, then that is what she needs to do. I could tell she was listening, though she said that she and Venera never had time alone and she didn't want to talk around the kids. But then she came up with the idea of writing her a note right before she leaves on Saturday, stating that her feelings were hurt, and then expressing hope that things will be better when she returns from Bulgaria. So that is her plan. And she knows things will be great when she visits them down the line and holds on to that positive note. We knew there would be hardships and I asked if this was going to taint her experience and she said "No, nor has it gotten me to the point of wanting to throw in the towel and come home." That was good to hear.

Jen leaves on Saturday to travel to Bishkek. She flies out Sunday and goes through Turkey. She has a seven-hour layover, but Turkish Air provides a hotel voucher and meal ticket. She said it will be great, because she can have a regular shower and soft bed. And the same will happen on the way back. Luckily, she will get home in time for Ian's birthday on Saturday. Kathryn and Jen have been arranging his party for three months and ordered some felt slippers that her ladies will sew. The tricky part was measuring his shoes when he wasn't looking! But now it is two weeks before and the ladies haven't started. She says they have the strangest mentality. They put things off until the last minute, and then they stay up late into the morning to finish projects. Even when there's a deadline, if someone comes into the office to chat, they stop everything and talk for two hours, or until the visitor chooses to leave. Jen thinks that friendships are of great value, but she usually says, "Hey, get your work done and then visit." Again, it's an American thing. She told Kathryn to hound them while she's gone to get the slippers done.

We told Jen that Peter Jennings died and she said a big "Oh, noooooo," as if he was a close personal friend. Maybe it's just because he is a part of home. We told her about our parish festival, Dominic's fishing trip in Door County, and Heidi's party for her upcoming graduation from Aveda. We asked her what language they speak in Bulgaria and she said, "Let's ask Grandpa; he can look it up in his atlas," but she said she knows it isn't Russian, although it has a strong Turkish influence. There will be interpreters at the seminar addressing the different languages present. She got an email giving hotel and food information for those who want to arrive early or stay later to take in the sights. The hotel is on a mountain and they plan to go on a hike after the sessions on Monday and Tuesday. They will also go into Sofia for an outing and to eat. Jen doesn't know if they will have access to the Internet, but she will on her way there and back in Bishkek and Talas.

We talked about her plans to travel home and she told us that when the VanHecke's travel agency checks things out, she could either fly out of Bishkek or Almaty, Kazakhstan. It amounts to about the same travel distance, but Almaty has more frequent flights. So we will see what options they come up with, and planning it now makes it seem closer. Jen got her final package of dehydrated food from the Dixons. She got two padded envelopes on July 29th, then a box of food on her birthday, and now one more padded envelope. It has been a godsend because of the situation of limited meals with the family.

We asked if there was anything else she needed and she said, "Yeah. Could you send me 'backs' to my earrings?" I thought she said, "Tacks to use as earrings?" Unfortunately, I don't think it was the connection—it was my ears. Before I divulged the mix-up, she said, "I keep losing them and there is no place to get those metal backs." The light bulb finally went on over my head and I told her, "No problem; they will be easy to send." You can be in a third-world country, but a girl has to be a girl and look pretty. We forgot to tell her that we filled in our church raffle ticket book with only her name. Hey... you don't have to be present to win! The two-thousand-dollar first-prize would have been our way to visit her, but for now we won't complain and will look forward to our Christmas gift of her in December.

Pray for Jen's safe travel to another country.

Love,

Karen

August 13, 2005

In about eight hours I'll be eating airline food... I can't wait! Summer has turned out to be the season for camps as well as parental visits. However, the camps in Talas have abounded lately, and to my estimation have been a great success. First, Kathryn held an art camp in our village for two weeks at the end of July. Kids from both of the schools came for afternoon sessions every day and studied the color wheel, perspective, made papier-mâché creatures, created collages, painted to music, etc. Ian and I helped out frequently, and volunteers from the oblast, even Bishkek, came in to help as well. The conclusion of the camp was a gallery showing of all the students' works throughout the week. Parents and family were invited and prizes were given for the best work in each project, as well as overall ability in each age group.

The second camp in our oblast was organized by the three K-11s. The focus of the one-week daily camp was respect. Each day a new topic was tackled, such as gender roles, equality, and ecology. Every day consisted of an intellectual and challenging part, as well as a fun but educational part. For example, the ecology day (respect for the earth) included a scavenger hunt, which had the students not only looking for "nature" items, but picking up trash as well. I was only able to help on the last day, but the kids said repeatedly that they had a great week. The smiles, hugs, well wishes, and exchanges of phones numbers and email addresses were evidence of a camp well done!

"Turning twenty-three... a milestone to remember, just like thirty-seven and fifty-four!" The above quote is from a volunteer in the oblast (for all you fellow volunteers... of course it was Willie!), wishing me a memorable twenty-third birthday in the Kyrgyz Republic. It was a good one, and as I told another volunteer recently, "You know, I've had worse birthdays in the States. So this year just determined for me that it's all about who you are with, what you are doing, and not necessarily about where you are." My birthday celebration actually started on July 30th during a visit to Taraz, when Kathryn and Ian treated me to lunch at the nice Georgian restaurant that we frequent. My host mother also made me an early birthday meal.

Currently men are working morning to night, every day of the week, on building an outdoor kitchen and *banya* in our backyard. This is also adjacent to the current kitchen, so Venera wanted to have dinner the Sunday before the actual day, since the workers did not show up. We had *plov*, my favorite! And a delicious cake that she makes. On my actual day, Kathryn pranced into my room singing "Happy Birthday" and invited me to her house for a pancake breakfast. As custom, the person celebrating the birthday brings lunch to the office. So I made some pasta salad, bought some bread, pop, and watermelon, and brought a box of chocolates along as dessert. The women filed into my office not long after I arrived and congratulated me with roses and kisses. My favorite coworker, Baktigul, came into the office kitchen while I was slicing watermelon to give me a nice grandmotherly hug (in lieu of the traditional hand-hold and peck on both cheeks) and then proceeded to give me twenty-three celebratory pulls on my ear. I told her that in America we give spankings, so I liked this tradition a little better!

Lunch was enjoyable, with toasting (traditional at any Kyrgyz party—and for once I didn't have to make a toast, since I was the guest of honor!), and the women gave me a tea set. After work, I came home to talk to my American family. It was good to talk to everyone and great to hear about how my birthday buddy (Dominic) celebrated his twenty-first birthday just two days before mine. Once the conversation was done, Kathryn, Ian, and I headed to the river where we had a bonfire and made s'mores (courtesy of a package from Grandma and Grandpa!). My birthday candle was placed in a s'more; however, with the wind, I didn't need to blow the flame out myself. All in all, it was a great birthday in Kyrgyzstan.

About three weeks ago, I received a phone call from my program manager's assistant, Tahmina, who wanted to tell me that Peace Corps Bulgaria would host a conference on human trafficking (Aug. 15th to 16th). I don't have easy Internet access, so she wanted me to know that members of the newly formed Gender and Development Committee, of which I am one and of which she is the supervisor, were invited to submit letters of interest for this conference via email. Staff at local HQ would then decide who would attend the conference with Tahmina. I wrote a letter stating why I thought I was a good candidate for the conference (human trafficking is a problem that finds its root in severely unequal gender roles, which I see on a daily basis through my primary assignment and secondary project) and then faxed it to the office, since the deadline was only three days later.

Unfortunately, there were problems with the fax and I found out that HQ did not have the correct number for my office once it was too late to do anything. By the weekend, I decided that I wasn't going because it was unlikely that they had received the fax, and even if they did, they were unable to get a hold of me, due to the incorrect number. The following Monday, I received a call from my program manager for separate reasons, and she congratulated me. When I asked her why, she said it was because I was chosen for the conference; she was surprised I hadn't been contacted already. The Peace Corps is paying for all expenses, and in preparation for the conference, I made the trek to Bishkek last week. I completed some paperwork for the conference and met with an organization that provides shelter and rehabilitation services for Kyrgyz citizens who are victims of trafficking. I also met separately with a volunteer who works in this same area, to pick her brain about the issue and her views as a volunteer. I came back to the village with a folder of statistics and information that I need to take to heart before my departure on the 14th.

Looking over my distribution emails made me realize that I haven't mentioned much about my host family. While living with my family has been an overall good experience, it has been much like a roller coaster. After a confrontation with my host mother this winter, I thought we had everything straightened out and that, from that point on, we would both communicate openly with each other. But the agreement to maintain open lines of communication did not last long. While there are many stories and details I could get into, I will just say that overall, living with my host mother soon became very stressful for me. Often other volunteers would tell me to move out, that my living situation would affect my experience as a volunteer greatly. Other volunteers even got caught in between many misunderstandings and hostile situations. Finally, with Kathryn's insistence, I consulted with Peace Corps staff, who thought it would be best for me to move.

After three unsuccessful weeks of looking with my director, the Talas TEFL manager came out and, within an hour, had found a place for me. In Kyrgyzstan, many families have compounds where there is a main courtyard and a few smaller buildings besides the house. My new house is located in a compound, where I have a small house consisting of one room and a kitchen. I am still in the setting-up process as I write this. I moved on Wednesday and have been working on making the place my home. I look forward to being able to cook my own meals and having the privacy of an apartment while also having the immediate support of a family if I have a problem or emergency. Hopefully, this will work out better than my last situation.

The only immediate negative side of moving has been being far from the center and far from both Ian and Kathryn, whose homes are on the other side of the village. Realistically it's not like I was moved to another village; it's maybe a twenty-minute walk to Kathryn's, and thirty minutes to Ian's. But not being able to stop by Kathryn's on the way back from work, or on the way to a nearby store will take a little adjusting.

Off to Bulgaria I go! I can't wait to pass on the details once I return.

Much love,

Jenny

CHAPTER 15

Bulgaria Bound

She knew she was meant to be there when they passed out a kit entitled *The Quest for Success; Preparing Our Students to Think Critically about Opportunities at Home and Abroad.* It will help her assist students in making educated decisions about their futures and provide valuable information about how community leaders and other concerned adults can support the youth as well.

August 22, 2005

It was so nice hearing Jen's voice, and it was amazing to think that she had been to another country since the last time we talked. Now that she's back, she's dealing with the transition of living alone. But that has never bothered Jen; we think it was one of the attractions to being an RA in college—no roommate! The hardest part is being forty minutes (walking) from Kathryn and Ian. And since it is not safe to walk that distance at night, they will have to rearrange their visiting times.

The first thing we asked about her place was if there was a *banya* or pit toilet near. She said they have a *banya*, but the mother (I forgot to ask her name) said it isn't working right and needs some repair. That could take a while, being in Kyrgyzstan, but Jen knows she can always *banya* at Kathryn's house until it is running. There is a pit toilet. Jen said that it looks as if it might fall over at any minute, but it is not as bad as the one at her work, so she's happy. But she is considering getting a chamber pot for her room. She figures that when you live alone, you can do what you want (with your pee), and it sure will be nice come winter.

As far as a phone goes, Jen is buying a cell phone from another volunteer. Unfortunately, it is Sadie, who has decided to go home. She is the one who was in southern Kyrgyzstan and then sent to Talas. She had to be sent to Thailand to have her wisdom tooth out, and while she was gone, she decided that she wasn't happy, that she had given it a chance, and that she needs to say good-bye. So Jen is buying her cell phone, which is of good quality and reception. She will buy a card that will give her service as she goes along. So she will have a phone wherever she goes and can now call us. SO much easier. It's a whole new world. We are going to try her new number next Monday.

Her director at her work thinks it's a good idea to have a cell phone for safety as well and will be coming to see her place and arrange a contract with the family. She also said that she will contact the police to let them know that a volunteer is now living there. Jen said her bedroom is a shambles because she hasn't gotten the dresser they promised her. It is one of those things that requires patience. When Jen asks, the landlady says, "Oh, yes; tomorrow." About three tomorrows go by and then when Jen asks again, she says, "Oh, my stomach hurts. Maybe tomorrow." But Jen knows this is normal and it will eventually happen, because she got all the other furnishings she was promised.

Jen's trip to Bulgaria was a wonderful experience. She said the flight over was a bit tough because they left at 3:00 a.m. from Bishkek and she had just had a hamburger around 1:00 a.m., so she really didn't sleep beforehand. Whether it was motion sickness or the meat, she's not sure, but Jen got sick to her stomach on the plane. She then felt better, but had to deal with the lag of losing three hours when they landed. In Istanbul, Jen was able to visit the Blue Mosque and Obelisk before heading back to the hotel. She had something light to eat and then rested in her room. She slept for four hours and then caught the one-hour flight to Sofia. Upon arrival, Jen was amazed by how so many people knew English. It seemed so European, as opposed to a third-world country. Jen found out that Bulgaria was two years away from joining the European Union and would have the Euro. There were two volunteers from Bulgaria who picked up Jen and the Kazakh volunteer, paid for the taxi, helped them exchange their money, and took them to the hotel.

In Sofia, she saw every fast food imaginable, and the odd thing was, so many Dr. Scholl's stores! I guess it's a perk for foreigners who are touring with achy feet? There was also advertising for American rock groups like Korn. She felt like she was in a different world. The place where they had the conference was a ski resort with very nice accommodations and most of the seminar was in English. It was filled with very positive and uplifting information: no graphic films on the evils of sex slavery or human trafficking. They referred more to "safe migration," because the bulk of the problem involves people who are extremely oppressed, who are trying to leave their countries, and who are willing to do anything, including selling their bodies or even body parts. People might be asked to sell their child's kidney in order to get access out, only to have the people sell it on the black market and leave the family high and dry.

The seminar gave out information kits to use with influential people in villages, as well as schools. It is to teach them about the dangers of empty promises. There is advertising saying, "Come to Germany... no passport needed." Locals need to be told not to believe these offers and that they ALWAYS need to have a passport whenever traveling—something is definitely wrong with any ad that says otherwise. So many get lured into a possibility of hope, only to have it not be at all what they had thought or been promised. Jen feels good about using this kit and providing safe guidance for those in her small village.

It was funny to hear how the volunteers living in the city of Sofia were so interested to hear about other volunteers' daily lives. They were horrified at the conditions that the others lived with, because they all have the usual modern conveniences of indoor plumbing, hot running water, showers, flush toilets, etc. They admitted that at times they wonder why they are needed there, especially when the country is so close to its European transformation. I guess I'd like to think that if I had to be away from my daughter, it should be for a good reason. Jen said something they all agreed with: "Any place that has a McDonald's, Dunkin' Donuts, or Kentucky Fried Chicken does not need the Peace Corps." Jen thought having access to fast food was nice, but what she ate was hard for her system to take, especially in a crash course of just three days. But it was a taste of home.

Jen got back in time to help celebrate Ian's birthday, though the slippers she and Kathryn ordered barely got done in time. Even though they were a bright green, he loved them. They felt bad, because he looked like an elf, but he reassured them that he liked them, despite the color. Erich and Willie's gift was a VCR tape with recorded baseball and basketball games from home. Even though they were old, the guys had a blast sitting around watching the games. Then they went to the river, since it had been such a hit for Jen's birthday.

Jen is planning on going to the bazaar this weekend, so she will be at the Internet site. She did get Heidi's Aveda graduation announcement, which made good time. I told Jen that I had a few tears at Mass that morning, thinking that she wouldn't be there to share in this landmark. She said, "It's just a taste of how it will be when I miss Dominic's college graduation." To avoid getting choked up, I told Jen that at 6:30 a.m. that morning, the temperature had been the same as my age! She said that she's so used to the heat that when they had cooler temps, she didn't notice, but she knows fall is around the corner, just as it is for us. After Heidi talked to Jen, I finished our call on my drive to work. She asked if I could take a note, even though I was driving. I said "Oh, sure. Let me find my pen." I was digging here, checking there with no luck, even though there were three pens in the van last week. All of my noises of struggle and saying "Hold on... hold on," prompted her to say "%^$#**" and "$%#@" in Russian. I said, "What does that mean?" She said, "My God, my God." I had a good laugh at that one, and it must have helped, because the van didn't go off the road, I found the pen, and was able to pull over and take notes. We got disconnected, but in my heart I wished "My God, my God" back to her.

Love,

Karen

August 27, 2005

I had the opportunity to attend the "Trafficking in Persons" conference held in Sofia, Bulgaria. Volunteers and staff from Albania,
Macedonia, Moldova, Mongolia, Kazakhstan, and Kyrgyzstan
were able to attend. I, along with Tahmina Maralbaeva, represented the Kyrgyz Republic. I definitely had to adjust back after
being in first-world settings for only a week. The trip overall was a
great success, the seminar was extremely practical, and my little
"vacation" time during layovers in Istanbul was an unexpected and
pleasant surprise. The following is part of the article that I wrote for
our volunteer newsletter, the "Teahouse." I think it will give you the
bare bones of what the TIP situation is like in the world.

According to the U.S. State Department, Trafficking in Persons
(TIP) is defined as, "modern-day slavery, involving victims who are
forced, defrauded, or coerced into labor or sexual exploitation."
Annually about 600,000 to 800,000 people, mostly women and
children, are trafficked across national borders. The profit from
labor or sexual slavery funds organized crime and the growth of
TIP. In the *Trafficking in Persons Report*, the Department of State
assesses governmental response in each country with a significant
number of victims.

Two years ago, volunteers in Bulgaria recognized the prev-
alence of trafficking in their country and decided to address the
problem as best they could at the grassroots level. Consequently,
a TIP committee was organized through volunteer initiative. With
the support of their administrative and programming staff, the committee compiled a TIP kit for each volunteer to use in either classroom or seminar settings. The kit, entitled *The Quest for Success;
Preparing Our Students to Think Critically about Opportunities at
Home and Abroad*, is meant to assist students in making educated
decisions about their future, and show how community leaders and
other concerned adults can support youth.

During the conference, the three "Ps" of trafficking were discussed: prevention, prosecution, and protection. As volunteers, we
are not involved with prosecution, and protection (rehabilitation)
is the focus of only a handful of volunteers who work in women's

crisis centers or shelters (such as Sezim in Bishkek). However, prevention is the area in which all volunteers are able to participate. Mainly through education, in the classroom or through seminars, volunteers are able to educate HCN (host country nationals), especially at-risk groups such as girls, the impoverished, and the unemployed. Some simple things that volunteers can do are: teaching girls about self-esteem and encouraging confidence, as well as discussing respect with boys in the classroom and through clubs, camps, and casual social interactions. Network NGOs who work in the area of TIP, through volunteers who work with such organizations, help HCN recognize viable skills they can use to gain legal employment. Also, volunteers can teach basic computer, sewing, and secretarial skills through clubs or seminars. Donating clothes and toiletries to women's shelters/crisis centers at a COS (close of service) is an easy and helpful thing that volunteers can do, because victims of trafficking return from destination countries with nothing in their possession.

The Bulgarian volunteers did a great job making the conference applicable to all countries and interests. There were breakout sessions in which we were able to choose one of three topics that we would like to learn more about: for example, ways in which to address TIP in the classroom, how to involve men in solving the problem, and learning more about the at-risk groups. Very quickly I, along with the volunteers from Kazakhstan and Mongolia, realized that the issues facing Asian countries are at times more specific to the "culture of shame" and cultural norms. We are thinking of hosting an Asia/Central Asia conference in a year to address the specific issue of how to address TIP specifically without addressing the "tradition" of bride kidnapping and widespread gender inequalities.

On the lighter side of the trip, I was able to experience Bulgarian culture, with traditional folk music and dancing, "fire dancing" or walking on coals, and traditional food. Like I said, I had an unexpected layover in Turkey. I knew I would be flying through Istanbul, but did not realize that I would be buying a visa and staying at a hotel courtesy of the airline. Although jet lag and some stomach problems prevented me from seeing much of Istanbul during the first layover, the second overnight layover gave me ample time to see the sights. I was just a short tram ride from the area of Istanbul that is ripe with historical sites, like the Blue Mosque, the Grand Bazaar, the Basilica Cistern, the Aya Sofia, and many more. I was impressed with the amount and level of English spoken, as well as the hospitality I was shown by complete strangers. I must have had a tattoo on my forehead that said, "Talk to me, I'm an American!" because that's what everyone said when they approached me: "You must be an American."

Take care,

Jenny

August 29, 2005

We called Jen at Kathryn's house. When we had the automatic half-hour disconnect, we called back on her cell phone. The reception was great. She is planning on having it with her during the day but not on. She will keep it on in the evenings, so anyone that would like to call around 8:00 a.m. our time can reach her at 7:00 p.m. her time. No need to set up a time that way. Welcome back to the land of normal!

Her place is slowly taking shape and she has most of what the new mother promised. She still needs a worktable for the kitchen, but the mother gave her rugs, a dresser for the bedroom, and a dresser for the kitchen storage. Her name is Altynai, which in Russian means "gold." The eleven-year-old boy is Nursultan and he is in boarding school because Altynai can't seem to discipline him enough. And the five-year-old girl is Asel. We asked if she was going to get the mandatory window bars, but she said they're only necessary if a volunteer is in an apartment and living on the first floor. They're not needed if you're associated with a compound or there's a house nearby. But then she heard that the lady was planning on having them installed at her place and the Peace Corps stepped in and said, "Okay, but they will be put on your volunteer's cottage first." I think they have a good idea of the pace of things around there. So although not required, she is getting them because the new family wants them, too.

I asked Jen if the 1,000 som was a lot to be paying for rent and she said, "For the summer it is, but come winter time, it would be very inexpensive, because the coal alone could cost that." Some people fluctuate their rent, but Jen said she is keeping it the same. Besides, come October, the Peace Corps will be paying for all housing expenses. She found out it was approved last week. That means more money in her pocket and so she will only be paying for one and a half months.

She is sending us a package that has three CDs of pictures! It will have photos of Bulgaria and Turkey. Can't wait. She mailed it in Talas, because she can trust it going out better there. She says they actually weigh it and tell her how much and put the stamps on. In Pokrovka, the ladies shake it and say, "Um, about fifty som." She only got one package and that was from us. It had hair accessories she is going to use with her GenGirls and the face cream and pictures for Venera. Jen has visited her once and gave her some tea she got in Turkey, but it was very uncomfortable. The boys were not interested and Jen said that Venera seemed fake in her attempts to be welcoming.

But Jen's Aisalkyn greeted her with love and Jen gave her a "zerbit" on the cheek, and she gave one right back to Jen. I told her that it may get better as time goes on, and if not, it doesn't matter, because she doesn't have to tolerate it anymore. She talked about how relaxed she is now when she eats. She doesn't worry about what food there will be, or if it will taste good enough to eat so that she isn't hungry an hour later. She can eat as she wants, always knowing what she is having and that she won't be critiqued for how she eats or how much. So it is an American cottage.

Jen found out that her groups of close friends from college are planning a camping trip together. She thought that was so cute until she heard some complaining about sleeping on an air mattress and not being able to shower for two days. Her response was "Oh, please!" She said that no matter what rustic conditions the volunteers have, they usually find themselves thinking of other volunteers that have it worse, not how it is better back home. Must be a good coping skill, because when they discuss how the volunteers in Africa have to live in mud huts, their place suddenly becomes a palace.

Jen still talked about her travels to Bulgaria. She told us that when she was in the Turkey airport, she saw a girl drinking Gloria Jean's coffee and reading an Istanbul tour book. She had to be an American. But Jen wasn't feeling well, so she didn't approach her. After they boarded, they ended up sitting next to each other, and she asked Jen, "Are you American?" Jen said, "It's funny how we can pick each other out of a crowd. Yes. Are you going to the trafficking conference?" She said, "Yes!" She was the representative from Kazakhstan and it made for wonderful conversation while flying.

Jen gave us a wish list and it mostly involves kitchen utensils that don't exist in Kyrgyz cooking, like a muffin tin. She wants to make muffins, because all they have is flat bread. Bazaars don't offer much in American appliances. But they did have hamsters! She got to thinking how nice it would be to have a pet. He could live in her house, she reasoned, but then she started to think of how cold it gets in the winter and how he might get too hot next to her heater.

Her yearning was totally resolved over the next few days, and it started with a trip to the toilet at night. There in the path was a small hedgehog. Her flashlight kept her from stepping on him. It was no big deal, but not something that would happen to her in Chaska. A few days later, when she came home from work, there was a box in her sink with two hedgehogs in it! Again, not something that happens in Chaska. She has no idea where they came from, but I was upset that they got into her house. She said, "Mom, the sink is outside! Then, in winter, I move it inside." (Duh, Karen... it's not hooked up to pipes and plumbing.) She thinks some kids were playing with them during the day and left them there. She said she touched one, and it was not soft and cuddly like a hamster! The next day they were gone, box and all. The differences between home and there that she encounters on a daily basis must be mind-boggling.

Love,

Karen

September 6, 2005

Hope you all had a nice Labor Day weekend. We called Jen's cell phone directly and got through on the first ring. Kind of cool. She shared with us that on Saturday they got together with the volunteers in Kirovka, and the boys played Frisbee golf. Now granted, it is quite hilly by the reservoir, and their markers are rocks, but they played eighteen rounds and made it as close to their course back home as possible.

She also helped Ian set up his new classroom. School started last week, but most kids haven't shown up yet. That's due to a combination of harvest still happening (they're needed in the fields), and the fact that they don't care for the boring review that happens the first couple of days. The teachers still never know which group of kids they will have or when, so they have to prepare their lessons for the advanced, medium, and extra-help class. It's frustrating, but they're more used to it.

I asked how her hedgehog friends are doing and she said it's the weirdest thing, because Ian was going to the bathroom at night and also ran into one. He took a picture of it and said, "Ironically, it was in a hedge!" The locals are saying they have never seen so many as this year. I asked Jen if they were blaming the Americans for bringing them and she said, "No." There is actually a Kyrgyz word for *hedgehog*, so they've had them before and don't think the volunteers are making up stories of monster sightings on the way to the bathroom.

Jen told us about another nighttime happening. One night Jen heard male voices outside, only to find her landlord talking to some men. All of a sudden, she didn't want to go outside to the bathroom. If a woman makes any eye contact with a man, it is interpreted as her wanting to visit and go to bed with him. I guess it is the standard way of thinking, given what they see on TV. So Jen cut the top off of a jug and is using that for her nighttime bathroom needs. The hedgehog will miss her, but better to be safe than sorry.

I talked to Jen about having her cell phone on in the mornings while getting ready for work, so people can call her at around 9:00 or 10:00 p.m. our time. She agreed, but said if they can't get through, they should keep calling, as she may be outside or washing up. She only has a ten-minute walk to work now, so she has more time at home in the mornings. Jen will be going to the Internet café this Saturday, so she'll be able to get emails!

Unfortunately, she didn't get any packages since we last talked. I wondered if it was her change of address and she said that the street address really doesn't mean anything, since she picks up all of her mail and deliveries, and Ian even mailed some things to her from Turkey and it got there without a street address.

When I told her about Hurricane Katrina, she said she had heard about it, but only because someone was watching the BBC and stumbled across the story. I'm sure the Peace Corps sent emails, but she hasn't seen them yet. She said it made her sad watching the news coverage, because she felt as if there suddenly was a third-world country within the United States, with all the desperate people who are going without.

She will be getting bars on her windows soon and her landlord cleaned out the *banya*. Guess it was a storage bin for a while. So how have they been showering? I didn't want to ask. Probably the river. They just got a hot stretch of weather and people aren't willing to heat the *banya* for bathing, so it's just cold water. Jen said she heats water in a bucket and then takes it in there to bathe. Dan asked about the family that lives in the big house. She really doesn't see them too much, which is okay, but one night a black cat was jumping by her window, trying to get in. Jennifer screamed a couple of times, and the mother came running to the cottage and said in Russian, "Jennifer, Jennifer are you okay?" Jen told her that a cat had scared her, but it was reassuring to know that if there's any trouble, she is right there, ready to help.

Jen made another trip to visit Venera and met her sister walking there as well. So they chatted and that set the pace for the visit. She gave Venera the pictures of the kids we made and some face cream. It was the Kyrgyz Independence Day, so Jen didn't have to work. Jen said she had to be overly friendly, but it made for a better visit. Venera showed her the new construction of the *banya*, summer kitchen, and fence. She told Jen she has to use the *banya* next time she visits, and even gave her some onions, peppers, and tomatoes out of her garden. Maybe time does heal all wounds. But when she started yelling at the workers in the backyard and then the boys joined in, Jen thought, "Okay, it's time to go!" This just reminded her of how much she loves freedom and having control over her surroundings.

We told her that there was a huge banner hanging on Main Street that said, "WELCOME, Russian Delegates!" She said "WHAAAAT?" Not sure why they were in Chaska, but I teased her that it was too bad she wasn't here to sit in on their meetings. We had a good laugh about that. As I hung up, I thought how we don't need delegates to visit. We carry a little bit of Russia around with us all the time.

Love,

Karen

September 12, 2005

Even though it was gloomy and rainy today, Jen's voice was chipper and bright. I told her the reception is so wonderful with her cell phone and she said, "That's because I'm calling from the neighbor's next door," and then gave a goofy evil laugh. Crazy girl. But there does seem to be more of a calm to her voice, since she got her own place. I asked if she is eating enough. She said "Yeah; I have three fried eggs with sautéed onions and peppers for supper." And Ian, Kathryn, and she made a bunch of pizzas, so she may have some of that later, too. They take a flat bread called "naan" that is baked in an oven(which looks like a Frisbee) and cut it thinner. They add pizza sauce they make from all the tomatoes they have, and put on onions and peppers. Guess pepperoni is out of the question.

She says she can't eat a lot in one sitting, but does get hungry again, so she eats again. She has noticed that, in general, European countries do not have the huge portions that Americans do. She said she can't stand the feeling of being so full that she wants to puke and has realized that she ate too much a lot here at home. Now she eats because she needs to. Speaking of food, I asked if she has a refrigerator, kind of knowing the answer. She said no. The big house has one she could use, but the last time she was there, it was unplugged. She says she keeps her eggs in a metal bowl that she puts against the wall and that keeps things cold.

She was desperate for entertainment on Saturday night, so she watched the Mass tape we sent. It is not of a traditional Mass. It was a musical performance at Vatican City but was pretty bizarre. She said, "At first it was like a train wreck that you can't stop looking at, but shouldn't." There were parts that depicted certain portions of the Mass, and some parts in Latin seemed recognizable from her theology classes, but for the most part it was strange. Her plan to attend daily Mass when she comes home for Christmas was even more confirmed. What you'll do when you don't have a Blockbuster in your village.

Jen won't be going to the Internet site until early October. Dominic and Sara called and got Jen in the morning and had a nice long talk before she went to work. Jen went to Ian's school with Kathryn, because they were having a bake sale. She knew that it wouldn't be the traditional kind of bake sale we have at church. It could have anything from watermelon to meat patties (and she wouldn't want to ask what kind). Each class tries to sell items to raise money for the school. In each room she went to, kids were beckoning, "Miss Jennifer, Miss Jennifer, you buy from me." She bought something from each class. Ian suggested they see who could eat the most. She snapped back, "Are you crazy? That's like having a foot race with someone in a wheelchair." In fact, Ian devoured the food he bought before reaching the next classroom. Jen said it was kind of funny, because kids started selling their food to other kids so the whole idea of fundraising was counterproductive.

Dan likes to talk to Jen about different things. Last couple of times, they discussed what her plans might be once she returns home for good. She said she had checked into www.peacecorps.gov for a fellowship in international affairs or nonprofit management. She also mentioned lounging around for a time doing absolutely nothing, but we all know that will last about a week. We have begun getting flight arrangements for her for this Christmas from our dear friends who own Norseman Travel in town. It's exciting to start picturing us at the airport, waiting for her plane to land and her to walk toward us. Jen said her friend Melissa talked about how her mother was shaking and screaming and ended up going through a customs railing and being in an area she wasn't supposed to be. Jen told Melissa that somehow she can picture the same thing happening with her mom. Do ya think?

Our conversation ended with the realization that this Thursday marks the one-year anniversary since she left. She said that most volunteers look at their in-country date as their anniversary; hers would be on the 20th. I said, "I don't think so, missy. Your anniversary date is when you left us and we couldn't touch or kiss you anymore." She didn't argue with me. In some ways, it seems like yesterday. I clearly remember standing in a circle as a family, hugging, crying, and holding on for those last minutes. But in other ways, so much has happened. We lost family members, many people have married, and holidays have held anemptiness without her. But the saving grace is that she is happy and under God's care, and our love continues to grow, no matter how far away she is. That is what helps me as a mother to let go and be okay with her decision to serve. But the next three months can't go by fast enough.

Love,

Karen

September 19, 2005

Our call to Jen found her, Ian, and Kathryn celebrating their one-year (in-country) anniversary. Kathryn had gotten some bacon from America (don't know how that worked; maybe we could send beef!) and they had bacon and eggs for supper. Jen went into the bedroom to talk while they were finishing up the dishes. We talked about how they usually have a dinner get-together once a week and Kathryn said she felt bad that they were cooking there all the time, but discussed how nice it is to be able to cook and clean up any way they want to. Kathryn's host mom is a clean freak, and on top of that, certain things have to be done a certain Kyrgyz way. It doesn't matter that they could be done a different way, with the same result. It HAS to be done the way she wants. Jen can also remember being corrected by Venera on cutting the carrots. You would have thought she robbed a bank! So in Jen's place, they have the freedom to do whatever, however, and it is so relaxing. Then Jen said, "Hold on. Where is that music coming from?" She started to giggle and whispered to me that the door was closed, but she could hear Ian teaching Kathryn the Kyrgyz national anthem! He was singing away and telling her what the words meant. They sing it at his school every day, so that summer he had made a special attempt to really learn it, so he could sing as well. They don't sing it at Kathryn's school.

Jen sounded so chipper, even before we got to tell her the good news that we had booked her flight for Christmas! On December 16th, she arrives in Minneapolis at 1:00 p.m.! She returns on January 13th at 9:00

p.m.. She flies out of Almaty, Kazakhstan (which is about a six- to eight-hour taxi ride) the day before, then to Amsterdam, and then directly to Minneapolis! Thank you, Norseman Travel, for getting such a direct flight. On returning, she will have to get a reservation to stay the night and travel back to the village the next day. Ian and Kathryn said there is a hotel that has a service that will pick you up from the airport and bring you back to the hotel, which is a godsend, especially when traveling alone. It means no taxi drivers trying to rip off an American.

Jen told us that the post office is moving, and so one doesn't really exist for now. The good news is they are moving to an apartment building across from her work; the bad news is they didn't prepare for the interim. The old post office is locked up—they are expanding the telecom center that was inside, but it's all locked up. So she may have packages waiting for her, but doesn't know. She thinks it has to open soon, since every two weeks people go there to get their pension checks. Can you imagine a business in America, especially a government agency, shutting down for a couple of weeks, just because of moving?

They are trying to go to the Internet café this weekend earlier than planned because of the "bean holiday." No kidding. Kathryn's school is closed all week because it is the bean harvest. So with no class prep, Kathryn suggested they go to Taraz. Ian was open to that, because the Internet is so slow in Talas that he can only send two emails a visit. So Jen may get to use the Internet soon and maybe could let us know if the post office ever opens!

She got some material to use as curtains over her open dresser. They are blue and white striped. She said, "I don't know why, but I took a liking to them." The ladies sewed and hemmed them so Jen could hang them. Jen squealed when we told her that we received her package with her three CDs of pictures on Wednesday. It had pictures of when she was still living at Venera's, going to Turkey and Bulgaria, and also her new place! We still aren't through them, but the picture of her holding a sign in red and green letters that says, "See you in December" is my screensaver at work. Our favorite video clip is of Aisalkyn taking a bath in a washtub outside.

Jennifer started up her GenGirls club again and was sitting at the day care waiting for the girls to arrive when she had the thought that she might see Aisalkyn playing outside. Sure enough, she was there and ran over to Jen, plopped on her lap, and just stared at her. They spent about a half hour like this, and Jen kept asking her if she wanted to go play, but she said, "Nyet." Only one girl showed up, and it was just to tell Jen that there was a conflict of info about the meeting date. So Jen said good-bye to Aisalkyn and went home. Then she had a terrible thought. What if she goes home and tells Venera that Jen was at her school? Not knowing why, she might think Jen is creepy and hanging around just to see her. But then Jen thought, "Oh, well. There's nothing I can do."

But a week later, Venera stopped into the office and said that Aisalkyn had told her that she had seen Jennifer. She told Venera, "Jennifer is back from America." She must have figured that since she hasn't seen Jen in a while, she must have gone to America. It wasn't too far-fetched; earlier she had thought that Jen had gone to the war when they were consolidated! Venera called Aisalkyn a liar, but she said that Jennifer was there for her "club." She said the word "club" in Russian, and Venera understood; there is no way Aisalkyn would know that word on her own. So Jen's bond with that little four-year-old girl continues, as ours does with her.

Love,

Karen

September 25, 2005

Jen had planned to go to Taraz this weekend, but since they have to re-up their visas, they won't have their passports for a couple of weeks. I asked Jen if that was dangerous and she said they still have their Peace Corps identification, so things would be okay; but they can't cross the border. So they went to Talas. Turned out to be a bummer of a decision. There was a citywide electricity outage, and every Internet site they went to was down. But they plan to go to Talas again this weekend.

Jen figured out that the post office is open now that she found the front door. The back door looked like the main opening, but on the side is the front door with a cardboard sign that says *Pochta*, which means "post office." Foolish her. Jen finally got Father Larry's package! Took over seven weeks. She also got a padded envelope from us that we mailed seven days earlier. But the biggest surprise was two big packages from Uncle Paul and Aunt Patty that came in seven days! Jennifer says that has to be a record. The fastest has been five days for a package from Willie, but his dad sends things from the New York post office, so they thought that was the reason it came so quickly. Uncle Paul and Aunt Patty's package was a godsend because it had long johns and wool socks. Jen's mornings and nights are getting very cold, even though the days are warm, just like here. But the nicest gift was the comforter and sheets that also were in the box. Being on her own, she doesn't have a host mother's bedspread anymore. Great gift idea!

Even though the post office has moved, it still has some of the mean old ladies. When she came to help Kathryn pick up two big boxes of books and school supplies from a sponsor from America, one lady said, "Oh, is that a TV?" Jen replied, "Yes, of course." There is such an attitude toward Americans being rich. Another thing Jen has noticed about Kyrgyz people is that they don't have the same respect for personal space as we do. They think nothing of standing very close and asking you how much you make at your job or how much you pay for rent. And if you don't answer, they assume they know. Kathryn tried to explain to people that it's not appropriate to ask such personal questions, but they don't get it.

When handing a package for Ian to Jen, one lady said, "Here, this is for your boyfriend." She boldly said, "No, he is my friend." Jen and Kathryn must be on a rampage, because each time they receive packages they have to fill out papers to receive them. This last time, the ladies said (in Russian) that they couldn't pick them up that Thursday—they would have to come back on Monday. Jen translated to Kathryn and she figured that they just didn't want to process the paperwork, so she said, "Please tell them NO. We will take the packages and they can check over the paperwork, and if there is a problem, we will be back on Monday." They handed over the packages. But there are also two nice ladies that have helped Jen many times.

The police at the station she has to walk past every day are also very nice. Because she had to register through the Peace Corps that she moved her residence, they are aware of her being new in the neighborhood. Nice for a parent to know. They shout out to her, "Jennifer, how are you? Was everything nice and quiet last night?" That is even better for a parent to know.

Jen brought a pair of jeans to be taken in to the ladies at her work. They are baggy on her, and when she washes them (which isn't very often), they bag out even more because she doesn't have a dryer to shrink them up and make them soft. Her friend at the office, Baktigul, said she would work on them; her way of doing that was by having Jen wear the jeans and pinning the excess on the outside in order to measure how much to cut. No problem. The ladies gathered around to help and Jennifer joked around with the ladies about how white her stomach is compared to her arms and face. She said, "Oooooh, I'm a ghost; you can't even see me." They had fun and laughed until Baktigul started taking her pants down, and her underwear came down, too. Jen had just been thinking, "What if she pins my underwear to the jeans?" A few ladies started yelling, "Jennifer, Jennifer!" She yelled back, "Let go of my underwear, Baktigul, let go of my underwear." She cut her loose. Jen went into her director's office and Gulnara asked what all the fuss was about. Jen said that Baktigul wanted American underwear and was trying to take hers off her body. Even though she spoke in Russian, she could hear the Kyrgyz ladies listening in the other room and laughing all over again. She is not only learning Kyrgyz from them, but they are learning Russian from her... through goofy fun.

I told Jen it seemed like so many ladies names end in *gul*. She says it means "flower." And *bakit* means "happy." So the name of her friend that sewed her underwear into her pants means "happy flower." And many men's names end in *bek*, which means "strong."

Jen was telling me about her GenGirls group. They still are having the "bean holiday," but they plan on starting up next week. And then she squealed, "Oh, the electricity is on again!" It had been out for two hours. It reminded me how so many people were up in arms and late to work last week from bad weather that knocked out electricity. She puts up with it on a daily basis, even without storms. And when we got disconnected, it took me about five minutes to get her back. She said she ate a banana (a delicacy she got from the bazaar in Talas) while she waited for us to call back. I told her that I just got some bananas, too, and so I would eat one and it would seem like we were together. It's the first time I've cried while eating a banana, but I smile at the thought of December 16th.

Love,

Karen

CHAPTER 16

A First Time for Everything

*"There is one way to understand another culture. Living it. Move
into it, ask to be tolerated as a guest, learn the language. At some
point understanding may come. It will always be wordless. The moment you grasp what is foreign, you will lose the urge to explain it. To
explain a phenomenon is to distance yourself from it."*

–Peter Hoeg

October 3, 2005

Back in America, I always had multiple birthday celebrations. Seeing as my brother's birthday is two days before mine and he also
had celebrations with friends and family, we always had a week
of birthday festivities that never seemed to stop. I thought my one
day in Kyrgyzstan was jam-packed with activities and had met the
quota set in the States. But I was surprised a few weeks ago when
my former neighbor, Nazira (one of Kathryn's students), asked me
to go to the disco with her for my birthday. She said she wanted to
celebrate with me since she couldn't on the actual day because she
was busy helping her father with his fields. I agreed, realizing that

I was really just an excuse for Nazira and any other girls coming along to go to the disco in town. I would gladly be their excuse any day, especially after seeing Nazira's excitement grow as we got closer to the disco. Many parents don't let their daughters go, or go often, because they are worried—not about their behavior, but about the behavior of the boys. Nazira and all of her high school classmates are at the prime age to be kidnapped; therefore going out after dark is risky enough, let alone going to a big dark space with lots of boys who could take a liking to you and then plot your kidnapping for the next day.

On a side note: the new twentysomething history teacher at Ian's school was kidnapped right from her classroom in the middle of a lesson the same week I went to the disco. Kidnapping doesn't only happen at night, but a guy's odds are better if he can get you at night. If you spend the night at the guy's house, it is assumed that you have had sex, consensual or not, which is shameful to your family. It's harder for girls to return home if they've spent the night, which is usually forced by matriarchs in the opposing family. Therefore, the later in the day the kidnapping, the less work it is to keep the girl overnight and the less opposition or support to return her to her family.

Nazira invited me to eat dinner at her house before the disco, which made me a little nervous. Guesting situations always make me nervous, since I am the guest of honor, a foreign novelty, and focus of attention. My Russian is tested to its limits... and I'm not one for public speaking in my native language. But when I arrived, Nazira and my "cousin" Chinara had prepared a table for three especially for us. We had a great two-hour discussion, mainly in Russian, since neither girls' English skills are exceptional. We spoke on subjects ranging from school, to parents, to sex education, to broaching the subject of love and kidnapping. Through this girl talk, I found out a lot about these girls and their thoughts. I am really interested in using some Kyrgyz textbooks from the Peace Corps to talk to the girls about sex and Kyrgyz stereotypes about gender roles in GenGirls, and so I sought their opinion. I don't want to be seen as the radical American coming in to teach the girls about what might be normally taboo, but the girls were very supportive of the idea. I plan on screening the texts and reviewing them with select groups of girls before introducing anything. I am constantly surprised by how modern all of these girls are once they feel comfortable to share their thoughts and feelings in a safe environment. There was some serious bonding between two sixteen-year-old Kyrgyz girls and one twenty-three-year-old American "girl."

At the disco, the woman collecting the entrance fee (fifteen som... pretty steep) refused my money, which is strange, since I've paid several times before to get in. Once inside, I greeted the DJ, Muktar, a local taxi driver with whom I have ridden several times. He is a good man and constantly thanks me for going to the disco as often as I can. The girls told him that it was my birthday, and he subsequently dedicated two songs to me, announcing it was my birthday over the microphone. He kept saying, "We congratulate you, thank you for coming to Kyrgyzstan. We will miss you when you are gone!" Then later he chose a slow song so he could dance with me himself. I think he seized the opportunity of Ian not being present, and just wanted me to have someone to dance with.

Now, Muktar is a married man, with a build similar to my father's, so it was just like dancing with my dad, which was really nice. He was very concerned when he asked if my parents had called for my birthday and then wished me a happy birthday in English before returning to his DJ booth. Then before leaving, he gave me the twenty-five som that usually goes to the birthday person or student of honor (like a kid that just won a boxing championship, or a girl who just won class president). I felt bad taking it, since I make four times what the average Kyrgyz person makes in a month, but I figure I'll just spend it on ice cream for some students on a random day.

During the last two songs he played while we were there, I quickly learned why mothers are so worried about their daughters going to the disco alone. Two guys kept swooping in to stand next to or dance with Chinara and one boy kept pulling Nazira aside to dance alone. Since neither of the girls had boyfriends dancing with them, they were technically free for the taking. But I saw to it that that didn't happen. I turned into a protective mother pitbull, pulling both the girls into different spots on the floor so I was between them and the boys. I would then give the boys the harshest look I could muster. It was more of a workout than dancing for an hour straight. I felt I had to look after them, since their mothers had let them go only because I was going with them. I tower over the average Kyrgyz person, even the guys, so I can understand why I would seem to be the perfect bodyguard. Mess with one of my friends and I'll go crazy, doing weird stuff like reprimanding you in English and walking away! Whew, look out!

I think due to the male vultures, the girls were ready to leave just as my knees were giving out. I said thank you and good-bye to Muktar, who kissed my hand, and then the girls walked me home. It makes me laugh thinking that the girls whom I was supposed to protect quickly turned into my protection, so I wouldn't have to walk home alone late at night on a Saturday. I guess I'm writing you about my evening since it was so unexpected and was really one of those Peace Corps "moments" that make me smile. I look back, thinking, "I have made friends here. I do have a life outside of other Americans. I could do this on my own!" Now I just hope that Muktar doesn't remember this "birthday" next year, when September 18th rolls around.

Since I last wrote, I have experienced a lot of firsts; first time being recruited by a Jehovah's Witness (Kyrgyz witness in the bazaar, in English!), first bake sale in Kyrgyzstan, first sighting of a hedgehog in the wild, first homemade meal in my new home, first bride kidnapping of someone I know, first computer class I gave in Russian, first pizza I baked in my oven, first Kyrgyz Independence Day and First Bell ceremony. My friend Baktigul held her first dollar bill, and I have completed my first year in country. I'll give you a rundown on the more significant experiences. Seeing a hedgehog en route to the toilet late at night is one of them.

Unfortunately, in my village, the Kyrgyz Independence Day, August 31st, went by a bit lackluster. There were some activities in the "stadium" (an open, grassy field behind the government building), which had mostly ended by the time I made my way through the village. It was a big deal on TV, with lots of special concerts, and I heard in Bishkek there was a pretty sizable parade and fireworks. The explanation for our lack of events was that our mayor this year doesn't really like throwing big parties, so we get to watch them on TV instead. The "First Bell" ceremony is held on the first day of nationwide classes, September 1st. On the way to work that morning, I was very impressed by the sea of black and white (students' uniforms are typically black pants/skirts and white shirts) and formally dressed parents making their way to the public school (Kathryn's). Kyrgyz people are not typically "on time," as we Americans would say, and so to see a mass of people going to the school at least fifteen minutes before the ceremony was to begin made me think, "Well, this must be a really big day if everyone is going to be on time." Generally when someone says, "Come at 7:00 p.m." that means feel free to show up at 9:00 p.m.. I have the hardest time discerning when I need to be on time and when I need to uphold the standard two-hours later rule.

I went to the lyceum to observe the festivities, since it's a smaller community and I wouldn't hear the end of it from the teachers and students if I didn't attend, and because Ian was going to make a speech to welcome the new parents and students in Kyrgyz. I was the digital camerawoman, there to record the speech, which went exceptionally, and then I proceeded to hang around. The first day of school for Kyrgyz students doesn't mean they have to do anything. After a forty-five-minute traditional Kyrgyz history lesson, they milled about talking to friends. Ian's new classroom wasn't ready and he spent the rest of the day moving books and desks. Kathryn, on the other hand, turned down offers to go to a café with the other teachers. The first day of school is viewed as a teacher holiday; therefore, I saw a lot of drunken teachers later that day. I'm not passing judgment; it's simply very different from my experience as a student in the States and therefore not what I expected. However, the first day excitement and nervousness transcends cultures. Kids were wearing their newest uniforms and the new students were dressed to impress, with their parents doing the same.

Before going to Bulgaria, I was asked by my director to give computer lessons to women in the village. I jumped at the idea; created a curriculum for basic, intermediate, and advanced levels; and then translated it all with a little help from my director's bilingual son. What I thought would be a small group of women coming once a week turned into two women having private sessions once a day. They will be coming in for a month, and looking back, I don't think I could have handled more than one person at a time. Once, after two solid hours of struggling through particularly rough lessons (both because of my language skills that day and the area we were covering), I was ready to collapse. I picked up the extra chair in the office, and as I brought it out to the sewing room, I tripped on the doorjamb and then slammed the chair into a wall. Baktigul, one of the seamstresses, and I burst out laughing. She asked if I was tired from the lessons and I wailed, "They have so many questions!" My dad asked if I was qualified to be teaching computer lessons. I laughed and joked, "Dad, I'm an American; I'm qualified for everything here!"

Seriously, though, I'm teaching to use two spaces between sentences and one between words. I think I'm qualified for that. I had no idea that teaching something as simple as how to properly use the shift key would be so rewarding. I don't think I've caught the teaching bug, though. Just giving these lessons has put me back at the level of exhaustion I felt when I first came to site. I, as well as almost all volunteers, slept twelve hours a night to keep up with dealing with a new environment and especially the challenge of communicating full time in another language. I slowly adjusted to the amount of energy it took to communicate (plus communication became easier) and went back to my usual six to eight hours. In the past few weeks, I have been catching myself sleeping closer to ten hours a night. It makes me laugh at myself just thinking that only two hours of intense language usage, with barely any listening on my part, can tire me out so easily.

On a fun work note, Baktigul commented that she had never held a dollar before. I looked at her and said, "I have three dollars in my room. I will bring one tomorrow." It was like Christmas morning to Baktigul when I followed through on my promise and the photo I took proves it. Normally, Kyrgyz people don't smile in photos, but who knew that something as simple as a dollar bill could change that age-old tradition.

One year being in this country has arrived surprisingly quickly in hindsight, albeit torturously slowly at points during last winter. When I was at the TIP conference in Bulgaria, I was one of the "oldest" volunteers, having almost a year under my belt. Most of the group had only been in their respective countries for five or six months. I told Ian and Kathryn this and they asked how that made me feel. My response: "Old, but really good that I was able to sympathize with where they were at and tell them how things only get better and better." I know that in the past year I have grown in ways that I never thought I would—emotionally, intellectually, and spiritually. A quote that captured my attention a while ago is only starting to make sense now: "There is one way to understand another culture. Living it. Move into it, ask to be tolerated as a guest, learn the language. At some point understanding may come. It will always be wordless. The moment you grasp what is foreign, you will lose the urge to explain it. To explain a phenomenon is to distance yourself from it." This is from Peter Hoeg.

Looking back on my first months, I see that I was always analyzing, constantly searching for an answer. "Why would you do that? Why would they say that? Why is that so important? How does that make any logical sense?" I've stopped questioning, internally and audibly, and have lost the "urge to explain." You simply take your shoes off when you enter a house. You honor the bread by taking a piece of it, even if you won't join the meal, or by not throwing it out, or by making sure it is right side up. You ask how someone's health is immediately after you greet them, and as a "girl," I must ask my elders first as a sign of respect. You can't jump into business; you must ease your way into the conversation by talking about tomatoes, or local elections, or what have you.

People don't form lines, so you have to be vocal in stores. People and events are much more important than keeping a schedule or working. Work will always eventually get done. Both host and guest have respective roles to play. I've found that, while I can explain all of these aspects of Kyrgyz culture in some way in my mind, that's not likely to be the reasoning behind them for Kyrgyz people themselves. I don't know that I'll ever truly understand any of the reasons for the culturally appropriate actions that I take here. But I've come to realize that seeking "understanding" often distances me from simple knowledge and participation. In my mind, being an active member of the community is much more important than thinking I'll have everything figured out if I just stand back a little bit longer.

An exchange with an older Kyrgyz woman struck me the other day. And it instilled a stronger desire in me to focus on participation instead of finding understanding. This woman was sitting at our office when it was time for lunch. Naturally, she was invited to stay and share what we had. She sat between Baktigul and me (the oldest and the foreign "guest," who should be sitting in the places of honor across from the door), and asked me if I was from America, in Kyrgyz. I said yes and everyone laughed at my sudden fluency as she continued to say something in Kyrgyz. Baktigul translated for me and the woman said that she saw Americans in movies, on television, in books. Americans and America were held up as models when she was a child and she greatly respected them. "Now I am sitting next to an American; we are looking in each other's eyes and sharing a meal. I never thought I would do so." I smiled and took another fork full of potatoes and thought, "Until I joined, I had never heard of your country or people. So what does that say about me and mine?"

One final thing: my parents just booked my flight home in December. I will arrive in Minneapolis on December 16, 2005, and will leave again for Kyrgyzstan on January 13, 2006. I am sure I will send a couple more distribution emails before then, but will email you when I am in Minnesota to set up times to visit. It's so exciting to finally have dates in place... December will be here in no time!

Peace and love to all,

Jenny

October 4, 2005

We didn't get any emails from Jen again on Saturday morning, so we decided to call her that night. It is such a blessing with her having that cell phone so we can reach her whenever. We just didn't know how two trips to Talas could result in no Internet. She answered right away and actually had some company over, a volunteer who was passing through and needed a place to stay for a few nights. Like Jen, she also had to learn Russian, not Kyrgyz, and I think it was exciting for Jen to have her first houseguest. So we quickly chatted to make sure all was okay, and the best part was that Grandma and Grandpa got to say hello and tell her how much they're looking forward to Christmas. And she even got to hear from her rodeo golf partner, our nephew Ryan.

Jen told us she couldn't email the first time she was in Talas due to lack of electricity, and although that same situation was totally possible again, the second time was because the Internet was down. But they were told not to worry; the person who could fix it was on their way. Three hours later... no repairman, and they needed to leave so they could get their taxi on time. So no Internet access. It was odd that they were turned down two weekends in a row in the most reliable city.

The next batch of volunteers has arrived in Kyrgyzstan and will be replacing the K-10 group. Their two years are up and with Jen having one more year to go, they are the hosting group. Ian and Jen will be traveling to the airport on Tuesday to pick up a few people who will stay with them for the week to observe the life of a volunteer. Jen did the same thing, but only after being there for a couple of months. Maybe they have decided they need to visit actual sites before starting their language lessons. The new people won't necessarily be assigned there; they are just being sent out to locations to see what life is like. Hopefully, they won't be scared off by the primitive conditions in Pokrovka. But the good news is that Jen will be able to try the Internet again while there picking up the new volunteers. So hopefully we will be hearing from her during the week!

Love,

Karen

October 11, 2005

We have changed to calling Jen on Sunday at 9:00 p.m., our time, which is Monday morning, 8:00 a.m. her time. It works out better for both her and us. Jen told us that she had spent the night at Kathryn's house and taken a *banya*. I asked why she didn't take one at her big house, and she said they don't have it hooked up yet, meaning there's no hot water, and there isn't any electricity or coal hooked up to heat the stored water in the water tank in the shower. When she wants to wash her hair, she heats up a pot of water and then takes it into the *banya* to shampoo. Hope the situation changes soon.

My other concern is that her cottage (that's what we're calling it) has two rooms and is in a U shape. She has to go outside to go through the entryway to get to the other room. So when she leaves her bedroom, she has to go outside in order to get into her kitchen. When I heard this, I told Jen I was upset; I had thought the rooms were connected. She said, "Mom, I have to go outside all the time. No biggie." I guess she's right. She walks in twenty-degree-below weather to work. No warm car. She walks to Kathryn and Ian's house. No warm car. She walks to the taxi stand and market, and most importantly she walks outside just to go to the bathroom. I guess I was seeing it from my point of view, not hers.

We were so thankful for Jen's emails Tuesday morning, which meant Jen, Ian, and Kathryn were able to sneak in and send their email before picking up the volunteers who had just arrived in country. Don't know if it is a Russian language or a European thing, but Jen seems to drop the word "the" in certain places. For example, she says, "We will be going to Internet" or "It has been nine months since I have been in country." I don't think her English teacher will care, and I just say it back to her the same way.

Their village was assigned one volunteer each, and they were there to observe and learn. They all would be taught the Kyrgyz language. These volunteers have been there around two weeks, so they are just starting their language lessons. At Jen's mid-service training they discussed the benefits of visiting permanent sites early to reduce the fear of what the big assignment will be like and allow them to ask questions.

The girl Jen hosted was also named Jennifer! She brought her to her work and introduced her to the ladies. She had to elaborate on how not everyone in America is named Jennifer. This girl only knew the basics of saying hello and "My name is..." in Kyrgyz. Jen had a computer class with a few ladies and the other Jennifer helped. Even though Jen has officially learned Russian and not Kyrgyz, she knew more Kyrgyz than this volunteer, and she tried not to let her know. From there, she took her to both Ian's school and Kathryn's. Then there was a disco school dance at Ian's, so they attended that.

The most asked question was about food. Jen made a pizza using Spam as the meat and the new Jennifer asked, "Can you get that here?" Jen just laughed out loud and then said, "Ahhh... no." They took them down to the river and had a bonfire with s'mores. The girl said she just wanted the marshmallows and again asked, "Can you get these here?" Overall, Jen thinks that the three volunteers they had will do well. But I said, "Jen, you must have seen yourself in them."

Another of Jen's adventures is that she has been asked to come and speak to the newest group in Bishkek in November. She needs to relay the info she got from her trip to Bulgaria about human trafficking and gender studies. She has also been asked to pass on some of the things she's learned on her own, including some dos and don'ts that she didn't learn in her initial training, such as: you don't look a Kyrgyz man in the eyes because he thinks that American girls are trying to send the message that they are available; you have to cut vegetables in a certain way; do not say the word *sick*, as it means the same as the F-word in English; never point your finger at anything; it's a sin not to like tea; and people will think that drinking cold water will make you get ill. She has a list of all the things she wished she had known ahead of time and is excited to go speak to the sixty rookies. The organizers feel that hearing this information will be more effective coming from a volunteer in addition to Peace Corps contacts. That's what happens when you make a suggestion at a training session. She also will use that time to check in with headquarters and visit the doctor for good measure.

Ian's director has asked Jen if she will teach an English class three days a week for three hours each to some classes. From day one, Jen has said how thankful she is for NOT being a teacher. But they explained that she wouldn't have to do any grading or paperwork. She is still thinking about it, but Kathryn said, "You can make it as fun as you want! Actually it will be an extension of the GenGirls." And Jen told us that, aside from her partnership project grant, being able to influence these girls to believe they can do what they want and be empowered is extremely rewarding. If she can make a difference with even one girl to rise above anything or anyone that suppresses her opportunities, she will be fulfilled. Jen said that since it is slow at her work right now with respect to her work on the grant, she is open to serving in another way.

Many people have inquired how much luggage Jen can have; when she goes back after Christmas, they want to load her up with goodies. I asked Jen about it, and she said she has a plan. She has the two suitcases that she went there with, and one fits inside the other. She will only pack one but put it inside the other. Then on her way back, she can fill the other. She said she is bringing few clothes home because she donated lots of hers that had gotten too big and couldn't be altered. She brought them to a shelter Willie was working at. She hopes to do some budget shopping for clothes that fit her the right way while home.

When Dan got on the phone, he told her that she is a "two-digit midget." She was confused by that comment, but I know from Dan being in the service that he meant that she was now a short-timer, meaning that she would be going home soon, in under one hundred days (three digits). He also told her that he had been duck hunting lately, which means he's been looking at the skies. At about 4:30 one afternoon, he was able to see the moon, since it's so late in the fall. He knew it was about 3:30 a.m. for her, so she was most likely sleeping, but if she had been awake, maybe they would have been looking at the same moon. I told Dan, "In sixty-five days, you can look at the moon together." As tears filled his eyes, my ears were filled with the sweet song, "Twinkle, Twinkle, Little Star." I will never hear that song the same way again.

Love,

Karen

October 19, 2005

We were surprised to get some emails and pictures from Jen on Saturday morning. They decided to go to Taraz instead of Talas, since their access to the Internet has been so iffy lately. They went to their usual telecom center, but Ian doesn't like it as much, so he said he was going to scout out a better place. Jen needed to go exchange money, and when she got back, Kathryn told her that there were program changes at the telecom center and they no longer would accept jump drives. Jen's whole method of dealing with emails depends on jumps drives. She was so frustrated, but when they met Ian at the restaurant, he had great news. He found a place just five minutes from where they were that had Internet access like in America. It was at one of the universities in Taraz and Jen said it ended up taking her an hour to send what would normally take three! They are so pumped, and because they have permission to go across the border to Kazakhstan twice a month, that is where they will go now. It's closer and more bazaar goods are available.

Since she had travelled across the border, I asked if she had gotten her passport and visa back. She said yes, but unfortunately they only renewed the visa until December 25, 2005. It was some Kazakhstan government thing, not due to the Peace Corps or Kyrgyzstan, so she is working with headquarters to see how she can get that changed, or she won't be able to enter back into the country after her return in January. Oh, shucks!

Jen has accepted the teaching position at Ian's school. It will be three hours on Tuesday and three hours on Thursday and it involves more than she thought. She decided to do it because she really didn't have any good reason to say no. Ian promises to be as much help to her as she is being to the school. One of the teachers left and so others were adding hours on to their already-busy schedules, and it was getting to be too much. This is a temporary situation until they find another teacher. They call a certain class a "form," not a grade. She got the ninth form, but really wished she could have had the eleventh; unfortunately, it was taken. There is no twelfth grade, as they graduate after the eleventh. Once the eleventh form heard that she had the ninth group, they came to her and asked, "Why didn't you pick our class? We want Miss Jennifer, too." But she told them that the director had assigned her the ninth class and she didn't have a choice. Ian teased her about playing hard to get at first when she was trying to decide but now is everyone's favorite.

Jennifer is disappointed that the donations for her grant are only at $300 out of the $3,000 that she needs before the monies are given and construction can begin. I told her that the *Chaska Herald* was interested in doing a follow-up story on her and at that time she could make the appeal for donations and refer to the Peace Corps Partnership website. I told her, "Who knows; maybe they will bring a camera crew here for pictures too!?" She giggled.

Jen will be getting a hot plate from Kathryn's host mom. Right when Jen was moving out, she offered her many kitchen things. Jen figured she would wait with the hot plate until it got cold and she wanted to cook in her bedroom, but as we talked, she decided she better ask for it now, since Kyrgyz people move at a slower pace than we do. She didn't get any mail this week, but one of the ladies who works at the sewing center is now working at the post office, so she feels better about getting her packages.

Jen heard through her director that Venera has been asking when Jen will come to visit. Seems strange to ask other people but yet not invite Jen directly. But Jen explained that since she is the younger person, it is her responsibility. She then told me that when she gets home at 5:00 p.m., she cooks her meal and then only has one hour of sunlight left to go anywhere. If I know Jen, she will work it out on a weekend or use a special holiday (seems like they have so many there) to make her appearance.

Many times when Jen travels with Ian, people refer to Ian as her husband. Kyrgyz people can't comprehend a woman who is not married with many children by the age of twenty-three. Jen gets mad at this, because in America, women are allowed to be single. But not there. Many times when getting into a taxi, the driver tells her to go in the back with her husband. Traveling with Ian is a good safety factor, but also creates assumptions. Women assure her that she should go along with it so she doesn't get bride kidnapped. Anyone who would attempt to kidnap a Peace Corps volunteer with the United States embassy behind them would be pretty stupid. But she just tolerates it, because "When in Rome…"

Recently, they went to a concert in town and had good seats in front because someone saw that the Americans were there and offered the seats to them. Jen thought that it was a very kind gesture, even though she doesn't like to be treated like a celebrity. But as the night went on, she was wishing they had sat in the back. As the music played, she had one, two, three, then four little girls on her lap. That was fine, but with each new addition, her chair started to tip. A few minutes went by, with more tipping. She told Ian, "Pretty soon this chair is going to break." He didn't seem to take her seriously, until BOOM. The chair collapsed, they all laughed, and Jen ended up standing for the rest of the concert. It's ironic that something like this has never happened to her before until she goes halfway around the world and loses seventy-five pounds. Guess the chair wasn't "made in America."

As I ended my call I said, "I love you and not that I'm counting, but I will love you even more in fifty-nine days." I'm sure she smiled on the other end.

Until next Sunday,

Karen

October 25, 2005

Jen's reception is so clear on her cell phone, so we had a speakerphone conversation and it felt like we were just hanging out in our living room, talking together. We will be in fifty-three days. Not that I'm counting. Jen still has a bit of a cold, but she doesn't think it's anything serious, even though it has been around for a while. She explained that Ian has a cold too. Probably because their filtered water is so precious, they tend to share their Nalgene bottles. Guess the people germs are better than contaminated water.

Jen got a card from Dominic and a copy of her ticket information from us. She suggested that we make a big calendar to put on the fridge from December 16th to January 13th and block out family functions; then if anyone calls, we can see what would be an option for a visit. I guess a busy social calendar is the price you pay for popularity.

Jen talked to headquarters about her visa situation and they are going to give her a separate "entry and exit" visa, because changing her visa now would require taking her passport back. They wanted everyone to be on the same schedule as the new trainees, but that wasn't taking into consideration those who would travel.

Jen says they had some nice warm weather on Saturday, but that she spent the day indoors making applesauce. It's their new food find, and they were determined to make it, even though they were interrupted by many power outages. They remembered how last fall the outages would happen with no rhyme or reason. In the summer, they had "scheduled" outages. There is more electricity used in the summer. In the winter, they depend on coal. Jen doesn't have any overhead lighting in her kitchen; only in her bedroom. So when she cooks at night, she wears her headlamp! Thanks to Uncle Paul and Aunt Patty for that. When she goes to pay her rent on November 1st, she is going to tell her landlord that she won't pay until she gets electricity.

It bothers Dan that her outhouse isn't as nice as the one at Venera's. He offered to send her a toilet seat. She said, "Dad, it just wouldn't be normal to put it over a hole in the floor." End of discussion. We asked Jen about the family in the big house, because she doesn't talk about them much. It's because she has lots of independence, which she likes. But there is the typical Kyrgyz trait of putting on a show when Jen has guests. The family left for a week and Jen had no idea where they were. But yet when Ian was there, she kept asking, "Was it difficult while I was gone? Was it too difficult on you?" People putting on a show and not being genuine is not Jen's favorite thing, but she is thankful for the chance to live there.

She uses the *banya* once a week at Kathryn's. She didn't want to wear out her welcome, so she offered to pay them twenty som. The mother said that she wouldn't take money from her, because she is so fast in the *banya* (just like her Grandma). But one time Jen couldn't use it because Kathryn let her know that "her family thinks they are already clean, so they won't be firing it up." Both Jen and Kathryn have different ideas of what being clean means, but when in Rome… We asked about the *banya* at her place, and she said she noticed they put a piece of linoleum in the bottom, but the plumbing is not working yet.

We commented on how different Jen looked to us in a picture of her kicking wool. "Kicking wool" is how they prepare wool for doing crafts at the sewing center. They take clean tufts of wool and lay them out on a straw mat, like the kind we used on the beach in Hawaii. Then they pour hot water on the wool and roll it up. They put the roll into a potato sack to keep it clean and put a rope around the whole thing, which is used for "steering." One person pulls the rope and usually about five kids walk behind and kick the bundle. They add more hot water, drag it down a road, and keep kicking for over an hour. This creates long sheets of felt that they can cut into patterns. Jen pulled the rope and also helped with the kicking. She told the girls to think of a boy that they didn't like and they could really kick hard. One of the ladies said she will make a good *kellin* one day. *Kellin* is Kyrgyz for "daughter-in-law," who ends up being the slave of the family. We are glad that Jen will be a daughter-in-law in America.

Anyway, we told her that she looks so different in the picture. Granted, she's looking down and has longer hair, but we still worry about her weight. She says that our worrying seems funny, and she told us about a recent outing when they had to walk over some water on a board; Kathryn went first and Ian said to Jen, "Okay, now your turn." Jen said, "Are you crazy? I'll break that board." Ian said, "What are you talking about? You guys are the same size." That is something that Jen still doesn't see.

We watched the first part of a movie tonight about human trafficking. Jen will be going to Bishkek on November 16th to speak to groups about this subject and she's trying to create a program in her village to warn girls about these dangers. We asked Jen when she is starting to teach at the school and she said, "Today!" (It was our Sunday night, her Monday morning.) She will be going there around 1:00 p.m. from work, so she has decided to eat lunch at the school. Don't know how risky that is, but maybe it will be a good way for her to connect with the kids. Gulnara thinks the schedule will work well because she teaches classes at the local center two days a week, too. This is supposed to be a temporary position, but I think her director knows it will be longer than planned.

We want to tell Jen about everything that happens here at home and that has been challenging, with some of the difficult deaths and yet fun weddings. So Dan decided to share with her about how he broke his ankle last Thursday. Her response of "WHAT?" was a loud one. When I was out of the room, Dan told her that he would be off his crutches this Friday. Unfortunately, the doctors say it will be two weeks from now. Luckily, Jen snitched on her dad and told me when I came back to the phone. Dan yelled, Jen laughed, and I was glad. He told her, "Young lady, when you come home... you are grounded!" She said, "You have no idea how good that sounds to me."

Love,

Karen

October 31, 2005

Jen answered the phone singing "Happy Halloween" in a weird voice. She was mimicking a tape we had when the kids were young that we played for the trick-or-treaters. Old memories die hard. We had daylight savings on Saturday and "fell back" an hour, so we now are at the exact time, only twelve hours apart. It was 9:00 p.m. Sunday our time and it was 9:00 a.m. Monday her time. It makes it so much easier to figure out what is what.

Jen had to walk to the neighboring village to get her flu shot last week, with her whining all the way there about how it was going to make her sick, how she had heard that they are injecting people with the actual flu virus, and on and on. Finally, Ian said, "You already are sick, so what are you worried about?" And she does still have her cold. She says it's better, but she has had it for three weeks. We told her to get it checked out, and she said she would when she goes to Bishkek on November 14th.

Jen got a box of goodies from Grandma and Grandpa and things from the first-grade classes at Guardian Angels. Most importantly, she got a NEW Flat Stanley. I asked what she did with the old one, and she said she thought she had thrown it away when she moved. I told her, "Don't let the little first-graders hear that." They got many pictures of her with him in her host country. So now she will take the new Stanley sightseeing soon, and will visit the class when she is home. The class from last year is in second grade now, but they will be just as excited to see her.

Ian's brother keeps sending him videotapes of all different kinds of sports. When he was watching a baseball tape, Jen told him that the Twins had won the World Series twice. They then had a debate about which years that had happened, so Dan settled that for her and then asked how her teaching was going. She said, "Good!" She has one group for two lessons and then another group for one lesson, and then they flip-flop the next week. Learning English at the school for the kids is like taking an extracurricular activity, so there aren't any real textbooks to follow. The private school where she teaches makes English lessons mandatory. It is their drawing card, and now with two American volunteers, there is quite the hoopla. But it isn't as important at the public school. Just as some kids choose to take Spanish or French here in the United States, some kids there study English as an extra language.

Jen told us that she creates her lesson plan by hearing the problems the kids are having. Next week it is dealing with verbs, like the difference between "to give" and "to take." Last week, she was trying to help them understand the phrase "I am interested in..."They talked about saying, "I am interested in playing football. I am interested in watching TV." Jen asked them to then make questions out of those statements. "Why is she interested in cooking?" or "When am I interested in taking a walk?" One boy finished early and was very eager for Jen to come and check his work. He kept wiggling around as he said, "I'm done... I'm done." So Jen went over to his desk and he had written, "I am interested in shooting wolves." She started to laugh for many reasons. First, that wasn't even one of the examples she had written on the board. Second, she doesn't think there are wolves anywhere near Kyrgyzstan. And third, Ian had told her that this boy has a tendency to come up with odd takes on the assignments. He kept asking, "Did I do it right? Is it okay?" Jen had to say, "Yes, you did it correctly!" So many of them never remember to put "ing" on the end of their words, and he got it right when he wrote "shooting." Small victories. Would she want to teach in America? She says no. That would be too hard, with all the regulations and guidelines. What she is doing is just having fun with kids while teaching.

The GenGirls still meet about every other Wednesday, and this last week Jen used some booklets about dating and self-esteem. Jen knew it went well because the older girls couldn't stop talking. They mainly were speaking Kyrgyz, but Jen said she would rather they do that, even though she doesn't understand everything, than be so hindered by their English that they don't say much. And she has such a trust with them that she knows they aren't saying things they shouldn't.

Jennifer helped with the Halloween concourse (or competition) they had with the students at Ian's school. They carved pumpkins, played scary skits (the prizes were the last of the jewelry and hair gifts that Sara had sent) and all came dressed in costumes. This was something that had to be taught, because they don't celebrate this holiday. The volunteer before Ian had started this celebration. Last year, Jen, Kathryn, and Ian helped, but it was done in November, because in late October there was a mumps breakout (something our school kids don't have to live with, but a fact of life for a country that doesn't have much in the way of vaccinations). Jen says she knows that polio has been eradicated, but she sees older men whose leg deformities and walking troubles had to have come from polio.

Jen's director, Gulnara, made a negative comment about Jen teaching at the school instead of being at the sewing center. She was indicating that things weren't getting done in her absence, and Jen shot right back that she couldn't do anything without Gulnara there, and that she had been gone a lot as well. People from the organization to which Gulnara had sent a grant proposal for their computer, fax, and desk were coming that week to see if they had used the funds appropriately. Gulnara was upset that the paperwork for them wasn't finished yet. Knowing how everything is handled at the last minute, Jen asked, "And why has it taken so long to get done?" Gulnara got quiet, but wasn't mad at Jen. Gulnara seemed to realize the truth in Jen's words, but just had to blow off some frustration because she is so overwhelmed. We were glad that Jen spoke up for herself, and actually felt comfortable enough to do so.

We discussed how nice and warm she is in her cottage since using her space heater. Just like here, there is frost every morning, but it gets nicer during the day. Nevertheless, she still wears her thermal underwear under her tights because it is so cold in the buildings when she does not do much but sit. We talked about who would have the first snow, her or us, and then she said, "Look at it this way; I will be home for a month, so that means I will only have about two months of the cold here." Thinking of her coming home makes everything seem so much better. It is the cure-all that I have used many times these last few months.

Love,

Karen

November 5, 2005

In mid-October, trainees from the K-13 group came to visit volunteers at their sites. It was an opportunity for them to see what volunteer life in Kyrgyzstan is like. We were surprised to find that all three of us would host a trainee. We met them at a large café in Talas, just as we did when I came to Talas for my visit. Only four volunteers were there waiting for trainees, as compared to the group of fifteen that were waiting for my group. We joked that what we lacked in numbers we made up for in enthusiasm, and oblast pride was evident as conversation quickly picked up. When I told our trainees that we would be leaving and they got to look forward to another hour-and-a-half ride after the six hours they had already spent traveling, they cringed but gamely piled into a taxi.

When we arrived in the village, we kept them busy with job shadowing the first day, followed by a self-defense session with GenGirls and a pizza party at my place. The second day we did some trainee swapping, participated in a baseball-focused sports club, and then went to the river for a bonfire with s'mores. The last day, Kathryn and I took the trainees out to Frisbee golf course in Kirovka, which followed up with a disco at the lyceum. It was funny to realize that our trainees were all twenty-two or twenty-three and I felt at least ten years older than they. We laughed at the fact that when all three of them were walking around either barefooted or in stocking feet on the concrete patio that connects my room and kitchen, Ian, Kathryn, and I internally freaked out. That's just something you don't do here; even indoors, you have to have something on your feet most of the year, due to the belief that the cold that comes from the ground is evil.

They definitely peppered us with questions, questions that at the time I thought were a little dumb, but I'm sure I asked the same if not similar ones when I first arrived. One that stood out to me was, "Can you buy Spam here?" But my personal favorite, one that made me burst out laughing before I realized the person who asked was serious, was, "Is there toilet paper in the outhouse?" Well, if you consider newspaper or your hand toilet paper, then yes, I guess there is. My mom asked if I could identify with their questions or could see myself in them when I first arrived. Training and being that new just seems so long ago, almost as if it never happened and that I've always been this Kyrgy-fied. I know that's not true, but it's startling how Kyrgyz I am as compared to the newbies.

It was difficult to be the go-between and translator for three days, trying to accommodate the ever-adjusting, very American Americans and the confused HCNs. I told my trainee Jennifer to let me know when she was hungry because 1) I don't eat as much as I used to and get hungry a lot less, and 2) I'm on Kyrgyz time and am used to eating late. I had to explain to the women at work that not everyone in America is named Jennifer and that we had to go to a café because Jennifer's stomach was not on Kyrgyz time. They seemed to understand and didn't mind that we were being bad guests by not eating at the office. I don't know that I'll host a trainee next year, though. It was a great experience, but if I already feel that I am unable to identify with where they are, then what will happen next year?

I never noticed before but, in my training village, there is a holiday much like our Halloween where children are allowed to go door to door singing for food and candy. I was the only one home the night that they came this year—persistent little buggers! I thought it was only one night during the season, but frequently kids have come to our gate and I hear their songs when I am walking home at night. One night, I was talking on my phone as I walked down my street and after warning the person on the other end of passing cars and tractors, I jokingly warned, "There's a group of kids doing some Islamic trick or treating. I'm a little worried that they will approach me for my phone." They didn't, and although my phone wouldn't be as filling as bread, it would be a much cooler goodie!

Kathryn and I were walking through the center at midday when we noticed a large flatbed truck and a crowd of people outside the government building. We went over to see what the fuss was about when a friend of mine from another NGO said that they were giving out flour and oil through some Arabian Islamic aid organization. There was an imam (Muslim clergyman) overseeing the handout. Kathryn got this huge smile on her face, ever the Christmas-season lover, and exclaimed, "Jenny, it's like a church fruit basket giveaway for Christmas, only it's flour and oil for Muslims! How cool is that?" It did kind of blow my mind; I had never anticipated other religions having seasons of charitable giving, like Christians have at Christmas. I shook my head and replied, "Tis the season! No matter when and where it is!"

Last November, Ian and I were privy to a concourse (competition) in which half of the boys at the lyceum were dressed in homemade dresses. It was shocking, but we soon came to realize that nothing gets more laughs or higher scores from the judges than a boy dressing or acting like a girl. We were once again spectators in the fall holiday concourse and were prepared for the silly cross-dressing. It was postponed last year due to an outbreak of the mumps. The students did wonderful jobs creating team posters and badges, singing, dancing, and acting in skits. A Kyrgyz concourse is a big draw and a regular event in schools. Students traditionally prepare for singing, dancing, and skits, and the teachers judge. Every time there is a special event or holiday, there will be a concourse: the start of the school year, the end of the school year, secular holidays, the director's birthday, anything you can think of. Over the past ten months, I have seen a number of concourses, but none with quite so much drag as the fall holiday.

As my mom may have told you, Ian's director cornered me today and asked me to teach. I, someone who has always been opposed to teaching English, told her that I would think about it and talk to Ian. I have lots of reasons for not wanting to teach: wanting to be able to focus on my Russian and my primary work and have people take me seriously as a businessperson, and just generally desiring not to teach, plus a a fear of public speaking, which especially includes a classroom of high schoolers! We had a good conversation, in which Ian was all for me helping out at his school, and willing to help me get started. The conversation boiled down to Ian's comment, "You came in here hell-bent on not teaching, I don't see how that's changed." I explained that while I am waiting for the partnership grant to be funded, I'm doing basically nothing right now. Sure, I've got computer lessons to give, but that only amounts to two to three hours a day. I read the rest of the time I am at my desk. I didn't come to Kyrgyzstan or join this organization just to have more leisure reading time. As I told my trainee, I feel that the greatest impact I am making is through GenGirls, not through my office. So, when offered the chance to fill up my week some more, to help out Ian, and to help out the kids who I have grown to love, I took it.

Thanks to a crash course in English grammar and learning the dynamics of the class from Ian, as well as some activity books and advice from Kathryn, I felt as prepared as I could have been before my first lesson. I've taught for two weeks so far, a few hours a week with two ninth grade classes. The kids are still in the "impress Miss Jennifer" stage, which will not last too much longer. Everyone calls me Jennifer or "Zshen-eeeee-fair," because they can't pronounce Jenny; it's a strange phenomenon.

The biggest challenge, besides the fact that both of these classes know limited English, is that they also know limited Russian. Since they study at a Kyrgyz lyceum, their Kyrgyz is much better than their Russian. When Ian told me that he had been getting blank stares due to the difficulty of what he was trying to teach, I told him that I also got blank stares—not because of the English, but because I was explaining a grammar point in Russian. Usually, though, one or two kids in the class translate the Russian into Kyrgyz for kids who don't get it. I don't have textbooks to work with or from, so the things that I teach or review with the kids are purely inspired by what they are struggling with in their lessons. But so far so good, and I look forward to continuing as long as they need me.

In August we decided as a volunteer group that we wanted to sponsor one last activity before our K-11 volunteers left. Naturally, a Halloween activity was suggested and we decided on an English light concourse. We wanted all schools to be able to participate and so English was not the emphasis; simply celebrating Halloween was the purpose. The kids had to come in costume and prepare scary skits, but other than that, we played games like pin-the-eyeball-on-the-monster, bobbing for apples, and a candy toss. It went well and the kids had fun, as did the volunteers. Now, I want to explain my costume, which was a Kyrgyz first-grader. In some schools it is mandatory for girls to wear uniforms that look very similar to that of a French maid costume. I decided to go as a first-grader, because my black bathing suit served as the basis for the costume. I got the hair puffballs and apron from friends in town, and the costume made itself. I will attach a picture of a real Kyrgyz schoolgirl as evidence that I wasn't exaggerating my outfit. We also celebrated Halloween at Ian's school with games, scary stories, and a dance. Halloween did not pass by unnoticed this year.

In about a week, I head to Bishkek to talk to the trainees about gender issues and cultural norms that they will need to understand

once they arrive at site. I'll also be speaking about the TIP conference that I attended in Bulgaria, so it should be an interesting
session. I look forward to seeing the trainees that we hosted, now
that they are a little less green.

Until next time!

Jenny

CHAPTER 17

Who Says You Can Never Go Back?

As they opened the door, she said she was met with deadpan expressions. When they finally recognized her, they starting shouting, "You are too skinny. You have long hair and you speak so well!" They had tea and cake and she said it was great to be able to talk so freely. And when she told them how she went to Turkey, she was a god to them!

November 6, 2005

We talked with Jen tonight, but we also called her on Wednesday night. I had checked her email account and there were some messages about increasing protests in Bishkek requesting the prime minister step down. And in one of the warnings, the warden named Jen, Ian, and Kathryn as requesting a day of travel to Taraz for Internet access and a visit to the bazaar. I was shocked to see their names, but it is a testament to the precautions that the Peace Corps takes. And maybe more so, since the last consolidation. But Jen assured me they have not been told they are on standfast, which is the first step, and if she is not allowed to travel, they will call her, because they know of her limited access to the Internet.

Sorry, but I'm just the mom, and don't want any crazy stuff in the capital to interfere with her coming home at Christmas. Dan got on the phone and let her know that after four years of hunting deer, he finally got a ten pointer while hunting by Grandma and Grandpa's garden. Don't think there is deer hunting in Kyrgyzstan, because if there were, there would be nicer meat to eat.

As we were finishing our call, the electric guy finally showed up to string cords from her bedroom into her kitchen so she'll be able to see after 5:00 p.m. and won't cut her finger again while trying to prepare food. She laughed as she relayed the "Three Stooges" routine of this process. First, Jen wasn't there because her landlady never told her the electrician was coming. Then when they arranged it, the landlady wasn't there, and then when they finally planned a date, the electric guy didn't show up. Now it wasn't planned and he was there. Hope it all turned out for the better, Kyrgyz style.

We asked Jen about the opportunity offered through the Peace Corps for a housing allowance starting in October. She said they have decided to start December 1st, so that all the new volunteers will be on the same program. In the meantime, Jen has been paying her host families out of her income as a volunteer. I asked why they had changed the policy to add assistance for housing and Jen said, "So that if you need to move or want to be independent, you can. Otherwise, you may be stuck in a situation that wouldn't be the best."

The Academy of Holy Angels is doing an alumni feature about Jen in their next magazine. Jen wrote up a quick article and we sent about ten pictures. They just sent us a sample of what the publication will look like and it is beautiful. We had to convince Jen to do this because she doesn't like to be in the limelight, but it means more exposure for the Peace Corps and her grant proposal program. We can't wait to see the actual article. Who knows how many ways people can be inspired.

Jen got our package with different kinds of muffin tins. She also got Grandma and Grandpa's package with pouches of muffin mix. Jen had said she'd never seen any muffins in Kyrgyzstan and missed them, hence our shipment. The funny part is that we were the only ones who knew that. So Grandma and Grandpa's random gift ended up being the answer to her prayers.

They decided to make chili and thought they could use the Jiffy corn-bread mix she had. Sounds good, but as Ian was reading the instructions, he saw that it needed milk and an egg and they knew they couldn't find milk on the spot. Jen only had one egg and wasn't willing to give it up, so Ian said, "MUFFINS IT IS!" They made the chili from scratch and were happy that the muffin mix her grandparents sent only required water. Their decision about which pouch to use was funny. Ian read each one and the "Berry Ber-ry" said it was "BURSTING WITH FLAVOR." Since they had the chili, they thought they couldn't handle so much flavor, so they would play it safe with the usual blueberry. Down the road, when they have a blah supper, they can choose the bursting-with-flavor option.

Jen asked us about Britney Spears' baby. She gets bits and pieces of news only from weird sources now that she lives in her new space and doesn't have a TV. So we turned her over to Heidi for an update on "pop culture." She also told Heidi she wants to get a haircut right when she gets home. We don't know how short she'll go, but love the idea that her sister will do it.

We talked briefly about how wonderful coming home will be, though some things might be hard. I was waiting for her to tell us of some worries she had, but she proceeded to tell me how frustrated she was when someone brought in cattails and told her the Russian word for it and asked her what the English word was. She kept looking at them and struggled and agonized as to the word. She described them to Ian and asked, "Are they called bobtails or cotton tails?" He easily said, "Do you mean cattails?" Relaying the story, she said, "Mom, I felt so bad that I couldn't remember the English name." In my mind I thought, "Oh, Jen; it doesn't mean that you are forgetting America."

During the Halloween concourse, Jen dressed up as a first-grader, Ian was the mom, and Kathryn was the taxi driver dad. But even funnier was what happened to Jen during the Halloween concourse. A while ago, Ian's parents sent them all a supply of pepper spray as protection. Ian never carries it with him, Jen has it in her backpack, and Kathryn holds it in her hand when traveling at night. During the concourse, they were teaching the kids about trick-or-treating and going from room to room. Jen was giving out walnuts (a special treat) but heard that Ian was giving out cornflakes (a delicacy for Americans there but nothing to Kyrgyz kids). To really bug Ian and get back at him for having a lame treat, she told her favorite student, Russell, to go to Mr. Ian because he would give him candy.

Russell came back and said, "Miss Jennifer, I went to Mr. Ian's room and he gave me mace." Jen was confused and immediately worried that Ian took Jen's pepper spray out of her backpack and did something. But then realized that maybe Ian was playing a trick on her; she couldn't believe that this eleventh-year student could pull off such a joke. She was impressed, because he seemed so distraught and upset.

At the end of the day, she wanted Ian to come clean with the joke and so she confronted him. She asked him if he pretended to pepper spray this poor kid to shock her. Now Ian was confused. She had to explain, "Russell was so upset that you gave him mace." He looked at Jen and said, "I gave him raisins." The Kyrgyz word for "raisins" is *maze*. Now she realized why he was upset with her: because she told him that Mr. Ian would give him candy and he got some lousy dried fruit. They had a good laugh about that. But we had an even bigger laugh from the question I asked her after her story. I said "Jen, why would a guy from Kyrgyzstan be named Russell?" She said, "Mom, his name is Rasule." Hey, I don't hear the best, and my phone was halfway around the world from her.

It's still hard to comprehend, but in forty days, I won't have to hear her over the phone. The distance between us will be small. Please help us pray for her safe travel.

Love,

Karen

November 14, 2005

We planned not to call Jen on Sunday night, as it would be her Monday morning and she would be traveling to Bishkek to speak to the new volunteers and go to the dentist. But then the phone rang this morning at 8:00 a.m. Her faraway voice said "Hello," immediately followed by "Everything is okay." She was at an Internet site and they had telecom service that was very reasonable. She said she felt lonely because she was in Bishkek where being an American is no big deal; you don't stick out and feel special like in a small village. More importantly, she wanted me to handle some of her banking for her trip home. After we got it all figured out, I went over it again, "I said okay, so you want funds... cash... for travel back home?" She said, "This isn't fun cash! It's to get souvenirs and travel without being so tight." I started to laugh and said, "No I said funds—F-U-N-D-S—not fun." Now who has the hearing loss?

She said they got snow for the first time today, just enough to cover the ground. I told her we were expecting snow tomorrow, and had a tornado watch on Saturday. She said, "What?" I told her it's been a weird fall season. Before we said good-bye, she said she was going to take a shower. I told her to enjoy the fancy hotel, with its soft bed and running water, just like home. She said, "Not entirely."

So we got the extra perk of hearing her voice when we didn't expect to. Only thirty-two more days until the real thing.

Love,

Karen

November 19, 2005

I was going to ask Jen how it went when she talked to the volunteers in Tokmok (the city where she had her language classes), but before I could, she said, "You will never guess where I went." On her way back to Bishkek, Jen went to visit her first host family! As they opened the door, she said she was met with deadpan expressions, and then when they recognized her, they started shouting, "You are too skinny. You have long hair and you speak so well!" They had tea and cake and she said it was great to be able to talk so freely. And when she told them how she went to Turkey, she was a god to them!

She also visited four other neighbor families, and was able to see her language teacher. The big news is that her Turkish family had been planning to take another volunteer, but the mother had another baby! The youngest boy is nine, so there is quite an age gap between him and the new little one. When the mother first was going to tell Jen, she made the motion of rocking a baby in her arms, but then realized that she could say the words now. They were so happy Jen finally came back; they let her know that Melissa visited and the first Ian had come back more than once. So now they had no reason to feel shame, since Jen came to see them as well, and I think Jen really enjoyed her time with them.

Jen told us that when she spoke to the volunteers, it was at the end of the day and the group seemed burned out. And she felt that some of things she told them they may not have been able to relate to, since they haven't been there long enough. But as I told her, she has to look at it as planting the seed, and they may remember her input when it applies to them and they need it the most. She told them about the definite difference in roles between men and women. For example, she told them about the first time she, Ian, and Melissa were invited to a family's house for dinner; they were shocked when the women were ordered into the kitchen and Ian was whisked off to the living room, where vodka was plentiful. Ian had given the girls an uncomfortable look, since he probably had been brought up helping his mom in the kitchen. And he hadn't quite understood at first why the men had vegetables with the vodka. But once he drank the poor-quality alcohol, he realized how happy he was to have that pickle to counter the taste of pure rubbing alcohol.

Jen also talked about her conference in Bulgaria and the dangers of human trafficking. She told the group she had learned that volunteers have to be a part of the plan for change by helping the desperate get jobs and showing them that they have choices other than selling their bodies or trafficking others. People need to find out what they are good at. Maybe it is leather-work, sewing, or computers. Jen told them that she had just taught some ladies how to use a spacebar properly, and people don't need to learn how to do complex spreadsheets in order to make a living so they can stay away from the false promises that lead to slavery.

Kathryn spoke about self-defense, since she is a black belt. She talked about being aware of dangers, having a plan, and keeping your personal space. It's good to know that the organization is open to using what other volunteers have gained and can pass on to the new recruits. Jen plans on leaving early Sunday morning to go back to Pokrovka. She wants to make sure she has time to get through the mountain pass. With bad weather, it can take up to a day.

It is really cold there now. As we spoke, she said she was in her long johns because she didn't have room to pack PJs, too. She also was wearing her fleece jacket and wool socks from Uncle Paul and Aunt Patty. I was amazed that she has to dress like that while inside the hotel, but she was amused at the idea that she looked like she got snowed in at a ski resort. I told her it must be a nice treat to be in a hotel. She said, "Mom, it's not a Hyatt. As a matter of fact, they ran out of hot water."

That reminded me to ask about her *banya* situation back at her place. She said it isn't set up and that's okay, because she just goes to Kathryn's once a week. She doesn't know when they will hook it up, but she sees the family in the big house leave and come back clean with wet heads. Guess they are saving on the cost of coal. It was 9:00 a.m. for Jen, and Melissa was going out to get some breakfast. Jen said, "Oh, get me some ##$%%." I asked her what she had asked Melissa. She said "In English, it is called fru-gurt (fruit and yogurt) and you drink it out of a carton." She also likes to get a dessert that is a piecrust with fruit in it. She likes the strawberry the best. She said that she usually eats it in four bites. She found out about a girl from her group of volunteers who had lost sixty pounds, only to find out she had gallbladder problems. It affected her liver, leaving her feeling full all the time and so she didn't want to eat. She had surgery in Thailand and is on the mend. Hearing this made us even more thankful that, even though gallbladder surgery had disrupted Jen's senior year of college a bit, she had it before going overseas.

While at headquarters, Jen weighed herself. She has lost five pounds since August, but felt that was pretty good. Don't know if I agree, but it does seem like her weight is stabilizing now and may be due in part to her doing her own cooking. When you cook for yourself, you know you will like everything on your plate and don't have to eat horse meat. I asked Jen how it was for her to be gone for the week from work and teaching. She said she told her GenGirls that she would have to cancel their time together and she taught one of the ladies at her work how to make copies so they could take care of some office stuff. But basically, everyone is so laid-back that if you're there, great. If not, they will do without. Can you imagine if we tried that in Minneapolis?

She has been busy helping two of Ian's students get ready for a contest for a chance to go to America. She is translating questions to help them study, since the competition will be while she is back home. I told

Jen it was time to say good-bye because my ear and my hand hurt. She asked why. I told her it always does when we talk. My left ear has the phone, while my right hand takes all the notes.

Love,

Karen

December 9, 2005

I'm here in Bishkek, the capitol, for an SOCD PAC (Sustainable Organizational and Community Development) meeting. I was invited to give some feedback on the structure and direction of the program as a "business volunteer." I thought I would send out one last distribution email before my visit home in just a week. Here's the rundown of the past month.

In the fall, I was invited to speak to the new group of trainees about gender issues in Kyrgyzstan, as well as trafficking at the Bulgaria conference. I, along with two other volunteers, discussed gender topics, such as what volunteers will be expected to do in their communities/homes based on their gender, what challenges they might face, and how they can best support volunteers of the opposite sex. The trainees had this session because the other volunteers and I did not feel that we were amply prepared during training to deal with varying gender issues. The purpose of this session was to speak honestly about what we face as American men and women, and to give the trainees an opportunity to think about how they would deal with similar challenges. Not that there is any one right answer, but having a plan of action is the best tool in facing experiences that might normally dishearten you, or threaten your safety (as Kathryn stressed in her self-defense session with the trainees). As I told the group, "How you might deal with something on Monday is not how you would deal with it on Wednesday. We are not here to give you the answers. You have to decide those for yourself."

The TIP portion of the session went pretty well. I created a handout and basically gave an overview of what trafficking is and how we can help stop it as volunteers. I felt a little rushed, because I only had thirty minutes to talk about something that has occupied hours of my time since I first started preparing for the conference in August. I hope to speak again at this group's IST (in-service training) in the spring to delve deeper into the topic. It should also help that they will have been at their sites for a number of months then, seeing Kyrgyz reality firsthand. I will also be speaking about TIP at our midservice training in late January. I really look forward to this session, because I feel I'll talk about a lot more without intimidating or scaring the volunteers.

On a side note, I was able to visit my host family and training village. I hadn't been back since last December, so the greetings I received were full of surprise, laughter, and lots of hugs. Not only do I look different, but I can actually speak with all of these families. I realized as I talked with one of the many host dads that I didn't really know anything about him, simply because I hadn't had the language skills to ask about much of anything. I got to see my host family the most, and spent time holding their new baby. I didn't realize how excited they would be, as a Turkish family, when I mentioned that I had traveled through Turkey. I think I drank a few gallons of tea after visiting four homes and I barely managed dinner that night after being fed at every one. It was a great visit and I am glad that I can say I have been back.

Teaching has been going well. I still haven't gotten used to kids calling me "Ajaykay," what they call their teachers. I've grown accustomed to "Miss Jennifer." I've finally become comfortable in front of the classes, both in English and Russian, with a little Kyrgyz thrown in for fun, and have found an instinct I never knew I had. When a lesson is going badly, I look to the kids to tell me what we should do. Not literally, but I try to pick up on what they don't understand or apply an activity that has gone well in the past and use it with whatever we are learning that day. I say "we" because I have found that my Russian has grown as I have taught them English. I routinely have, "Ohhhhh!" moments in front of the students when something has clicked in my mind when I translate for them.

I've picked up on their innate desire to win at all costs, and have used games as a way to drill into their heads new grammar and vocab. It's also cool to be able to turn a game over to the kids to test their level of fair play and English knowledge. Of course, there have been frustrations with the kids not understanding what I am saying to them in Russian. It is not only because my Russian isn't perfect, but also because their Kyrgyz is better than their Russian. It should be; they go to a Kyrgyz private school where every lesson is in Kyrgyz.

Last week when I gave my first test, I literally had a student half-way through the period exclaim, "Oh, this is a test!" I wanted to wring his neck and bash my head against a wall at the same time. But through it all, I have Ian and Kathryn to lament to: Ian especially, since he knows the students individually and can share my frustrations and sympathizes because I've taken on the brunt of lessons with his least favorite classes. In other English news, three students—two from Ian's school and one from Kathryn's—from Pokrovka made it to the third and final round of a competition to study for one year in America (FLEX). They will find out in April if they will go to America this summer. We're all holding our breaths, crossing our fingers, and waiting in anticipation for April to come quickly.

GenGirls is going well. We've been plowing through the Kyrgyz booklets that cover topics from drinking to rape, friendship to drugs. So far the girls have been really into just reading the questions in the booklet, discussing each one, and then reading the answers provided. Sometimes conversation goes further, when someone thinks the answer is wrong or just lame. I've struggled with whether or not I should insist we talk in English only, because usually I sit there while they speak Kyrgyz to each other. I can understand the gist of what they are saying in Kyrgyz, and even more when they occasionally switch to Russian.

The only input I have is guiding which questions we will talk about and asking additional questions if I think it's necessary. While I would love to be in on the conversation completely, I've decided that it's most important that these girls share their thoughts and feelings about serious topics without a hindrance such as language. I know many girls would not speak at all if the discussion were only in English and they are the same girls who lead the conversation in either Russian or Kyrgyz or both.

Before I leave in December, I hope to watch *Dirty Dancing* with them. I have a copy with Russian subtitles. They'll have questions to journal about, and we will then talk during the following club meeting. I've also been helping out with a club for young students who basically don't know any English. Kathryn's best student really wanted to start a club for beginners and teach them how to make books as well. Kathryn didn't have the time, so I offered my services.

Basically, I stand in the background, help with the crowd control of twenty plus elementary students, and assist Albina, the club leader, with English spelling. I'm basically an adult figure and translator for the Russian kids who come. Albina can lead this club on her own, but would like someone as a wingman, which doesn't bother me in the least.

Well, that's all in news from halfway around the globe. I hope to see many of you during my visit home, which is just a week away.

Peace!

Jenny

December 9, 2005

Greetings from the comfort of the Peace Corps headquarters, where free Internet access abounds, as well as books and indoor plumbing. It's heaven on earth! I wanted to take a few minutes to remind you all about the Partnership Program Grant that I wrote, which was posted online over the summer. To date, only $400 of the necessary $3,400 has been raised to complete renovations on what will hopefully be a multipurpose facility. I NEED YOUR HELP!

Only through your donations can this grant be funded. Partnership makes it possible for friends and family of those serving in the Peace Corps to personally contribute to projects that their loved ones are facilitating. What I find amazing about this opportunity is that you have the chance to enhance life for people who have become my colleagues, friends, and family on the other side of the world. I strongly encourage you to take the time to check out the Partnership program at www.peacecorps.gov. Click on "donors" on the main page, then on "current projects." My project is listed under my last name, under the Kyrgyz Republic. If you are unable to contribute, please help me in spreading the word and pass along this email to those who might be interested.

Thank you in advance from me and the women of History Sources!

Jenny

December 11, 2005

Merry Christmas! A quick note before the big day. This Advent season, we are called to "Prepare... make ready for the Lord." That's how it feels at our home, but in addition to celebrating our Christ child arriving on December 25th, we are celebrating our oldest child coming home on December 16th! No present under the tree will compare.

It was so bizarre to say to Jen on our last call, "See you on Friday!" She still had a bit of a cold, but hopefully it will be much better by travel time. She is busy getting ready and we even planned out her first supper at home. No McDonald's for a while. Lots of fruits and vegetables. Who knew! Couldn't get kids to eat them before. But when you don't have access, I guess they sound good.

Jen has an eight-hour drive to Almaty through Taraz, Kazakhstan. Then she leaves there at 4:00 a.m. Thursday, which is 4:00 p.m. our time. Begin the prayers then. She has a four-hour layover in Amsterdam and then a direct flight to Minneapolis. We hope she can get rest, but a plus is that she will gain twelve hours. And we get excited when we get that extra hour come daylight savings time.

We discussed how things may be different, but that they will be okay. She worries about the attention she will get because of her weight. She said the boys at their service training were all of a sudden more interested in her. I told her, "That's how boys are, but just like the extra looks you get in Kyrgyzstan because you are a white foreigner, people are going to give you attention here at home because they are so glad to see you, no matter what shape or size."

Our conversation at the farm on Thanksgiving Sunday was brief, and we passed the phone around to family members. Jen was shocked to hear about a turkey fryer fire! She said, "Why didn't anyone tell me?" So I recounted the story to her. The Corbys had already eaten their Thanksgiving meal and the garage was saved, but the turkey fryer was a goner. It never ceases to amaze me how important the little things are to her. And even though it seems that I ramble on about every little bit of news, some things still fall through the cracks. When she's here, she will experience our craziness firsthand.

Jen wants to get her hair cut right away, courtesy of her sister's talents, and then go clothes shopping to get things that fit better. Then there's decorating the tree, enjoying Mass Sunday morning for the first time in fifteen months, and heading to my parent's farm. This is where we will have Christmas and New Year's. She will be able to have regular warmth, not just hot heaters in certain spaces and then cold spots in other areas. I am upset about our drippy toilet, but maybe after using an outhouse and peeing in a hole for so long, the drip-drip noise that drives me nuts will be music to her ears.

The other day Jen was at her home reading when she heard a man outside say, "Can I come in... okay?" He didn't wait for an answer, but just opened the door and started speaking in Russian, wanting to know where her landlady was. Jennifer said she didn't know, that she was not her mother, just her landlord. He was put off that she spoke to him in that manner, since he is the elder. But she thought, "Hey, you are the one barging into my room." She didn't fear being hurt; it's just another example of what we consider rude not being a big deal there. He continued to stress that her landlord was "Mama, Mama..." to which she replied, "Nyet, nyet, and leave now... this is my home." He seemed to think he had free access to Altynai's land and buildings, and that Jen should keep track of her. Jen told me, "I didn't want to be disrespectful, but what did he think I would say? 'Hey, stranger, come on in and have some tea?'" This is why she normally locks her door whenever she is in her place.

Her landlord knows she will be going home soon, and Jen is trying to work out a different payment arrangement, since she won't be there to run up the heat. Lord knows, they don't have to worry about water pipes bursting!

I will send an update while Jen is home and I'm sure you all will hear from her as well. Thanks for all the concern and support over this last year. Our hearts are brimming with Christmas joy! As Jen would say, we wish peace to all.

Love,

Karen

CHAPTER 18

Finally Home on Leave

"Speaking Russian and living in Kyrgyzstan will always be like swimming to me, whereas speaking English and living in America are like breathing. I can swim, but if I had the option to walk up on shore and simply breathe, I would definitely take it."

–JEN

January 18, 2006

Happy New Year! Christmas came on December 16th this year for the Lawrence family! Jen's flight was one hour late, but our group, including Grandma, Grandpa, Aunt Sue, and Elizabeth (cousin) was ready and waiting with a welcome sign, flowers, and an American flag balloon to make it all festive.

As we waited, I kept looking at the glass doors and stairs where she would come through once she got through customs. I longed to see her getting closer to us with each step. There was a nervous energy and everyone seemed to be talking at the same time. I checked the doors again. Nothing. It became harder and harder to wait, but I tried to stay relaxed.

And just like that... she was there! It was such a shock, since I had just looked away for a minute. She was lugging her carry-on suitcase down the stairs, and as soon as the glass doors opened, she let it go.

We ran to her and could finally hug after fifteen months apart! Without planning it, we hugged all together in a huddle, which was pretty much the same way we hugged as a family when we sent her off. People stared, but we didn't care! It was a good thing.

I loved how she held her sister around the neck as we walked to get her luggage, but things seemed a bit tentative, too. That threw me off guard, but I just tried to downplay it. When we got into the van to drive home, I put the flowers I had been holding on the floor between the seats. Jen said, "Mom, no!" I told her they would be fine, but she said, "No, it is on the cold ground. You don't understand." I know that whole "cold is evil" mentality, but her response threw me off. I quickly picked them up.

At one point on the drive home, we talked about the terrible cold and the huge snow we had just gotten and she immediately put her foot up on the dash and pulled up her pant leg to reveal the longest leg hair I've ever seen. It was not the sight I wanted during our first hours together. I began to think that my expectations of her finally coming home were WAY too high. I was confused and I didn't count on feeling that way. I tried to push away the frustration.

On the drive home, we passed Katie's apartment that had a big banner hanging out on the balcony, "Welcome Home, Jen." And coming into the driveway, there was another banner and balloons from Megan. I was so anxious for her to see them, but I think it just left Jen feeling overwhelmed. We enjoyed spoiling her with food: fresh pears were her choice. Everyone was talking and laughing in the kitchen, just like old times.

But with major jet lag, Jen was in bed by 8:30 p.m. and we retired around 9:00 p.m.. I got mad at myself for feeling a bit letdown that things didn't seem how I had them pictured in my head for so long. I went to bed and hoped that my emotions would be better in the morning. And my prayers were answered. Jen got up at 4:30 a.m. The funny part was what happened in between.

Dominic and Sara were watching TV and, at about 10:00 p.m., Jen came upstairs and walked past them. Dominic said, "Hey, Jen; are you having trouble sleeping?" No answer. She went to the bathroom and then came back out. Again Dominic said, "Are you okay, Jen?" No answer. She went halfway down the stairs, stopped, came back up, and went into the corner cupboard. Then she went downstairs.

In the morning, Jen asked if I had put a box of cereal on her nightstand. I was totally confused, since our "witnesses" weren't up yet. Jen told us that she had woken up at 2:00... chewing! She finished chewing and swallowing the cereal in her mouth and went back to sleep.

When we put all the pieces together, we realized she had been sleep-eating, but we were even more amazed that she could wander around the house in her sleep after being gone for so long and still knew where the food was. For some strange reason, NOW I felt better! This goofy event somehow helped me stop evaluating everything and just enjoy. It didn't have to be picture-perfect, and I never felt disappointed like that for the rest of her stay.

It turns out that this was not the first time that she's eaten in her sleep. She told us that she would sometimes put bread on her nightstand so that she could have a quick breakfast in the morning. That way, she wouldn't have to go out into the cold to get to her kitchen. It made sense, but many times she would wake up and realize that she had already eaten it in her sleep because she was so hungry. It was so sad to hear this. That is one of the biggest struggles I have with her serving. She is cold and hungry and I can't do anything about it.

Speaking of hungry... we solved that problem with every food we could imagine and Jen gained about twelve pounds while being home! It was fun to see the things that she was so excited about, like lettuce, ice cream, yogurt, and any fruit or vegetables—but especially lettuce. Not to mention showering, flush toilets, and WARMTH everywhere she went.

One morning, Jen got up, said hello, went to the bathroom, came out, grabbed a Pop-Tart, and sat down on the couch. I looked at her and said, "Look at how fast all that happened. I can't imagine how you usually get up, put on a coat, hat, and boots to go outside in zero degrees, and then work around it to go pee." Jen looked at me and said, "And then I come inside and get my stove going to heat water so I can wash my face." Everything in America goes so much more quickly.

Jen was very careful not to overdo it with the food, though. And she did have some problems with milk at first. It's something she's not had overseas and so she really enjoyed having a bowl of cereal with milk, as opposed to eating it dry. It didn't agree with her initially, but soon it wasn't a problem. And there wasn't as much of a problem transitioning to life back in Minnesota as Jen thought. She worried about how it would be coming back to America. But getting pampered with a haircut at the salon with Heidi right away Saturday morning went great. Shopping the next day was fun and going to Grandma and Grandpa's on Sunday was even better than before she left. We had a family portrait taken that evening, which became our Christmas card. What we didn't know is that the kids planned to have a portrait taken of themselves as a surprise for us for Christmas. Aside from our reunion at the airport, it was the best gift.

We decided that the best present Jen received was a manual washing machine capsule from Aunt Sue and Uncle Bill, and the best gift she gave was the Kyrgyz wool tree ornaments and slippers for Grandpa. Jen did an excellent job of managing her time seeing friends and family, and that even included speaking at our parish Masses and at a Catholic high school. She even spent time at St. Mary's University and spoke to three classes about language barriers, cultural differences, and her overall experience while in country.

The final touch was a follow-up interview with our *Chaska Herald*. They came to the house and took a picture with Jen; the "Welcome Home" sign that Elizabeth made for the airport was in the background with some Kyrgyz souvenirs in the foreground. We are waiting for the press on that one.

But unfortunately, all good things must come to an end. As we prepared to go to the airport and we were sitting in the living room, Jen started to cry. This was from someone who doesn't shed lots of tears. As we all cried together, we reassured Jen that it was okay for her heart to hurt, because it shows how deeply she loves. She reassured us that her tears weren't from not wanting to go back (although the thought of the cold might have swayed her) but, "Because we've had such a great time together. We've had such fun."

That was reassuring and we agreed that it was good to get it all out before we got to the airport. But we all continued to cry driving to the airport. Jen asked Heidi to come from the backseat, to sit with her and Dominic, so that all three of them would be in one seat, just as it had been when they were kids.

We needed to regroup when there was confusion about her ticket from Amsterdam to Almaty, and when we learned that her bags were a bit too heavy. But all that got figured out, and then we were back to dealing with our emotions. Jen even commented, "What is wrong with us?" I think God would reply, "Absolutely nothing!" She boarded the plane and all four of us just walked away, crying. Stepping onto the escalator, I looked back and saw Dan consoling Heidi, and Dominic struggling to see where to step with so many tears in his eyes. I just let him be. The ride back to the empty house was quiet, except for all the sniffles. No words would have really helped.

I reassured myself that having Jennifer home so we could all be together was worth this hurt. It's just the price you pay and we wouldn't have changed a thing about our Christmas with her: Midnight Mass, a picture with Great-Grandma, and so many treats to eat. Any worries and extra planning didn't really matter, because it all fell into place. She might have been gone for a long time, but in so many ways it picked up from when she left. Even though it is hard for me to think of my child being cold or hungry, the truth is... she's happy. And for that we are thankful. It will help make the next ten months or so go faster. Our hearts can't wait to go to the airport again!

We finally had our Sunday call to her and were glad to hear she had arrived safely, but she had tears again. She said that she just misses us so much. She's worried that it is going to be like starting all over again and that it will be difficult to accept being away. We tried our best to convince her that her arriving back there isn't the same as it was when she first arrived last September. She knows too much and has done too much to go back to that time. We tried to convince her that it will get better every day, and that it's very normal to get more homesick when she hears our voices. She said, "I guess. I will be teaching at Ian's school three days a week because they are closing my office for two months, since the heating costs too much to keep it open." I wanted to say, "WHAT heating?" But instead, I just thought how being busy with the students will be a godsend; the ladies will function out of the director's house and their homes, so all will be well on that end.

Ian and Kathryn decorated Jen's home right before she got back, and included a gift of a tree. It was from a lady Jen had given a Russian/English dictionary to, to help with her English. It was just three spruce branches held together by a clothespin, but made the room look festive. But she didn't get to see her room that night because she got back so late and stayed at Kathryn's. A big part of the delay was that she had to help push the taxi driver out of a ditch during the drive back to her village. There was so much snow that the car slid off the road, which isn't too surprising, but having to help the taxi driver push is not something you would usually have to do in America.

They had the coldest weather while she was gone. I know she is thankful for all the warmth we gave her here. Warm home, hearts, and love.

Love,

Karen

January 24, 2006

Dan made the call to Jen and when she answered, he said "*Buenos noches.*" It was the right greeting, but the wrong language; Jen gave him an A for effort. Jen told us that she went to visit Venera and the kids to bring them some gifts she got from the dollar store while back home, and that she had a hard time connecting with Venera. It turns out that Venera was on her vacation (doctors get four weeks a year and they have to take it all at once). Jen had stopped by on Thursday, but they weren't there. She left a message with the cousin who lives down the street. When Venera finally called her back, she was not very enthusiastic and her voice was pretty monotone when she said (in Russian), "Hello, Jennifer. How are you, Jennifer? You came here on Thursday—we were not here—I'm sorry. How was your coming?" (Asking about her "coming" was the same as asking about her return trip back.) Then when Jen answered, she kept saying, "What? What? I couldn't understand you because of your American accent." At this point, Jen wanted to give her gifts for Venera's family to the GenGirls.

They arranged a time to meet and Kathryn came along for the gift-giving. Jen had gotten the boys a snow globe and glow-in-the-dark bugs. For Aisalkyn, Jen got a little doll and purse, and Venera's gifts were a photo album and perfume. The boys were the same: according to Jen,

Madim can be a stick in the mud (having a Kyrgyz man's mentality), but Kadim is so silly and cute. She told us, "I just love that kid." Jen said that Aisalkyn was quiet and kept looking at her. She soon found out why.

There has been a strange turn of events. Four men now rent out Jen's old room! They are doing some construction work at the bank and needed a temporary place to stay. Aisalkyn said, "When the men leave, can Jennifer come back and live with us?" She still thinks that when Jen left, it was because she had to go back to America. As Jen told us, it isn't her place to explain it to her and evidently Venera hasn't. Jen misses the kids, but each visit solidifies her decision to move out on her own. I wonder if Venera makes food for the men?

Speaking of food, Jen had spent the night at Kathryn's and when we were talking, Kathryn was making breakfast. I asked what they were having. Jen said, "Pasta." I thought, "WHAT? The normal breakfast food is mostly supper leftovers. I guess they agree that breakfast is the most important meal of the day." Jen had some stomach pains when she got back and was worried about it. But everything has simmered down. We figure she brought back enough American food—Spam and all—that she will be able to ease back into Kyrgyz food.

Jen's schedule includes meeting with her director from the handicraft center on Tuesdays and Thursdays, and then teaching Mondays, Wednesdays, and Fridays. But this day she was going to Kathryn's school as a guest speaker! She said she is always at Ian's school and feels bad that she hasn't helped Kathryn more. When Kathryn was going over her lesson plans and didn't know what to do, Jen offered to come to the class. I asked what she was planning and she said, "I'll just speak about America." Not sure if that will be in Russian or English. Kathryn is now seeing a Russian tutor. She has a good friend that is half-Russian, but she also sees how important it is to know Russian in addition to Kyrgyz. Jen let us know that Kathryn is feeling so much better since Jen got her the antibiotics for her sinus infection. She still was blowing her nose a lot, but it was more normal now. What doesn't seem normal, at least to us, is that Jen said Kathryn finally took the huge bag of used Kleenex into the backyard and burned it. Yuck! Talk about spreading the germs by smoke.

Jen will be traveling on Wednesday to Bishkek for her midservice training. That means: nice bed, running water, Internet, good food, and...

oh, yeah... training, too. She will be speaking on Thursday to the group about her trip to Bulgaria. She is glad she won't have to speak to all sixty volunteers at once. They can sign up for different groups, so she will have small groups of those who want to hear about her trip.

Our good laugh of the conversation came when I told Jen that Dan and I went to see *West Side Story* at the Chanhassen Dinner Theatre for his work Christmas party. I told her that the part when Maria is running toward Tony and he's shot caught me totally off guard. The gunshot was so loud that I started scrambling and practically crawled up Dan's back as he faced the stage. Jen got to giggling. Pause. Giggles. Pause and laugh. It was as if she could picture the whole scene in her mind. I think that is the key to being away from home successfully: being able to still imagine it. And if I had a nickel for every time I did the same, I'd be rich.

Love,

Karen

January 28, 2006

I'm back in Kyrgyzstan after a wonderful trip home to see family and friends and to enjoy as much American cuisine as possible! To all of you I had the chance to see, thank you so much for juggling your schedules and possibly traveling so we could get together. For those of you who I unfortunately did not see, I look forward to coming home for good and enjoying time with loved ones at a more leisurely pace.

Instead of giving you a rundown of all that I did and saw, I thought I would describe more in detail what I thought and felt about coming home. Months in advance I was anticipating culture shock; after all, I live on the outskirts of civilization. The worst of the culture shock began and finished in the Amsterdam airport. I was struck by the varying shapes and sizes of all the people in the airport. Kyrgyz people tend to be built in cookie-cutter fashion according to age and gender: teens are petite and thin, middle-aged and older men and women are "thick" or just plain overweight, yet are somehow still miraculously smaller than me. At five feet, six inches, I tend to tower over everyone here, so to see people bigger than me, both in width and height, was fascinating.

Being grilled about my luggage, who packed it, when I last checked it, etc., was another stage of culture shock. Although militias carry AK-47s at border posts, I am much less intimidated by them than I was by the unarmed flight attendant before boarding my flight to Minneapolis. While waiting with all the other strangely dressed (i.e., not Kyrgyz or Russian!) passengers, I grew more and more uncomfortable. I felt like I didn't belong and longed to be out of the boarding lounge and hanging out with the guy in a turban I had seen earlier. At least he seemed to know what it felt like to be a foreigner.

A military officer sitting next to me leaned away from the aisle and into me, barely grazing my arm, and apologized for "being in my lap." I had to laugh! The last time I crossed the Kazakh border, I was so tightly wedged in the pack of people at the fence, I commented that the only way I could possibly know the people around me more biblically would be by taking off my clothes. Ian then proceeded to literally pull me out as I took my first real deep breath in thirty minutes. The point being: personal space bubbles have not existed to me in a long time!

Surprising things bothered me once I was stateside. The number one thing being the change in local news anchors. It just didn't seem right to be hearing the news from people I had never seen before in my life. Where had all the familiar faces gone?

Also, I had a hard time sleeping the first few nights. I couldn't figure out why until I realized I had grown so accustomed to sleeping under four blankets that without the additional weight, my mind was preoccupied with worrying about being too cold. It just didn't seem right that I could keep warm under only two blankets. In fact, I had a problem with being too warm constantly. My body has seemingly adjusted to the constant cold of living in ill-heated Kyrgyz buildings and homes.

Conversation was at times awkward. In a group setting, I kept wondering if the conversation should focus solely on me, or on commonly shared experiences by the group (excluding me). Neither was completely comfortable, which is why smaller groups of two or three, or one-on-one conversations, were easier to handle. Questions could be deeper and focus could be shared. In a group setting, all that English was somewhat overwhelming as well, and I found that I was only able to successfully focus on one conversation at a time. I have become so used to tuning out anything or anyone but the person I am talking to so as to comprehend the Russian that juggling multiple conversations or a task and a conversation was nearly impossible.

I was surprised at how annoyed I grew with children who didn't respect their parents or adults. In Kyrgyzstan, respect for elders is one of the golden rules and something that has been ingrained into my thoughts and actions. When I heard the slightest whining from a kid in a store, I grew instantly impatient and annoyed. It got to the point that I reprimanded one of my twentysomething friends for "sassing back" to his mom on the phone. I later found out that this sassing is part of a playful banter that they share. On the other hand, the mindset that I've developed that somehow, due to my age, I am entitled to certain courtesies caused me to go against the typical Minnesota-nice behavior. If someone were visibly younger than me, I barged past them through a doorway. I even blatantly cut in front of a kid where two lines merged together... just after receiving the Eucharist! Why was I acting this way? That was frustrating but trust me, it was nothing compared to the shock I was bracing myself for!

I was also startled by the habits that stuck with me, ones that I didn't even realize had become habits. Many of them involved eating. I nearly pounced on my mom when she offered me a sandwich with lettuce the first day I was home. Lettuce isn't something we can find readily and I reacted the way I would have had Kathryn or Ian returned from Talas with a bag of lettuce in tow.

Also, communal eating stuck with me. I got caught a couple of times eating from a serving bowl and then putting it directly back into the fridge instead of scooping up an individual plate. I ordered a salad from the only fast food place that I ate at, and not surprisingly, couldn't finish it. I insisted that my brother help me with it, since I knew he would still be hungry after his meal and I didn't want the salad to go to waste. He was hesitant; in America, you tend not to eat from someone else's plate while they are still eating. I bullied him into eating the way we eat in Kyrgyzstan, from one bowl or platter at the same time. It cuts down on dishes and fills multiple hungry stomachs faster than waiting your turn.

I kept catching myself eating with my hands. I didn't realize what I was doing at a restaurant when I picked up a handful of lettuce and began to bring it to my lips. I froze, trying to decide if I could just tilt my head back and throw the lettuce in my mouth, or if it would be better to put it back down and use a fork. That would have been a no-brainer in KG, but being in a restaurant using my fingers on some "not so finger food" caught me feeling out of place.

When on the phone, it took me awhile to get the hang of giving and receiving immediate responses. When I get a call from America, there is a three-second delay I always have to wait for, and I didn't anticipate the waiting to be so ingrained in me. The first couple of phone conversations were strange, but I eventually got the hang of it.

I don't mean for this email to be a depressing list of all the odd things that were awkward or challenging for me. But these are all the quirky things that still stand out to me as I straddle two cultures. I write this after being in country for only two full days. The night I arrived in the village, I ended up staying with Kathryn, since my room was still very cold. I unloaded my backpack and then sat across the room from her as we began to catch up. She looked at me, frowned, then said, "Come over here!" and patted the bed where she was sitting. We ALWAYS sit on her bed together, whether we are talking or doing separate activities. ALWAYS. I had the three-foot bubble going around me again. I'm slowly weaning myself from it, but caught myself twice today sitting farther away than usual from both Kyrgyz and American friends.

Last night, the three of us Pokrovkans made dinner and looked at my pictures from home. As we ate, I watched both Ian and Kathryn eating the baked onions that we had cooked with the chicken. My immediate thought was, "I can't believe they are eating those onions, sitting in chicken drippings!" My second thought was, "I can't believe I actually care, since two months ago, I would have been doing the same thing for the nutrients I could gain!" It's a slow process of losing the unnecessary American quirks and habits that I picked up over the course of a month. Kathryn commented that even my Minnesotan accent is back—something I slowly lost due to spending so much time with a Colorado guy and a New Hampshire girl, as well as annunciating my English slowly and clearly for Kyrgyz students.

Jumping back briefly to my state of mind during my vacation. I find myself using two words: "coma" and "marathon." After numerous home videos, sharing pictures I had not yet seen and stories I had not yet heard, I realized that my visit was much like waking up from a fifteen-month coma. To me, that wasn't so bad. It was fun and interesting to catch up on family events, pop culture, and the lives of my friends. Due to my "coma," I had the ultimate excuse for laziness one day. My dad came home from work and hassled me for doing nothing. I looked at him with shock in my eyes and very passionately answered, "Dad, the pope died today!" Yes, my grandparents had taped the pope's funeral and the announcement of the new pope just for me. It was an emotional four hours spent in front of the television.

During the first few days home, my mom was constantly offering something else to drink or eat just as I was bringing food or drink to my lips. While I commented on her acting more like a Kyrgyz mom than an American mom by pushing food on me, I reminded her that my visit home was a marathon and not a sprint. I would eventually get to all the food and drinks available to me.

Something that I did more at a sprint than a marathon pace was watching movies. I took in as many new releases, old (but new-to-me) releases, and in-theatre movies as I possibly could. I looked forward to my long flights due to the number of movies I could ingest. Even though I noticed all these cultural and behavioral differences, I still felt at home, much more relaxed and myself than I have since arriving in Kyrgyzstan. It proves that while I am Kyrgy-fied, I am still not Kyrgyz, and America will always be my first home.

On the other hand, I am happy to say that returning to Kyrgyzstan has proven to me just how comfortably I function within Kyrgyz culture and in another language. Taking a break from Russian has actually greatly improved my fluency in conversations. Before December, I was stuck in a rut of beating myself up for not being better, not studying more, and for generally having stalled out. Returning and jumping right back into Russian without problems has been a great boost. However, speaking Russian and living in Krygyzstan will always be like swimming to me, whereas speaking English and living in America are like breathing. I can swim, but if I had the option to walk up on shore and simply breathe, I would definitely take it.

Here are some details about my everyday life since returning. I've been keeping busy teaching lessons at the lyceum, speaking in Kathryn's lessons, helping with the usual beginner club, and hosting GenGirls. I've spent time guesting, giving my friend's their gifts from America, and working on organizing the disaster that is my room after unloading three bags of stuff from home! It's been great just catching up with students, showing them my pictures, and answering their questions. They've had some good ones, sometimes thought-provoking and oftentimes difficult to answer.

Nonetheless, I've been busy and will be sending this email to you from Bishkek when I go to our MST (midservice training) seminar from the 24th to the 27th. I will be presenting on the TIP conference I attended in Bulgaria last August and talking about what we, as volunteers, can do to combat trafficking and gender inequalities in Kyrgyzstan. You will read this after I have presented... hopefully it will go well!

Much love,

Jenny

CHAPTER 19

Back to a Different Normal

"Miss Jennifer, Miss Jennifer. We miss you." Some kids were hanging on her and blowing kisses. Then they asked, "Will you teach us today?" She told them, "I can't, because you have a new teacher." Then they said, "But she's not you."

January 29, 2006

When Jen answered the phone, little did we know she would be talking from Kirovka. The reception was terrible, and at one point, we thought she might be sleepwalking and talking. But she was the first one up and was trying to be quiet and find her adapter, because the phone was saying "low battery."

The situation was this: on their trip back, they went through the mountains, because Taraz had gotten a bad snowstorm. Unfortunately, a semi had jackknifed in the road, so they had to sit and wait for them to put chains on the semi so it could get going again. It caused them to be too late to get a taxi back to Pokrovka, so they stayed with Erich in Kirovka.

They will be heading out today, and she should be back in time for her first lesson at 1:00 p.m.. Her news from the midservice training is that

Washington denied the Peace Corps' request for early dismissal for Jen's K-12 group in October. Even though there will be a two-and-a-half month overlap because the K-13's are coming earlier, Washington is not allowing any changes to their COS (close of service). They can take an early out, but it would mean some changes to their exiting benefits. Jen will cross that bridge when she gets to it. Maybe her project will be so busy with construction that it will be nice to have a few extra volunteers.

Jen's speech regarding human trafficking at the conference went well. A larger group signed up to hear her share about her trip to Bulgaria, which was good; they even formed a committee that will help pass on the prevention information to other villages.

Unfortunately, with their recent snow and ice storms, Jen fell down outside the hotel and now has a bruise that looks like three stairs on her butt cheek. One of the girls who saw her fall sent someone to tell the hotel that the stairs were icy, and then stood there to warn another girl who was coming out. As she said, "Watch out... this is where JENNYYYYYYYYYYY fell!", the second girls' feet went out from under her at the same spot. So they were comparing their aches and pains later that day.

They were told another revolution is possible in March. Even though the final elections were in July, the first elections were in March when there was the uprising, and in honor of the "anniversary," there may be demonstrations or some violence again. It helps to be forewarned, and we know how well the organization favors being extra careful.

Jen will be going to an Internet site on February 14th when she is in Naryn, about twelve hours away. She is going to speak at a "Diversity Week" in Melissa's (one of the girls from her early language class) village about her time in Bulgaria. There also will be presentations about running crisis centers, and Jen is going to get information about that, so if Gulnara ever wants to create one with the new office space, she can.

In checking up on Jen's project on the Peace Corps website, Jen saw that $325 in donations has come in since she was home. Maybe it's because the interview with the *Chaska Herald* came out this week. I looked like a crazy person at the gas station going through the pages to see if it was there. Finally, on page six, there was a picture of Jen with the sewing ladies and another picture of a yurt. I started reading, but saw that the text began with only part of a sentence. Then I looked above and it said, "Continued from page 1." I hope nobody heard me when I said,

"CONTINUED FROM PAGE ONE?!" I wanted to call Jen right then and tell her she'd made the front page. In the front right-hand corner, there was the start of the article that read, "Answering the Kyrgyzstan Call—Chaska Resident Serves 2 Year Peace Corps Assignment."

I did get a strange look when I asked for five copies, but I figured I could just point to the article and say, "I'm the mom." So nice to have an excuse for crazy behavior.

Love,

Karen

February 6, 2006

While we were trying to call Jen on the cell phone, she called us on the home phone! She must have purchased minutes for her phone, but the lines were having problems, so she told me to call Kathryn's, which we did. Unfortunately, it was like the old days of calling Venera's house, with a phone with dangling exposed wires. There was such an echo delay and static. We're so thankful for Jen getting that cell phone from the leaving volunteer.

There's not much going on for her, because the school is on a semester break this week. The kids probably liked it, since they were having such mild temperatures. Jen was wearing only three long-sleeve shirts and no coat one day. She even got to watch a movie because she didn't have the space heater on. Her electricity won't let her do both at the same time, but she said she knows that will change soon and winter will be back.

Jen is going to use this week to meet with her director every day and resubmit a grant proposal for the cafeteria at Kathryn's school. When they sent in the proposal for her group of History Sources sewing, they also put in funding requests for the cafeteria construction, but it wasn't addressed, so Jen is going to help her director translate and write the grant again. Her concern is for her project and how she wishes she could start the construction in the spring. She talked to someone at headquarters and asked what would happen if the funds didn't come in. The lady said, "We've never had a project not be funded."

Jen learned there's a global fund that monies go to when people donate and don't specify a specific cause. And if a project receives more money than is needed for their project's completion, it gets put in a pool for other causes to use. So that was encouraging for Jen. After all her work, it would be nice to reap the satisfaction of seeing her efforts completed. Not that the next volunteer couldn't finish what Jen has started, but I'm sure she would find it so rewarding to see it turn out as she has hoped.

When Jen was at midservice training, she signed up to be tested in her language skills as intermediate or advanced. The lady who tested her said she would have given her advanced/high, but Jen had trouble with her changes in tense, like saying in Russian "We could have left on time" and "If you would have been on time." She said she understands the change in tense when she hears it, but still has trouble saying it correctly. Basically, though, she felt really proud. The tester said she speaks very clean Russian, meaning that there is no trace of a Minnesota accent. She asked the tester to repeat that, because, as Jen told her, her host mother used to critique her all the time about her accent.

Jen also learned that she puts emphasis on the correct word in a sentence. Russian speakers give a rise in voice when they speak a word that needs an answer, not just at the end of the whole sentence. Jen said the bottom line for her is that she can talk to her director for hours in Russian and not have any problems, but now her language level and improvement is documented in her file.

When she was in Bishkek for the training, she took all the clothes that no longer fit her. She asked that they be donated to this crisis center shelter there. I wonder about the women who will end up wearing this American girl's clothing. I guess that for Jen, donating two years of her life isn't enough. For that part of her heart, we are so grateful.

Jen will be going to the Internet café on the 14th as she travels through Bishkek to go to Naryn for Diversity Week. And then she'll do the same as she travels back again on the 18th.

Love,

Karen

February 12, 2006

When we called, Jen said she had been at Kathryn's for five days because her own electricity was out. But Jen's finally came back on, and she didn't want to stay and wear out her welcome.

Jen explained that this wasn't just a Pokrovka brownout; they're in the ghetto of town, so if bills aren't paid, the electricity gets turned off. But when they checked it out, they found a problem with the meter on their street that kept it from turning back on. Jen's landlord asked her if her space heater had caused it. She replied that she's had her heater on for quite some time—and even on higher settings—without any problems, so it wasn't that. Sure, blame the American girl.

Even though school is back in session, Jen will only have one day of lessons, as she is going to leave to go to Naryn. She and Ian are going the teach-them-about-Valentine's-Day route. They will teach them "the roses are red, violets are blue" saying and the Barney song, "I Love You." The magical lesson will be how to fold a piece of paper, cut out half, open, and voilà... a whole heart. She said they will totally freak out about that one.

She had a small GenGirl's session, and since she will be gone for the next week, she invited some to come over to her place and make cookies. About three girls came over, and when Jen asked them what to call what they were about to make in Russian, they answered correctly. Then she asked them to say it in English. They told her they were baking "cookie chips!" Jen had to correct and go over again how they are called chocolate-chip cookies.

We tried to catch Jen up on the Olympics. Without a TV, she doesn't get much exposure, but we told her that the athletes from Kyrgyzstan (only four of them) marched in with their kalpak hats on! Makes it all real. Kazakhstan had many athletes. Jen said, "Yeah, that's because they're rich and it's huge." She reminded me that during the summer Olympics, she was in Philly getting ready to ship out. That was when Sara called, all excited because Kyrgyzstan was in the opening ceremonies. At that time, we got just a quick glimpse of the athletes, but it was exciting to think that they represented the adopted country where Jen would soon be living. We also tried to catch her up about the Muslim cartoons that were causing riots. Even though she feels out of the loop, some things are okay to find out later.

We told Jen that donations toward her project had increased by $510.25. That is the exact amount she raised by speaking at church. It still is so touching to know that that the twenty-five cents came from a little girl who gave half of her allowance.

Jen got one package from the Dixons with food and one from Uncle Paul and Aunt Patty with a printer. Now she can print out her pictures there instead of mailing me a disc and then me hanging out at the Walgreens kiosk and mailing the prints back to her. So much easier this way!

When Jen first got home at Christmas, she needed to make copies of some pictures and then mail them off for a calendar contest that she learned about from Kathryn. Last year, Kathryn's parents got an International Peace Corps calendar done by alumni volunteers out of Madison, Wisconsin. All volunteers are encouraged to send in pictures to represent their countries. Out of thousands of entries, one of Kathryn's was picked! Not sure what month it will be, but Kyrgyzstan will be represented for 2007.

The picture is a field with trees lining one side—they look golden in the sun—and a guy in the background. Now she has to write up a description that shares some facts about the country and her experience being there. Jen said that when Kathryn's parents called to give the news, she screamed like she had won the lottery.

Jen took a quick, unexpected trip to Talas to get some grant-writing papers signed for Gulnara on Tuesday. While there, she dropped us a quick email. We knew she would get Internet access on her trip this week for sure, but that extra email was such an unexpected treat. She said that she went because Gulnara couldn't afford the taxi ride. Jen offered to go, because she can classify it as program travel and will be reimbursed by the Peace Corps.

The reason for Gulnara's lack of funds is that her husband left her right before Jen came home for Christmas. It has been a long time coming. He was having affairs with women and squandering their money, and she told Jen, "Even though it is hard, we are almost better off without him here." Jen's counterpart, Rosa, is having problems with her husband being with other women as well, but the wives are taught to accept it.

It only makes Jen enjoy Nurgul, who is Kathryn's counterpart, and her family even more. Nurgul lives four doors down from Venera's. She speaks very good English and her husband is the one Jen danced with in a picture she sent. When Jen showed Nurgul some pictures from home—one was of us at the farm—Nurgul said, "Your grandmother is a good Kyrgyz grandmother. Everyone is not wearing shoes." She was referring to the tradition that people take off all shoes at the door and put on slippers. She said, "It seems Americans always wear their shoes indoors." Jen explained that we usually wear shoes, but we take them off when we want to get cozy.

Jen was planning on staying with her good friend Melissa in Naryn; Melissa is having an early out in May. I'm sure she has a number of reasons, but one might be that her host family has been getting on her case lately, claiming that she is having too many guests over.

She told Jen, "Don't worry. Instead of telling them that you're another volunteer, I will just say that you are an American visitor. If they think you came all the way from America to see me, they will be okay." Jen said, "Well, you better tell me which way you're going, so that I don't speak Kyrgyz to them or somehow know exactly what to do with all the traditions." They had a good laugh.

Just as we were going to say good-bye, she started to yell a few sentences in Russian at someone outside. I asked, "Is somebody at your door?" She said, "A nude. He's been whistling outside my window wanting to know where Altynai is." I said "A NUDE!?" She laughed and said, "NO, A DUDE!"

It was great to share a laugh with her like we did when she was home, and since she has great reception with her cell phone, I have to admit, it was my hearing that created the confusion. I am thankful that she keeps her door locked, and wanted to know all that was said. She told me that he said, "Is Altynai there?" Jen said, "She is not here." He said, "Where is she?" Jen said, "I do not know... I do not know anything!"

This is the regular phrase she says; otherwise, she is constantly bothered. But I don't agree with her. After all she has been through, I hardly think she knows nothing. Even though we just talked, I am looking forward to her emails this week.

Love,

Karen

February 18, 2006

The last time I updated you I was in country for only a few days. After a full month, things continue to go well, and I've had some fun interactions with people within my community. First and foremost, the reason I was able to email you: our MST (midservice training) went well. It was a two-day, three-night stay in a resort on Lake Issyk Kul, "Warm Lake." The lake is true to its name; despite the cold, it was not frozen over. We were able to choose from a handful of sessions during each time slot, so as to get the most out of our training. The sessions were generally led by volunteers; a few were by staff members.

I presented during a gender and development session, which included information about the "Take Your Daughter to Work Day" that volunteers are trying to organize countrywide, as well as trafficking. I presented on the TIP conference I attended in Bulgaria last August. The thirty minutes I had went well and there were a good number of people present. At the TIP conference, we had all brainstormed ways in which we could combat trafficking. I feel that at this point in time, the most I can do, and really what all volunteers can do, is educate other volunteers and host-country nationals about trafficking itself. Some days I feel like a one-woman revolution, but sharing my knowledge with others lightens the load and turns it into a team effort.

The session went well, and we had a very productive GAD committee meeting that night. We are in the process of establishing an official committee with one representative from each oblast, but the ball is already rolling on some exciting efforts. Materials about GAD will be translated into Kyrgyz and Russian and then distributed to any interested HCNs. The possibility of a public service announcement regarding trafficking in persons is being looked into, as well as the collection of local views on gender roles and stereotypes for both the north and the south. Militia-sensitivity training in regards to domestic violence and sexual assault is in preparation stages. A GAD kit that will eventually be distributed to all volunteers is being put together and will include educational activities to do with HCNs.

Finally, a manual is being put together regarding volunteer encounters with local gender customs. On a fun side note from MST, a volunteer put together an impromptu disco on the last night. A lot of volunteers, including myself, were hesitant about going. You see, we haven't danced around Americans for a really long time. In a Kyrgyz disco, you are a god, you can do nothing wrong, and any dance move you bust out is instantly cool because the American is doing it. Yes, I have done the "Running Man" in public. People eventually showed up after some encouragement from a very enthusiastic volunteer and we all really had a great time. It was so much fun to look around and see smiling faces on people who I rarely get to see and most of whom I've never danced with. The best part of the evening was noticing that the energy level would dip with American songs and rise with locally popular songs. It was definitely the surprising highlight of MST.

On the way back from the resort, we came into Bishkek through a snowstorm. The snowstorm that didn't hit the resort hit the south, and prevented volunteers from the southern oblasts from flying back on Sunday. They were still in Bishkek on Tuesday of that week, waiting for flights. Our little group made it back to Talas all right, despite having to wait while chains were put on the tires of a jackknifed semi in the mountain pass. We were a little nervous that the semi would start to slide, but after it was righted and we passed it along with the long line of cars and trucks that had also been waiting, it was smooth sailing.

Once we volunteers were back at the lyceum after MST, the students were really excited. They said that life had been boring without Ian and me. At tea time the first day I was back, one of the girls looked at me very seriously and said, "Did you miss the lyceum's bread?" I thought I was going to die laughing. I expected her to ask if I had missed the students, but the bread took precedence. Actually, I don't really like the lyceum's bread. It's unique, but oddly so, because as you chew, it disintegrates into a very thick paste that chokes you as you try to swallow it. It's a fight to finish the bread, but when you're hungry, it doesn't really matter. I went to the place with the outdoor bread oven where I usually buy my bread, fresh and delicious. The Turkish guys who work there asked why they hadn't seen me in a while. When they joked, "Did you go back to America?" I answered with a smile, "Yes." They came back with, "Did you tell everyone hello from the bread guys for us?" I laughed, "Of course I did!" They replied, "Good for you!"

Also, at the store closest to my house, the woman who works there asked where I had been. When I told her I had been in America and she asked how things were. For a split second I wanted to answer, "Horrible! The indoor plumbing, hot running water, ample food at all times... it was just awful!" But I answered, "Everything was good!" as I paid for my things.

Recently I was showing Kathryn's counterpart's family my photos from home. Nurgul, her husband, Talai, and their two children have been trusted friends since moving here. They have routinely said they would have willingly housed Kathryn, me, or both of us if they had a spare room. After a while, the attention turned to my computer. "How much did this cost?" asked Talai. I said, "One thousand dollars, but it was a gift when I finished at the university. My whole family gave it to me." Later, when I thought we were focused back on the pictures, the young son looked at Nurgul and asked, "Mom, how much would Jennifer's computer cost in som?" She replied, "Forty thousand som, dear." He asked, "Isn't that the cost of two horses? She could take two horses back if she sold her computer in Kyrgyzstan!" We all had a good laugh at the idea of me riding off into the sunset with my two horses.

The reason I am emailing you now is because I went to Naryn Oblast to speak during "Diversity Week" activities. A university TEFL volunteer organized the second "Diversity Week" in which volunteers speak to university students who study English about a variety of topics. Presentations ranged from talking about family, hobbies, home states (my focus—go, Minnesota!), religion, etc. If volunteers had anything planned, it usually went out the window, and volunteers who didn't have anything in particular planned (like myself) still had great sessions.

This was all due to the students' enthusiasm and interest in asking questions. I began talking about Minnesota, but then was asked questions such as, "Where is your favorite place in Kyrgyzstan?"; "Are you interested in different religions?"; "What is important to you?"; and "What did you do before you started Peace Corps?" It was a wonderful opportunity to share who I am and how I view being an American with the students, as well as a way to get to know volunteers better.

Peace,

Jenny

February 19, 2006

Our conversation with Jen started out about the Olympics and how Kazakhstan's hockey team only lost to the United States by one point! Even though she is for America all the way, I think Jen was a little proud of her next-door third-world country.

She told us how her travel back from Naryn took eight hours, through the mountain pass, because of snow. Erich even ended up having to help push the *marshutka* with other Kyrgyz men when they got stuck. Par for the course. Jen had the taxi stop at Kathryn's home before heading to her place and Kathryn told her that their electricity had been out from 9:00 a.m. to 5:30 p.m. that day and so they had just turned on Jen's heater. It would be far from warm, so she told Jen to stay with her.

She had some more news. Kathryn said, "You don't have to worry about going to lessons today, because you are done being a teacher." Jen immediately panicked, thinking she had done something wrong and been fired. I'd say that you would have to be paid in order for that to happen... The real reason, Kathryn explained, was that they found another teacher to take over.

Even though Jen knew her position was temporary, she was relieved to hear the reason, and Ian will have a much lighter load. Kind of the pits to have it happen while she was gone a week, but that was just how it happened. I asked her if she thought the kids would be mad and she said, "They better be." I know they will be upset with anyone who replaces her.

Our biggest concern is that, with the History Sources office being closed due to high heating costs, and now not teaching, Jen will get homesick from not being busy. But even before I could say anything, Jen started listing off all the things she still can do. She has more projects with GenGirls, she's still helping Albina teach younger kids, and, more importantly, she has to get going with starting up a gender and development committee. Along with this, she wants to raise awareness about women's rights and teach girls about self-esteem, so they will not believe that they can get a free ride to America without visas. This last issue has been on her mind and in her heart for some time.

They want one representative from each oblast to meet in Bishkek from March 13th to 15th, and she thinks she will be chosen. They are even working on making a public service announcement. Participating is one more way for her to feel that she has made things better in the area. With all the backward thinking and traditions winning over common sense, she sees how the school kids with whom she works are the ones most open to the change. It's the best place to start.

It is Men's Day on Thursday. Kathryn and Jen are going to make the annual macaroni and cheese dinner for Ian. He said that's all he really wants. Food. They are all waiting on the medical officer to visit, for another check on their housing conditions. This is good, because both Ian's and Jen's have changed since the last one. The doctor checks to make sure the water is running, warm, and far enough away from the outhouse. The doctor also makes sure the housing is warm enough (I think that might be up in the air for Jen) and that they have electricity.

I asked if she was able to use the extension cord that Uncle Paul gave her and she said she hadn't yet. In fact, she is going to wait until the doctor has come for fear she would blow a circuit and affect her inspection! We had a good laugh about that one. She said her big package with her manual washing machine arrived at the post office while she was gone. Thanks, Aunt Sue and Uncle Bill for getting it as a Christmas gift, and thanks to Uncle Paul and Aunt Patty for sending it. Will be fun to hear about her maiden voyage cranking away the stains!

Jen explained that they do inspections periodically because Kyrgyz people always say yes when asked if things are in working condition. In the summer, who is to know if a heater works well enough? I guess I am thankful that the Peace Corps knows people there and protects their volunteers.

Peace Corps officials have also been upfront with the volunteers about the possibility of another riot on the anniversary of the government building's takeover last year. Funny how they don't protest because of the anniversary of the elections they felt were so wrong, but because of the pride of what they did that day. There will be a planned standfast (absolutely no travel, so Jen is hoping she can still go to Bishkek on the 13th through the 15th) that week. They will be notified for sure.

It doesn't seem like it, but it is almost a year since Easter Holy Week brought us lots of scary days. No communication, until those wonderful words, "We are safe... I'm okay... Mom, can you hear me?... I'm okay!" It was one of the best Easter Sundays we've had.

Pray for Jen's patience in not being so busy and having to wait for her grant to go through so she can begin work on the building renovation.

Love,

Karen

February 26, 2006

Jennifer's place survived the inspection by the Peace Corps medical in-spector, who turned out to be a nurse. She told Jen she had everything set up so nicely and commented that she must enjoy the privacy of living on her own. One strange thing was that wandering turkeys sat outside her window and gobbled away the whole time the nurse was there. Jen said they just showed up one day (amazing they are alive and not some-one's supper), but since she's usually gone during work hours, she never experienced them. They just wouldn't give up and were like barking dogs outside her place. Only in Kyrgyz land.

She talked to the nurse about a reoccurring low-back pain that she's had ever since she slipped on the icy steps at the midservice training. It hurt at first, but then went away for a couple of weeks and she thought all was good. Then an eight-hour *marshutka* ride brought it back. She is to do a regimen of Advil for a week and include some stretching. If that doesn't work, they are going to do an x-ray or MRI when she goes to Bishkek on the 14th, just to make sure it's nothing more serious.

Men's Day went without too much fanfare, but this year Jen and Kathryn decided to make sugar cookies for guys special to them. And because they turned out so well (they were made from scratch!), they put on some sprinkles that Uncle Paul and Aunt Patty sent for Halloween. She didn't think the men would mind or have a clue that the black and orange were Halloween colors! She made up a bag and brought them to Madim and Kadim. Venera wasn't there, and Jen whispered to the boys that they were for Men's Day and only for them. She figured that as soon as she left, they would be devoured, but she found out from Gulnara that Venera told her they kept the bag sealed and waited for her to come home so they could show her what Jennifer had brought them. That must have been as sweet as the cookies for Jen.

She had another sweet thing happen. She had to bring something to Ian and ran into kids that were shouting "Miss Jennifer, Miss Jennifer; we miss you." Some were hanging on her and blowing kisses. Then they asked, "Will you teach us today?" She told them, "I can't, because you have a new teacher." Then they said, "But she's not you." Jen chalks it up to the fact that she didn't really know what she was doing, so her lessons were probably crazy freak shows to them. But I think she doesn't give herself enough credit.

Kathryn decided to be the winner of the Polar Bear Club this year and this time it wasn't to impress the GenGirls, but because of a bet with Erich, the volunteer from Kirovka. The bet is for who will swim in the river the earliest. Last year when she took the plunge, it was April 14th. This year, the weather was nice, so Jen and Kathryn decided to go for a hike. Then, just like that, Kathryn checked the water and said, "It's not too bad... I'm going in." Jen documented this on film as proof to Erich. Jen said that she took some clothes off, but I didn't ask for details. When they broke the news to Erich, he questioned them about the validity. Did she just jump in or did she swim? The bet was for swimming. He asked Jen if she had done actual strokes. Jen replied, "I'm out of here. If you're going to keep changing the rules so you can win, I'm not going to be in the middle of it." They had a good laugh. The things volunteers do for fun.

Jen has been working with Gulnara every day for a few hours. They've been planning on opening the office March 1st, but Jen doesn't see that happening until the middle or end of March. Some repairs were supposed to happen before that, and they haven't been done (surprise, surprise), and she doesn't know when they will. Then Jen cheerfully said that it doesn't bother her. She got to thinking after we talked last about being patient and enjoying the downtime. She's realized that many business volunteers work very limited hours in the day, while she has always worked eight. And the teachers have the summers totally off. So she told herself not to feel guilty (it makes me wish we didn't raise her to be so productive), and said, "I'm just calling the shots and doing what I want and it's okay." I was so glad to hear that homesickness doesn't seem to have entered in. But she did say that if she gets shipped home because of any violence due to the revolution's anniversary, she will be okay with that, too.

Dan tried to update Jen about his elbow surgery. She didn't like that he had downplayed it in a previous conversation. I think he finally realizes how important it is for her to know about everything going on back home and that not sharing even the tough stuff really isn't protecting her.

She told us that she received a W-2 and is trying to decide what she should do. We couldn't remember how we handled it last year, but as she read more, it seemed that she wouldn't have to file unless she made over $7,000. Her W-2 says $2,700 for the year. When she saw that number, she was shocked and said, "Hello—I am totally under the poverty level!" I said, "Yeah, and you still are happy!" She replied, "Who knew!" But the sad part is that she is making four times that of the average Kyrgyz man. I guess that's one of the main reasons she is there. Blessed be the poor.

Love,

Karen

March 5, 2006

Jen was able to send us a quick email on Thursday because she had a trip to Talas with her director. It was for a women-in-business concourse (competition) in honor of Women's Day the following Wednesday. She said there were people from seven different counties and they were in an auditorium with a real microphone, so the ladies see it as BIG time. The microphone was the clincher.

It was difficult for Jen, because it was all in the Kyrgyz language and she had to keep asking questions. She finally gave up, because the longer it went on, the more it seemed to turn into a beauty pageant for forty-five-year olds! They paraded about, had to answer a random question without preparation, and showed their "talent." Gulnara showed handicraft-wears and spoke about the building renovation. It was a long day, and just when Jen thought it was over, it started up again, so she asked someone what was going on. They said in Russian, "Now it is the second part." Arrrrggggghhhh! Jen figured that this must be where they have the swimsuit competition, so she slipped out to go to an Internet site down the street.

Earlier that week, Gulnara had asked Jen if she would get up and talk at the concourse about the project, speaking in Russian. Jen said no. Gulnara then went on to explain more about the event. Jen said no. Then she told Jennifer (as Kyrgyz women are noted for) that Jen *would* be speaking. Jen looked at her and said, "I can help, but I am not getting up there and having my Russian critiqued and my accent pointed out." So Gulnara did her thing on her own, but Jen brought things out on cue and did tell the group at the end in Russian, "Happy holiday to all women in Kyrgyzstan." That small bit was a hit.

Gulnara got third place, but Jen wasn't sure what that even meant and if there was a prize or not. Apparently, the winner got 4,000 som. She was pooped after this sixteen-hour day, but she still went to an Internet café in Taraz with Kathryn and Ian the next day. She also will be going to Bishkek next week and is not sure if she will be home in time for our call.

The new group (K-13) is having its in-service training a bit early so they can get in and get out of the city before the anniversary of the revolution on the 24th. They planned for the gender and development committee to meet, as some of them are in the K-13 group. I'm not thrilled that Jen will be travelling when the safety of travel is so sketchy. But I'm just the mom.

She assured us that they've had no news of a standfast, and that one probably won't come until next week when she is already there. Great. If she only knew the degree to which we've had to stretch as parents. But she's also getting a back x-ray as the pain isn't getting any better. So I guess the medical attention makes the trip worth it. She said she will try to call us from Bishkek after she has her back examined.

Jen used her washing machine for the first time! She wanted to document this maiden voyage with a video, but she was by herself and thought she better have some practice time first. The christening went well with undergarments only. The only hard part was trying to screw the top back on when her hands were soapy. She cranked it for about five minutes and was convinced it was more intense cleansing than scrubbing by hand. So she has a new toy. Maybe she can earn some extra cash by charging other volunteers for its use.

As we were talking, Jen said, "Hey, we're having a pretty romantic conversation." I didn't get the connection when we had just talked about laundry. She said, "I don't have electricity and am using candles." That can be nice, but also means that she can't use her heater. It has been mild there, but rained that day and the temperature really dropped. I know she dresses for these times, but I wish I could send heat through the phone lines.

All of us homeowners in America always seem to have some home improvements we need to do and Jen is not immune. She kept hearing a sound. She explained it wasn't a plopping or a banging sound. It was a thumping sound and she just couldn't figure it out. Then when she went out to the bathroom before it got dark, she realized there was a hole in her ceiling! When she told us this, I thought, "Isn't it enough that you don't have electricity or heat?" Fortunately, the hole wasn't in her bedroom or kitchen; it was in the ceiling of the patio between. The roof is a piece of tin covering a layer made of mud and straw. Hunks of it were on the ground and water dripped through. She figured there was a leak in the tin and that the makeshift Sheetrock couldn't handle it. She had a good laugh over it, but plans on talking to her landlady. I told Jen to tell Altynai that she feels like Chicken Little.

Heidi then took the phone and they began having their regular girl chat; she was filling Jen in on the Academy Awards. Then she stopped talking and said, "Jen... was that a rooster crowing?" Jen casually answered yes. Then Heidi said, "A REAL rooster?" I could just see Jen rolling her eyes and wanting to say, "No, Heidi; it's the tape-recorded message on my alarm clock so I know when to wake up." But she just assured her it was real and Heidi basked in the enjoyment of hearing a REAL rooster across the miles. I thought about the turkeys that had gobbled outside her window and wondered if Jen ever thinks, "This volunteering stuff is for the birds!" But from her voice, I don't think that's how she sees it.

Love,

Karen

March 12, 2006

We needed to call Jen later than usual so we could hear how her doctor's appointment went. She was seen in a Kyrgyz hospital, and her 8:00 a.m. appointment actually was at 8:00 a.m. I worry whether the doctors even know what an MRI is because they kept referring to it as an x-ray. I told Jen to ask them and make sure. Jen said, "Mom, it was an MRI. I was in a tube!"

She called us the next morning to let us know that they couldn't see any fractures or problems with her spine, so it appears that her pain is all from the soft-tissue injury of when she fell on those steps. She was going to meet with them later to devise a plan. She sounded relieved that she wouldn't have to have medical help that would take her away from Pokrovka.

Jen said she has been going into the office and that the recent mild weather has helped it not to be so cold. They have three sewing ladies and things are steadily getting busier, but they haven't moved in the office equipment yet, and it will get busier when people need to make copies or send a fax.

Her latest accomplishment was creating a three-month calendar for documenting upcoming deadlines and events. She can also use it to record her schedule so each time she leaves and they ask, "Where are you going?" she doesn't have to say things like "To club at school." Under her breath she always wants to say, "Like I have to tell you EVERY Tuesday." Such a small, basic chore of posting a schedule seems to have created a whole new way of life for her coworkers.

She spends her time at school after hours on Tuesdays and Thursdays for clubs, and then on Wednesdays she has GenGirls. Sometimes, when she's delivering something to the school, Ian asks her to take his class so he can run errands, like going to the bank. Recently she was filling in for Nurgul's classes when Nurgrul had to attend a funeral. So Jen sees herself as a "substitute" teacher. She's not totally gone. Jen kept commenting how she was walking around Bishkek with a long-sleeve shirt and jeans. No long johns. She said, "Spring is here! That's why I'm just waiting for the snow." Is she a realist or just someone who grew up in Minnesota?

But her biggest thrill is that, now that it is warmer, she doesn't have to run her heater right when she gets home to give it hours to heat up properly. She can use her computer and watch a movie first, then switch to the heater until things are warmer. It left me thinking of how in America the little things are no big deal, but in her world, the little things ARE big things.

Love,

Karen

CHAPTER 20

Just When You Need It

"Only in Kyrgyzstan would I be a pillow for a little girl I just met that morning, have my hands warmed by another woman who I talked to very infrequently, and be invited to the wedding of the daughter of a coworker, all during the marshutka ride home."

–Jen

March 12, 2006

We're constantly amazed at all the people touched by Jen's adventure. Last week while grocery shopping, I was standing in line to check out and I saw someone who used to live in our neighborhood. She smiled and I smiled back. Then she budged past the others in line and said, "We so enjoy Jenny's letters." I was confused at first, knowing she wasn't on Jen's email distribution list, and then realized she was talking about the two local paper articles. I told her that we're proud of her, too, because her adventure hasn't been easy. I also told her that I would tell Jen what she said. She smiled again.

On another occasion, we had dropped off Heidi's car at the repair shop and I was waiting for Dan to come out so I could drive us home.

When he finally came out, he was smiling all over. I was confused, because he usually doesn't look that way when we take a car in to be repaired. He said that Father Conran was in the office; he was dropping off his car. He used to be an associate pastor about twelve years ago and still lives in the community. He said, "Hello, Dan. I just want to tell you that I think it is so wonderful what your Jenny is doing. I love reading about her. Too bad more kids don't do the same."

Just when we think it's no big deal, someone reminds us of how this journey that we thought was only ours has gone so far beyond that, and has touched so many people. I guess that is what the Peace Corps was thinking about forty-five years ago on March 1st. Happy anniversary!

Love,

Karen

March 12, 2006

So I arrived back in the village, finding myself with time on my hands. I was "let go" as a teacher and my office has been closed during the winter due to inadequate heating and simply not having the funds to pay for mounting electricity bills. Luckily, I have found ways to keep myself busy, both with my director and in outside activities.

When I returned to the lyceum recently to finish filling out the grade books, a group of girls that I had taught ran up to me to give me the customary greeting between females: a kiss on the cheek. I asked them how their new teacher was and they all made sour faces. I laughed and said, "Well, she's a good Kyrgyz teacher, right? She can explain things to you much better than I could, right?" One of the girls replied, "But she's not Miss Jennifer! I don't think any Kyrgyz teacher could ever be Miss Jennifer."

Maybe that's because Miss Jennifer takes off her shoes in class. She throws things across the room during activities and she uses Kyrgyz phrases and slang to catch students' attention. She teases students who are giving her a hard time in the middle of class in Russian. She plays games, sings songs, and is basically a walking freak show. Once, when Kathryn was giving me a hard time about being a crazy teacher, I shot back, "Who said I was a teacher? I tell the students that I'm their cultural experience."

Finally the office reopened and despite it being very cold in the building, it's good to be back around the women on a regular basis. When I returned from Naryn, my director jumped on the Take-Your-Daughter-to-Work-Day bandwagon and has promised to help me find the appropriate mentors for the girls who are interested in participating. It can't really be a true mother-and-daughter activity, as many women stay at home, are teachers, or work in stores. Those are the three things that the girls understand and don't need to spend a day shadowing. Therefore, we will be going to the bank, clinic, government building, etc. to find mentors. This will be a great help so I don't have to go through the painful process of speaking to people I don't know in my non-native language, over and over again.

Also, she thought of hosting a cultural exchange camp this summer. She pointed out that volunteers never come to Talas Oblast, the home of Manas (Kyrgyz Paul Bunyan), and that we should give them a reason to visit. So we are in the planning and finding-funding stages to organize a cultural exchange camp for students in the village and any interested volunteers.

We are in the process of writing an SPA (small project assistance) grant to renovate the public school's (Kathryn's school's) cafeteria. There is a cafeteria, but it is not at all functional. The school, with my director, has applied for grants to complete this project, but to no avail. We'll see if the Peace Corps can help us out. There are also plenty of odds and ends to attend to in the office. On the to-do list is creating a three-month calendar of events and deadlines and transferring the knowledge of how to maintain the souvenir catalogue from my brain to my director's.

Recently my program manager, Jypar, visited my site as a one-year check-up of sorts. During the meeting, I realized that I comprehended about 95 percent of what my director and Jypar were saying to one another. I thought back to a year ago when the meeting was held in English, Kyrgyz, and Russian, so that all involved could understand. Now the meeting was almost completely held in Russian and I was participating just as much as Gulnara, my director.

Reflecting on where I was a year ago—regarding language skills and productivity at work—and where I am now both encourages and scares me. I had a mental timeout during the meeting, during which the realization that I understood what was going on was a little too much to handle. I had a brief inner struggle. I thought, "Ahhhhhhh! I don't want to understand this conversation without even trying! Someone take this comprehension away!" Long story short, the meeting was very helpful, as I got some of Jypar's feedback on what I can do in the last seven months of my service.

Not only was Wednesday, March 1st, Ash Wednesday, but it was also the forty-fifth anniversary of the Peace Corps. In honor of its birthday (which is how we explained it to the students), we played a game of baseball with students from both Ian's and Kathryn's schools. After all, one of the goals is to share American culture with other peoples. We explained to the kids that baseball is America's national pastime, taught them how to play the game, and then let them take over. The final score was Ian's team, twelve; Kathryn's team, eight. I was the official photographer and cheerleader. Luckily, we have had an unusually mild winter, and with no snow on the ground, the game went off without a hitch.

Recently my director, Gulnara, was asked by the local government to represent our county in a statewide competition. The competition, held in Talas, was for businesswomen, and the grand prize was 4,000 som ($100). The women who participated had to demonstrate what they did in their businesses, in an auditorium in front of a panel of judges. In true Kyrgyz style, the entire presentation was put together in four days, from finding models to show off the dresses the women had sewn, to practicing a cultural skit, to gathering all the handicrafts and props. I was able to participate, and accompanied Gulnara on stage a few times. I was a model for a few handicraft items, and was able to wish all women in Kyrgyzstan a happy International Women's Day, March 8th.

I was a little nervous at first, but it was a wonderful day spent with women whom I truly care about and who care about me. The energy and solidarity that Kyrgyz women have around each other when there are no men present is powerful. I recently said in a magazine article that I have found my passion working with girls and women. After this competition, I realized that I have passion because I soak in their natural passion and compassion. Only in Kyrgyzstan would I be the pillow for a little girl who I had just met that morning, have my hands warmed by another woman who I talked to very infrequently, and be invited to the wedding of the daughter of a coworker, all during the *marshutka* ride home.

Recently, Kathryn and I were at our "bazaar," which really is only four elderly women who sit at a table selling small bags of carrots, potatoes, and onions. I was trying to buy some carrots when a woman selling an assortment of items came up to me. She started pushing a small bag of carrot salad at me, telling me to take it. I thought she wanted me to buy it and was being more forceful than the usual shopkeeper, and I politely refused her several times.

Then I actually listened to what she was saying. "Your mother is far away; please take this and eat for your health." I just about started bawling on the spot at such an unexpected, unprompted extension of kindness. I stood in disbelief, holding the salad as she walked away and then explained what happened to Kathryn, who was paying for her things. Before we left, I went up to the woman and gave her a kiss on the cheek, saying thank you. I later found out she is from Korea and her Korean carrot salad is a spicy specialty in the village. It was one of those moments that made me realize there are people here who understand what it's like to be so far from home.

Peace and love,

Jenny

March 19, 2006

We talked to Jen around 10:00 p.m., and since it was 10:00 a.m. her time, she was at her office. She told me that we might be interrupted, because she has to deal with people coming in to make copies. I asked her why they don't just make the copies themselves, like we do at Walgreens. She said, "Mom, nobody knows HOW to run a copier." And they surely wouldn't have a coin dispenser built in, so she has to take their three som per copy, which is less than a penny. Their office is only one of two places that can make copies, so it was busy.

I thoroughly loved listening to her switch from English to Russian. She greeted a handyman that stops in every day to check on things that need to be done. He had to check a hole in the wall that he filled in with plaster. During all this bilingual interaction, we did our usual talking.

Jen told me she got our little package with odds and ends and ate all three little Crunch bars right away because she was so hungry. I asked how her weight was and she said, "Well, I think I pretty much lost the ten pounds I gained at Christmastime, but things are stable." She still has episodes of sleep-eating. Whenever she is in Bishkek, she buys something special to have for her breakfast. She keeps it on her night-stand so it is ready right away in the morning. But sometimes she wakes up to go to the bathroom and on the way back starts nibbling.

We talked about her back. She said it isn't the best, but isn't getting worse. The doctor showed her the x-ray; the problem is from muscles that got so tight that there's pressure on the nerves that go down the spine. It's usually found in knees. She uses the muscle relaxants when it is safe (I guess she doesn't have to worry about driving), and they even gave her Bengay, which she thinks really helps. The pain is probably mostly from the fall on the steps, but it could also be from her neck problems from sleeping on third-world-country beds and pillows. Dr. Guse (our chiropractor) gave her a pillow you fill with water and that pretty much got rid of the neck pain. At any rate, everything is in her file and that will take care of any further help she would need once getting out.

We were interrupted by more Russian greetings. Then we went back to the old reliable. Then she said, "Mom, you have to help me remember something." I was thinking it must be a special date or event of our family. She said, "What was the name of the oldest son on *Bonanza*?" It's amazing how those goofy things can drive you nuts. I was happy to solve the puzzle: Adam.

Then Jen lapsed into more Russian. Then some giggling, and then scuffling. I just waited. Jen told me that an older man came in to have copies made and when she was on the phone, he just stood there like he was going to wait until she was done. Since she didn't want to end our conversation or have him stare at her for twenty minutes, she said, "It's okay; please let me make your copies."

She told him she was talking to her mom in America. He got a huge smile on his face and said, "Tell your mother, I will kiss you... but it is for her." She kept giggling in the I-can't-believe-that-just-happened sort of way. "Oh, don't worry, Mom; it was on the cheek... on the cheek! He's cute. Well, it was kind of gross. He smelled like tobacco." But the whole thing made us laugh. It amazes me that kissing when greeting is so commonplace there, but we can walk past someone and not even say hi.

The best part of our conversation was when she told me about her Saturday morning, which was our Friday night. Dan and I were driving with Uncle Paul and Aunt Patty up to their cabin around 9:30 p.m., and on a whim, Dan dialed up Jen and handed the phone to Paul. It was a surprise to both of them.

But the story behind the story was that she didn't go to Kirovka that morning with Ian and Kathryn. She just wanted to stay home, take care of her back, and watch the movie *North Country* that she got in Bishkek. But then she thought she really should wait, so they could watch it all together. She was agonizing over the decision, because she really wanted and needed to experience a piece of home and hear Minnesota accents. Just then, the phone rang and it was Dan. Ask and you shall receive... even halfway around the world.

Love,

Karen

March 26, 2006

First and foremost, Jen let us know that the anniversary of the revolution on March 24th came and went without violence. It could be because the president turned it into a holiday. He might be corrupt, but he isn't dumb. Whenever there is a holiday, it means a day off from work for the people. And a holiday and day off together, for Kyrgyz men, is a time to party and drink. And that took precedence over fighting. I'm sure many didn't forget about the "Tulip" Revolution, but it went without a violent protest and all are safe.

As we were first talking, I could hear that she was chewing. I asked if she needed to finish her breakfast, but she said that she had only two bites left, which made me curious about what she was eating. She said, "Egg McMuffin." There was a long pause as I waited for her to say, "Just kidding." Nothing. Then she said, "Well, my version of one." She explained that bread goes stale so quickly that she has to find creative ways to use every last crumb. One creation is her variation on an Egg McMuffin. She takes dry bread, puts cheese and onions on it, and puts it in the oven. Then she fries an egg and puts that on top. But this can only happen when she visits Talas or Bishkek beforehand, because those are the only places where she can get cheese "wheels" (similar to cheese slices). Pokrovka doesn't have any, but she heard rumor that they may be getting block cheese soon. Yippee!

We got to talking about Dan's birthday coming up, and I went downstairs so we could discuss some ideas in private. We talked softly back and forth for a while until Jen stopped and said, "Hey, why am I whispering?!" I started laughing so hard, and so did she. We kept laughing at how the other was laughing, and I thought, "How silly to do this long distance." But then I just hugged myself and held her voice tight in my ear. I told her I was pretending that she was here and we were being silly together in person. She said, "Awwwwww." I like when she does that.

Dan & I helped out with a benefit dinner for Amy M. and Jennifer wanted to know how it went. I told her that as I was handing out garlic bread, people kept commenting on the article in the Chaska paper about Dominic; it was about his Outstanding Senior Award. I told Jen that it was embarrassing, because she was just in the paper and now Dominic. And Heidi is the famous local salon haircutter. Jen quickly responded with, "Sorry, Mom. We'll try to screw up soon so we can be in the arrest section of the paper." No matter what language she speaks, her sense of humor is still there.

Jen had to sign a new housing arrangement with her landlady. Jen found it interesting that she could understand the Russian word for "lessee" and "lessor" better than she did, since she signed in the wrong place each time. Hopefully, it will still be legal.

Jen and Kathryn attended a going-away party in Talas for a volunteer who is leaving. Jen said that it was fun, but the best part was staying with some missionaries (they've been there for five years) for the night. It was such a treat, because they had cable. That meant CNN! They were glued to the news about what was going on around the world. Jen didn't feel so bad about Kyrgyzstan's government when she saw that Belarus was fighting over a rigged election and Thailand was trying to get rid of their prime minister.

There is a fine line between being a missionary and being a Peace Corps volunteer. It's a church and state thing. But they found themselves talking about the upcoming Easter season. They were telling the girls that if they're interested, there's a church that was set up for Kyrgyz people who have converted to Christianity. It is nondenominational and services are in the Kyrgyz language. Kathryn seemed interested, but Jen seemed a bit blah about it.

One of the missionaries asked Jen how she felt, and she said, "Not that there is anything wrong with attending an Evangelical free church, but Easter is my favorite holiday and it wouldn't be the same." One of the ladies asked Jen what faith she practices. Jen said she was Catholic. Then they told her some shocking news. The lady said, "Did you know that there are two nuns and one priest in Talas who are trying to build a church? They work in an orphanage and speak some English, but are Slovakian, so are fluent in Russian!" Jen about flipped off her chair! They have been there for two years. Jen said, "And I just find out about this now?"

Like I said, there is a fine line between being a Peace Corps volunteer and a missionary. Not that they wouldn't have told her about it... she just didn't ask. So it was meant to be that they spent the night there. She is so excited, because she will be attending a seminar with her director, Gulnara, in Bishkek, April 11th to the 15th, and on their way back they will go through Talas and she can take in an Easter Sunday Mass! She is going to tell her friend Erich about it, too, because he is Catholic. This might be a new reason to go to Talas. Only four hours to travel for Eucharist.

Love,

Karen

April 3, 2006

Jennifer was excited, telling us about the English competition they had on Saturday. There are two big ones a year that involve all schools that have volunteers serving. Pokrovka has always wanted to host one, but the volunteers in Talas always turn them down. So Jen had the idea that they should do it the Kyrgyz way. You don't ask, you just tell.

So they informed everyone that the English competition would be in Pokrovka, and they hoped they could come! I think she has figured out that two can play at that game. She said she and Kathryn worked so hard on it and it paid off. It was the most organized and fair school event they have ever had. It struck me how she used both those words. In America, we might not have something very organized, but being fair is pretty much a given. I guess school functions can take after the government.

There were six schools involved; their introductions to everyone were skits that talked about their schools and showed how good they were. Ian's school was the best. Their skit was titled, "What if the USA President came to Kyrgyzstan?" It was hilarious, especially the part where they were making the president *besh bar mak* (a local dish in which a sheep—all the parts, head, guts, and all—are cooked in a big pot) and he ends up with diarrhea! This might put Jen's stomach troubles into perspective.

Each group from each school rotated to different stations, and the one she most looked forward to seeing was the "snipe hunt" booth manned by Willie. They figured he would be a natural, because he is such an animated guy; his role would be to describe the animal—the snipe—to the kids and lead them around the gym on a hunt. Unfortunately, the first group figured it out in five minutes. They looked right at him and said, "There is no such thing as a snipe." That word must have a universal language all its own. So Willie turned his booth into a paper-rock-scissors competition, because he always beats the other volunteers. Jen said the kids had the most fun with him.

Ian's class took first, another school took second, and Kathryn's took third, so they were very happy and so were the schools that participated. Jen was in charge of all the prizes and did a lot of sorting and preparing before they had a small disco at the end. Maybe next time they will think twice before turning down the little town of Pokrovka for a party.

Since it was such a hit, Ian, Kathryn, and Jen went to their favorite café in town for dinner. Funny thing about ordering food there; it is unheard of to just order a salad. Back home, a salad can be a meal, whether it's a Caesar, Cobb, or just chicken salad. But there, it is not seen as a complete meal, even though Jen says the salads are so big. And Kathryn decided to bring her own tea, which isn't correct, but she didn't want to deal with strong Kyrgyz tea to which she'd need to add tons of sugar.

The waitress was very confused by their order. They ordered salads and hot water. She said, "You mean you don't want food or tea?" To help her feel better, Jen said, "Okay, you can bring us some *plov*," which is a rice dish, but that still got them a strange look.

To make matters worse, Jen had made no-bake cookies that day, which she brought along. They hadn't turned out too well (too sticky), and Jen said they should order some ice cream and put it on top to make a sundae. Now they had to explain to the lady that they wanted ice cream in a bowl; it's usually hand-held. The waitress was still confused and brought them ice cream in large teacups. They laughed like crazy while trying to mix ice cream and no-bake cookies into a teacup. Hey, when in Rome.

When they paid, they were told it was 136 som, but then someone came running after them saying it should have been 142. Ian said okay and gave her six more som. She said, "No, I need ten more." Ian was just going to give it to her, but Jen pushed his hand away and Kathryn specifically spelled out each number as she counted from 136 to 142. They weren't sure if it was a ploy to get extra money out of the foreigners, or the waitress just couldn't count.

Jen was part of another confusing situation when she went to get her check from the bank. She noticed that they had withdrawn 1 percent from her pay. This didn't make sense, and trying to find out why was even harder. She told us there have been new people at the bank, and she's noticed that getting her pay has become more formal. She used to have to provide her ID and sign a paper, and the clerk would then match the signature and go to another lady who approved it. Then they paid her. But lately they were asking so many more questions and were requiring her passport as well. And she was yelled at twice for the way she signs her name. (That's something that wouldn't happen in Chaska, that's for sure.) The local people usually only sign their last names. And Kyrgyz people don't have middle names, so when Jen signs as Jennifer Marie Lawrence (how it is on her passport), they think Jennifer is her last name and that Marie is her first, while not being sure why the Lawrence is there at all.

The bank cashier has called her Maria (not even Marie), which really bugged her. When they got on her case the second time, she explained, "That is my name. That is my name. How am I supposed to sign it?" They backed off. Don't mess with a tall white American woman when you take 1 percent out of her paycheck. She says it amounts to about one dollar out of two hundred, but it is the principal of the thing and she doesn't want them to take 2 percent the next time and then 3 percent the next. This from the girl who would get cheated out of food at McDonald's but would never go up to the counter to get it back. She put a call into headquarters and knows it will be taken care of. Another interaction with them has been a good one.

I noticed that Jen's partnership program wasn't posted on the website anymore. Last time I checked, it still needed $1,382, so for it to be totally down to zero seemed odd. I quickly called Jen during the week to tell her so she could check with the authorities. She got excited, because the exact same thing had happened to Kathryn's program. Her mom noticed it wasn't on the website anymore and about two weeks later, Kathryn got an email stating that her project was funded and asking her when she wanted the monies.

Jen has a call into headquarters and is excited to get going with the renovation. She has been very busy at the office and so it seems that the timing of not teaching right now is okay. She will not only be the catalyst to keep things rolling, but is totally in charge of receipts and disbursements. It became even more evident how important that is when her director said, "If we get everything done and have money left over, we can have a party with vodka." Jen had to explain that if there's any money left over, it goes back to the Peace Corps to help another area. No vodka here! There were other internal projects for which Jen wrote grants for Gulnara, but she still hasn't finished her part of the paperwork. She wants the help, but just can't seem to make the deadline to do her part. Again, when in Rome.

Jen said she will be sending some photos on CD soon, but is most upset about us not receiving the package with Dan's slippers. The ones she got him for Christmas were too small, so Heidi adopted them and Jen got another pair to mail home. It has been over six weeks and Dan says he can picture the guy at the post office with nice warm feet. What really bothers her is that there were thirty thank-you cards she wrote out to everyone she saw at Christmas and that she wanted us to mail for her, so they'd arrive at the recipients' addresses safely. Guess they weren't safe this way.

When Dominic talked to her, a man came to her door and asked where the landlady was; Jen yelled in Russian to close the door. He did and left. She had forgotten to lock it. It was no big deal to her, just an irritant. She is more upset with the pack of wild (small) dogs that live behind her. Dan could hear them barking over the phone and he told her that he felt like he was right there with her. He also told her that he now has Bishkek's temperature on his computer screen, and he was happy to see it was seventy degrees. Between the strangers, dogs, and "Dad spy," she is never alone.

Thanks to everyone who donated to her partnership program. That will make one of the main purposes of her being there happen. Wishing everyone a wonderful Lenten season.

Love,

Karen

April 11, 2006

We had to plan when we could call Jen for Easter. Jen's friend Erich tried giving up alcohol for Lent, but Jen said it isn't working very well. She gave up pop. I kind of laughed, saying, "Well, that's easy where you are," thinking about the icky carbonated Kyrgyz orange drink they have there. But she said, "You would be surprised how much easier it is to get Sprite and Coca-Cola." It seemed strange to hear her say Coca-Cola the way they do there, instead of Coke, as we say here. Just another friendly reminder that she is not with us.

Jen will be in Bishkek from the 11th to the 15th for an AIDS education seminar. There was a warden message that came down about some protests in the city on the 8th and 9th, but she is about a half hour outside the city, and so her trip has not been cancelled. Gulnara is a candidate to receive an organization grant for the oblast, so Jen is attending with her. There will be presentations, but Gulnara will also be interviewed, and if she wins, she will receive a bonus for running the project in their oblast. There will be about twenty other volunteers there and the seminar will be in Russian and English. No Kyrgyz. So Jen joked with Gulnara that she may need help with some Russian and that if Gulnara gets confused about anything in English, Jen will translate.

Jennifer received a box from the Dixons, but not Grandma and Grandpa's package yet. She said, "It will come, Mom." She wasn't that laid-back when it came to the package with new slippers that she sent Dan. We found out that it came back to her! Apparently, Ian had done Jen a favor and initially brought it to the post office to mail. The problem was that he is so immersed in Kyrgyz culture (maybe it's a teacher thing) that he addressed it upside down, with country first and name last, like you do when sending something to Kyrgyzstan. The U.S. postal system didn't like that and returned it to sender. At least the mystery is solved.

Jen was telling us about her friend Nicole in Kirovka who is losing her hair. The Peace Corps is giving her vitamin B supplements, and are really encouraging her to eat more vegetables. When they suggested her getting more spinach, she said, "You've got to be crazy! How do I get vegetables in Talas Oblast?" It is common belief that volunteers age more quickly in Jen's area than they do elsewhere. It's partly due to the fact that there are not as many life conveniences. Then Jen informed me of the gray hairs she found. There is no doubt she has matured in this experience, but hopefully the aging process will slow when she gets home with running water. I didn't want to make her feel bad and let her know that I have added a few gray hairs myself throughout this whole endeavor.

Jen got formal notification that her project is fully funded! It is such an exciting, happy time. She just needs to get the 1 percent withdrawal from her account taken care of so that the raised funds don't get tapped into. She was told the withdrawal is a new policy. If it were just her personal money, she wouldn't care—it seems like the new government's way of getting money—but when it comes to the partnership project's money, she is like a mama bear with her cubs. She's got headquarters working on sorting it out.

She's been busy helping Gulnara with the budget for another project for the school cafeteria. I asked Jen why she has to help with that. She said Gulnara is the one everyone comes to when there's a fundraising need. She has the connections. Jen doesn't mind the extra work, but when she's down to the deadline and has to go to the office from 6:00 until 11:00 p.m., because the electricity is out during regular work hours, she gets a bit testy. Hoping her renovation goes smoothly.

She loves her coworkers but sometimes gets upset with people who come into the sewing center. All of her advertising has made the business boom, so there are more people coming in. She said, "To the new ones, I am a novelty, a spectacle to stare at because I have light skin and light hair." Then there are the pushy ones who say, "Hey, German girl." She says it gets old, but in the same breath, she says she is so thankful for her ladies there who care about her so much that they even feel bad for how some of "their own" treat her.

Jen's back is getting better, but she says she doesn't go dancing every Saturday night. It seems strange to hear her say that, since she never went out to clubs when she lived at home. But I know their disco is different. She was more upset that she hadn't had a *banya* in over a week. She said it was too cold. It even snowed yesterday, but it melted right away. Hated to tell her that it was around sixty degrees here.

We told her about doing the readings for Palm Sunday and how Dan wanted to wear a toga as he pretended to be Pontius Pilate. She laughed, but then said, "Do you know the Russian word for 'toga'?" I thought this would be a strange lesson on a word I really wouldn't use in conversation, but I asked anyway. She said, "Toga." There was a pause and then her giggle. I asked what other words are the same. She said "computer," "box," "printer," "telephone"—mostly technical terms that are recent to the culture. But we had a laugh trying to figure out how "toga" fit into that category.

We got a CD of pictures from Jen on Friday. It's the first she has sent since she was home for Christmas. I told her about my favorite video clip of three GenGirls making cookies at her place, and how they had to pound on chocolate bars to make the chocolate chips. And my favorite picture was of her and Aisalkyn at Vernera's birthday party last month. They did a "year later" pose of a photo they had of Aisalkyn with her dollies. She had told everyone that the blond one looked just like her

American sister, Jennifer. Now it's missing arms and legs, and another doll doesn't have hair anymore. But both the girls have long hair, compared to their short hair before, and sure look a lot better than the dolls.

There is a priceless photo that shows Aisalkyn climbing into Jen's lap and looking directly in her eyes; Jen is looking back, dimples and all. I told her that it seems different, seeing pictures from her now. I have less of an ache when scanning over the pictures, not such an urgency and desperate feeling to see her and how she is living. She agreed with me. Seeing pictures of us now doesn't make her feel so homesick. It was a nice comparison and we did a good job of convincing each other that we are doing so much better now.

I heard a background noise that sounded like kids' voices. Jen said it was the landlord's daughter and her friends outside playing. She said, "She is not a cute girl." This didn't sound like our loving Jen, so I said, "What?" Jen then explained that this little girl has a terrible underbite and that she is not Altynai's daughter. Many Kyrgyz kids are taken in by unrelated families, and this young girl was probably rejected by her biological family for her looks.

This emphasis on appearance could be why she heard Aisalkyn's hair will be shaved this summer; Kyrgyz people believe if you do that, it will grow in darker. Aisalkyn has lighter brown hair, and they want her to look more like Venera and her sons. Rumor has it that she is not Venera's true daughter. Jennifer was adamant and said, "Well, I don't care; she is MY sister!

Last week, Jen heard a little voice that said, "Ooh... Jen-eeee-fear," and turned around to have Aisalkyn run up into her lap. When she told Kathryn about how sing-song her voice was when she said her name, Kathryn replied, "Jen, that is one of those moments when Kyrgyzstan loves you." That is our hope, too. Keep the possible protests in your prayers.

Love,

Karen

Gen Girls (a group Jennifer created to empower teenage girls) showing off the club t-shirts they designed. The eagle holding a globe represents the international relationship of hope and freedom they experienced as Generation Girls. Karen and her co-workers created the t-shirts and shipped them to Kyrgyzstan.

Children learning how to make friendship bracelets from floss at Talas Camp in 2007.

History Sources's office (where Jennifer worked) in Pokrovka.

A babushka (grandmother) practicing modern quilting.

Jennifer's coworkers at a handicraft seminar.

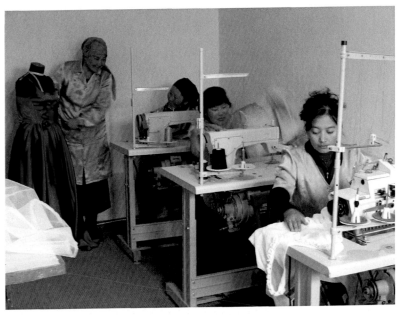

Sewing graduation dresses for local girls.
The blue smock is their work uniform.

Rosa, the woman assigned to mentor Jennifer, and Gulnara,
her director, hand processing wool for handicrafts.

Kyrgyz souvenirs on display during the grand opening of the sewing center.

Jennifer checking construction on the inside doors and walls of the History Sources building.

An arched window outside of Jennifer's work building. Aqua is the most commonly used color of paint throughout Kyrgyzstan.

Jennifer and her History Sources director, Gulnara.

The Kyrgyz national dish, besh bar mak, which means "with five fingers."
All sheep parts are boiled in a kazan (wok), served over noodles,
and eaten by hand. Although Jennifer understood the importance of the dish,
she never acquired a taste for it.

Jennifer giving a dedication speech at the ribbon-cutting ceremony for the History Sources center and public school cafeteria renovation.

Jennifer eating the sheep's eyeball at the renovation reception.
The eye is offered to the guest of honor, in hopes to be *seen* again soon.

Kathryn holding the original sketch of the mural she painted in the school cafeteria. A night sky joins the day with the Peace Corps dove symbol.

Family and friends welcoming Jennifer back home on November 19, 2006.

CHAPTER 21

---•●●•---

Lessons Learned

"One of the women piped up and said, 'Since you Christians don't read the Koran, then you are not good people. Kyrgyzstan doesn't need your help.' This is the first time in a long time that I have experienced such open hostility to the Peace Corps' presence in the country."

—JEN

April 14, 2006

I've been in Kyrgyzstan for about eighteen months, studying/speaking Russian, and there are still linguistic moments that leave me humbled. The other day I was in a store and wanted to buy some croutons to have as a snack. To me, flavored croutons are the equivalent of chips, especially since the chips here are like Styrofoam. I looked in the display case and saw two bags of bacon-flavored croutons, so I asked the girl for two bacon croutons. She looked around the case, visibly confused, and, even though the bags were right in front of her, she didn't once touch them. I, very annoyed, said again, "Two bacon-flavored croutons." She said something to a friend in Kyrgyz and they together finally got my croutons.

I paid, walked out, and then laughed later with Kathryn when we realized that I kept asking for bacon-flavored clothespins. Kathryn and I had just memorized the word in order to buy some clothespins at the bazaar, and since it is similar to croutons, I used what was still stuck in my head. I told some K-13s that it just goes to show you that no matter how long you've been here, how competent you are in your language skills, you still have experiences that humble you.

The last time I wrote, I was in Bishkek for our first gender and development meeting. We decided on a mission statement, goals, and objectives, and that each representative would be in charge of organizing an oblast committee. This committee would basically be the volunteers who are interested in working in areas of GAD and who would like to be informed about different projects or start oblast or nationwide projects. Right now, a major nationwide project that is underway involves collecting stories about encounters with the culture, lesson plans focused on gender inequality, discussion topics, and activity ideas for clubs and seminars.

Take Your Daughter to Work Day, which was adapted to Take Our Girls to Work Day, is well underway. In my village, my organization has offered to sponsor the day, find mentors, and talk to the directors of both schools in order to allow the girls to miss lessons on April 27th. We've hit the ground running with this committee!

In a surprising turn of events, my regional GAD meeting (held in a café in Talas) turned into the beginnings of an "Oblast Day." As an oblast, we decided to meet once a month as a way to collaborate on projects, brainstorm ideas for the classrooms and the office, and have a regular opportunity to support each other, no matter how far away from each other that we live. This started when the opportunity of having everyone together prompted people to talk about their work in general, and a great brainstorming session about Earth Day occurred. I'm looking forward to the next Oblast Day!

We celebrated the Islamic New Year, Nooruz, on March 21st by going to a nearby village to attend their village-wide party. Kathryn, some of her students, and I went to this village last year, and so enjoyed it that we invited Ian, Erich, and more students to go with us. Jilegone is such a small village that instead of having parties on each street, like our village, they have one party for the whole community.

In an open field, there were rows of table linens on the ground covered with *borsok* (diamonds of fried dough), candy, cookies, and bread. A stage was set up for the festivities and two MCs led us through a morning of traditional activities. They passed on the responsibility of hosting next year's celebration by giving a shaft of barley to next year's hosts. Skits, music, games, and speeches followed.

A traditional game involved tying the feet of a one-year-old child together and having children race to see who could reach the child and cut the string first. There was also ping-pong, a giant swing (called six frogs, probably because you can fit six people on this swing), and traditional wrestling. Wrestling in Kyrgyzstan involves tying rope around each competitor's waist and trying to be the first to bring the other to the ground—touching his back to the ground—while only using the rope. It was a beautiful day, the first after a week of cold weather and rain. I even got my first sunburn of the year!

One year ago on March 24th, I thought I would be coming home as I watched Kyrgyz people rioting on the streets of Bishkek on the television. I'm still here and the one-year anniversary of the revolution came and went without any unrest. I believe things were so peaceful because the president turned this day into a national holiday. Not many Kyrgyz people would pass up the opportunity to enjoy a day off of work and national festivities to organize another revolution. We had been warned in the winter that there was a "Revolution Committee" planning another revolution because they were not happy with the results of last year's change in government. Perhaps because the current president was threatening to use force instead of running away like the last president, nothing happened. We enjoyed a concert in our village, some traditional dance, wrestling, and a game, involving sheep vertebrae, that is much like marbles.

My primary responsibility, my organization, has really gotten busy. We just applied for a small project assistance grant through the Peace Corps. Twice a year, USAID gives our post funding. A committee of volunteers will review the grant applications and decide what group to allocate funds to. With the community's support, my director had written a grant application to Mercy Corps for funds to repair and refurbish the cafeteria in Kathryn's school (it's a space now in disarray due to the fall of the USSR, lack of money, and lack of management).

Since my organization's workspace was opened with SPA funds, my director asked if we could apply for a SPA grant for the cafeteria this year. The application was due on the 7th, so I had some stressful days leading up to the deadline, including having to work around a countywide power outage to complete the budget in time. But challenges like that make handing in an application that we can be proud of that much sweeter, not to mention if we actually get the grant. We will find out in about a week.

In very exciting news, my Partnership Project has been fully funded! It has been online for a little under a year, and we are so excited to finally start the repairs to the apartment that will be turned into an office space. Thank you to all of you who donated! Oddly, the funds needed were stuck at $1,300 for a long time and then suddenly my grant was pulled offline (meaning it was funded). Kathryn and I have come to realize that her Partnership Project actually made it possible for mine to finally be funded. Those that missed the deadline for hers floated their money to mine. As exciting as it is to finally get this project underway, I am even more excited to document the process and send thank-you cards personalized by my coworkers!

Peace!

Jenny

April 16, 2006

Happy Easter to all! We had a great holiday, complete with a "big people" outdoor egg hunt, courtesy of Heidi. It was such a hit; we are going to do it next year. But a bigger hit was Jen attending Mass on Easter Sunday. She said, "Mom... it was awwwwwesome!" There were about thirty people there, which comprised three volunteers and twenty-seven Russian Orthodox people. There was one woman who looked Kyrgyz, but they didn't want to push the issue and ask the priest if she had converted from Islam or not. Jen visited with the priest, Father Alex, after and found out he knew English. She got so excited that, as she talked to him, she went in and out of Russian and English. He was so happy to see new faces and Jen said now that she knows about it, she is going to try to go back once a month.

On Sunday night, she got the long-awaited box from Grandpa and Grandpa. The timing was perfect, because it contained some Easter goodies—so she got her "basket" on the actual day! It was like she was at our egg hunt with us. She told me there were three packages of Peeps and she would bring them to her next GenGirls meeting. She was tempted to melt them down and make Rice Krispie treats, but said, "I just don't know if I can stand all the screaming." Not sure what the verdict will be.

She also got a box from the Guardian Angels classroom. It was a Valentine's Day package. I asked why it took so long. Jen said, "Jenna sent it circus mail—it goes by boat." I asked, "Circus mail? Why do they call it that?" Jen asked, "WHAT?" I said, "Circus!?" (We've been in this position before.) She calmly said, "Surface mail. Surface mail—S-U-R-F-A-C-E." I should know that if there's a confusion of words and it isn't in Russian, it's probably me.

Jen's AIDS awareness conference went well. She said they were separated into different presentation groups based on language: English or Russian. That way, the comprehension was at the maximum. They were told that the term "STD" (sexually transmitted disease) has been changed to "STI" (sexually transmitted infections), which includes a wider range of illnesses. Even though there are only 100 reported cases of AIDS in Kyrgyzstan out of a population of five million people, the need for education is great.

They were told that there probably are more like 800 cases because of the deep shame associated with contracting the disease, and that most people don't get medical help. So their goal is to select certain students and teachers and train them to present seminars on the actual facts to continue education and understanding for the next generation. Sometimes, ignorance is not bliss.

Kathryn has been having so many problems with pain in her knee and hip. After lots of tests and blood work, the doctors have diagnosed her with arthritis. And this was not something she suffered from before going to Kyrgyzstan. They aren't sure if it's just situational, meaning caused by her current living conditions and the climate. The weather has been warmer there, so she is beginning her "bring your long johns to work" routine: she gets too warm walking there, but the building is still too chilly inside. Maybe her joints will get better once she comes home. At this point, she is being treated with regular use of Advil. Keep her in your prayers.

We were talking about Dan's returned slippers and I mentioned that I couldn't believe America couldn't figure out how to deal with the upside-down address. Jen said she figures the package went to Moscow and then France and got returned from there. France was experiencing major protests from students about the recent prime minister's new policies. Taxis, buses, and the post office were closed, as well as the universities. Jen's good friend Jessy is in France teaching English and was okay, but didn't have class for a while. I guess Kyrgyzstan is not the only country with civil unrest.

Love,

Karen

April 23, 2006

Heidi started our call to Jen. As I was figuring out what news we needed to pass on to her and what we needed to know or do for her, their conversation was full of, "And then HE said, and then SHE said..." It tickled my ears to hear my girls gossiping like that.

Jen needs us to contact Sara about the slippers that were ordered from the silent auction at St. Mary's. Sara was in charge of the annual benefit dance, and she put out the slippers that Jen gave Dominic for Christmas as something to bid on. The lady who won wants to order four pairs! Jen told us they have a large amount of wool that was prepared and ready for dying, and that it would be great to get the order going now. When you think about what it takes to do that (kick the wool, lay it out flat, water it down, roll it up in bamboo sheets, roll it down the street, and kick it some more in order to soften it), I could see how Jen wanted to get the order going. And with shipping involved, she wants the people to get them before winter! So Sara called Jen and they got the order worked out.

More importantly, Jen wanted Sara to pass on to us that she is in stand-fast mode. That means she is only allowed to be at home and work. Her plans to go to the Internet café this Saturday are now on hold. There is a political demonstration planned for the 25th and 26th, and then for the weekend of the 29th. Most of the unrest is supposed to take place in Osh or Bishkek, but the Peace Corps is being very protective and we are thankful.

I don't blame the Kyrgyz people for protesting their corrupt government, but I wish they would do it on their own time—that is, when my daughter is not there! That sounds selfish, but it's hard being the mom. It was hard enough to let go and trust that she could handle major challenges. As if having her hungry and cold isn't bad enough, the government unrest just pushes the envelope. Coping with situations like these is a lesson I continue to struggle with. She is an adult, choosing her path, no matter how scary it may seem to me. Whether this will lead to consolidation like it did last Easter, we don't know.

Jen sounded stressed as she rattled off all she has going on this week. Monday is Aisalkyn's fifth birthday. It reminded me how long Jen has been gone—Aisalkyn was a three-year-old when Jen went to live with them. It also was Albina's birthday. She is Jen's favorite GenGirl, who helps teach others how to speak English. On Tuesday, she is supposed to help judge an English concourse at Ian's school. And Thursday is the second annual Take Your Daughter To Work Day. She had lots more planning to do, and just trying to emphasize how important it is to be a working woman has been a lot to pull it together.

Love,

Karen

April 30, 2006

Jen's standfast has just been called off. I was anticipating it getting worse, so this was the best of news. With all the restrictions, I asked Jen if she was able to have her GenGirls meeting. She said, "You know, my work is with the people, and it's so hard not to be with them, so we still had club." Ian's family had their phone turned off from not paying the bill, so Jen told the warden he could reach them best on her cell phone. Knowing that she would be contacted, they also went ahead with the planned picnic with the school kids.

I told her I saw the warden warnings for over a week in her email account and she said, "Mom, don't worry. They call us right away, because they know we're so remote." Thank God. She told Dan she was "on vacation today" because she didn't have work due to a holiday (rather like our Labor Day), and that soon there would be Constitution Day and Victory Day. These people have more reasons to celebrate than we Americans.

We told her we ended up with six inches of rain (per Mom's trusty rain gauge) this weekend in Chaska. She excitedly told us about the terrible hailstorms they've been having. She was walking home from work when the hail started coming down hard. They were trapped, and she told Albina, "It's hitting my ears—oh, my ears. It's killing my ears!" Even when she cupped them with her hands, they still hurt. Jen said the hail pellets were the size of Excedrin tablets, but were even bigger the next night. She felt so bad for the farmers who had to race to cover their crops, her ears didn't seem like such a big deal.

Jen wanted us to pass along to Bea and Bob Hogan that she has been using the spices they sent like crazy! And every time she uses the garlic powder, she dances the jig and thinks of Maw-Maw and Paw-Paw, because it's way too expensive for her to buy there.

Now that plans are in place to get going on Jen's renovation project, she's excited, but also worried. She wants to keep a close reign on the funds, but also knows that she has to "let go and let God." Her director, Gulnara, reassured her that she has managed Peace Corps jobs before. In my mind, I thought, "When my daughter got there, you didn't even have a phone, fax, computer, or a chair for her to sit in. So I can see how Jen is having to learn a lesson in trust."

Another problem is that costs for the work have gone up since she wrote her grant, and they actually need more money than she requested. So she is busy putting together a plan to stretch the funds a bit. She hasn't gotten this far to not have it happen. This will help make her last seven months go fast. I say seven months, because she told us that her departure date is scheduled for December 2nd, but she will be allowed to exit thirty days prior to that without any change to her benefits. I know that when she leaves will depend on where she is with the renovation project. She has another volunteer coming in October to replace her, but if we know Jen, she will not be able to walk away in the midst of an important part of her project, so her exact departure date is still to be determined.

While we were on the phone, Jen started talking to someone and I said, "Is someone there? I will let you go." She said, "No, it's just Jesus." Now how do you answer that? Then I remembered and said, "Is Ian there?" Not that he is so heavenly, but I figured his beard must be growing in, since he lost the bet about swimming in the river. Jen said, "Yeah, keep talking." I said, "Me or him?" Jen said, "YOU, Mom." She told Ian to eat what he wanted; apparently, he had stopped by for a bite to eat.

She told me Ian has been having problems in his home with meals. Recently, they figured out that he hadn't been fed for thirty-six hours, partly because of his schedule and partly because of theirs, but it's not right. So Jen, Kathryn, and he had a movie marathon, complete with chicken for protein and vegetables, which are a delicacy.

I asked Jen how Aisalkyn's birthday party went. She said she felt bad that there wasn't a large crowd like there had been last year. Jen said Aisalkyn was wearing a First-Communion-type dress that seemed two sizes too big for her. Venera asked if Jennifer had brought her camera, but Jen hadn't because she came straight from work; she had been afraid that if she arrived late, it would be shameful. Venera told Aisalkyn that Jennifer would have to take her picture next time. Aisalkyn quickly said, "My dress will be too small by then!" Jen laughed, but I asked her if that was a bad thing. She said, "No; it just shows how much a newly five-year-old doesn't have the best concept of time.

I asked what she brought her. She gave some earrings and chocolate. I said, "Oh, I know how much she loves candy." Jen said, "Yeah...

that's great, but the chocolate costs more than the earrings!" Pretty sure Aisalkyn thought both gifts were as sweet as Jen.

Hoping for continued peace from protests.

Love,

Karen

May 5, 2006

Happy belated Easter! I had quite the experience on Easter Sunday; I was riding in a bus full of Kyrgyz people, balancing three bags in my lap and trying to maneuver around some kids playing in the aisle while wearing my Sunday best. This just wasn't a "normal" Easter experience. But it was my experience this year.

First, I want to relay a funny story about Lenten sacrifices. Last year, I didn't abstain from anything for Lent. My attitude then was, "My life is all about sacrifice right now; giving up what little comfort I have (i.e., chocolate, pop, ice cream) is just not going to happen this year!" But this time, I wanted to participate more fully in Lent, so I gave up pop. I was commiserating with another Catholic volunteer about caffeine withdrawals, since she gave up coffee. Holly, a three-times-a-day coffee drinker, announced to her class of high school students that she had given up coffee for Lent, a period somewhat like Ramadan but in the Catholic faith. A little later during the lesson, one of her students raised his hand and asked (with attitude), "Miss Holly, what is Lent and when is it over?!" Holly gathered from his question that the lack of caffeine in her system was evident in her mood that day. We laughed, as she said she had the only group of Muslim kids with a countdown until Easter— not because they were looking forward to the holiday, but because they were anticipating Miss Holly's return to coffee drinking.

My Easter Sunday began by traveling to Talas with a small contingent of Christian volunteers. We had stayed in a small village just outside of the city the night before and were dressed in spring skirts and dresses to attend a Catholic Mass in the city. By chance, some Christian missionaries in the city had asked what my religion was and when I said Catholic, they contacted the Slovakian priest and nuns in Talas who are in the process of building a church. Because I had just come from the AIDS seminar in Bishkek, I'd had three large bags with me. Whenever you go to the capital, you end up coming back with more bags than you left with, filled with food, supplies, clothes, or books. This made our group stand out on the bus from the village to the city even more than usual.

Also, the villages from Talas to the mountain pass leading to Bishkek do not see volunteers often, and we were the focus of attention when we stepped on the bus. At first we heard the rumbled whisperings like "Tourist; they are tourists. They must be tourists." Kathryn eventually engaged in a conversation with an older man and two older women. They asked all the typical questions, like "Where are you from?" and "What are you doing here?" and "Where did you learn Kyrgyz?"

Kathryn explained that we were going to the city to celebrate a religious holiday. The man began talking about how he had read the Bible and how he thought the Koran and Bible were very similar. However, one of the women piped up and said, "Since you Christians don't read the Koran, then you aren't good people. Kyrgyzstan doesn't need your help." This is the first time in a long time that I have experienced such open hostility to the Peace Corps' presence in the country. However, the man spoke up and defended Kathryn before she even had a chance to herself, and said that we are teaching their children and giving them a future.

Work has been very busy lately due to juggling two grants in different stages and organizing Take Our Daughters to Work Day for my girls' group. We received the funds for our partnership grant, which is a tale in itself. My director and I went to the bank to withdraw the funds from my account, and neither of us thought to bring a bag. I don't know how we thought we would be able to walk out of the bank with 142,222 som in cash without my backpack or a dark plastic bag. As my director was trying to stuff wads of cash into her miniscule purse, I rolled my eyes and ran out to a nearby store to buy a bag. As I walked back to the bank, I thought, "So this is how you rob a bank in Kyrgyzstan—no getaway car, just a getaway bag. If only I were being filmed for a promotional video right now!" Gulnara and I laughed as we walked back to the office, me looking like a football player with a bag of cash tucked under my arm, ready to take out anyone who dared to touch our precious package.

Take Our Daughters to Work Day on April 27th went extremely well. My director and our organization were the official sponsors of the project and I really couldn't have done all that I did without Gulnara's help. I asked her if she could help me talk to the different offices and organizations where we wanted to place girls with female professionals. We first went to the police office and went straight to the chief of police.

Lesson #1: You have to talk to the top bosses in Kyrgyzstan; they volunteer the services of their workers and the workers don't have a say in the matter. When we told the police chief about our plan, he first didn't understand why girls would need to observe working professionals or think about their futures. Secondly, he said that he would have to talk to his higher-ups in Talas for permission and would need an official letter stating all the information we just told him.

Lesson #2: Nothing can be casual in Kyrgyzstan. There is protocol and red tape to go through in situations like these, thanks to the lasting impact of the USSR. We formulated a letter and ended up using it for every organization. Most bosses were really helpful and happy to assist us in any way that we needed. The directors of the hospital, clinic, and government building were very responsive and surprisingly pleasant to work with. On the other hand, the director of the local court accused us of being spies who just wanted to report their work practices to someone else. That was right before he agreed.

Lesson #3: Unfortunately, many people don't understand why it is important for kids to think about their futures and professions, and to get hands-on experience, or at least talk to someone in the field they would like to enter. A few days before the event, I had girls coming to my office to beg me to put them in the site of their choice. The girls had filled out applications to participate, and included on the application was a list of the places they could go.

It seemed odd to me for a long time that all the girls wanted to go to the police station. It finally dawned on me that there are young police officers working there. The girls just wanted an opportunity to be around the cute guys who work there.

Lesson #4: Even when asked to think seriously about an opportunity to learn about a profession, some girls can't get out of the cultural frame of mind that they are only worth as much as the amount of attention they get from guys. I had one girl write on her application that she wanted to become a doctor, but what site did she pick? Not the hospital and not the clinic, but rather the police station. Because of all the hype about what site they would be placed in, I made a point of telling them at our prep meeting the night before that if they had their hearts set on only one site and would cry if they didn't get it, then I didn't want them to come the next day. The morning they arrived at my office to receive their site placements I said to them, "You are not babies, and you are not yet women, but you are young women. Young women don't cry when they don't get their way; they make the best of the situation and learn from it."

Lesson #5: These girls had never heard the word "women" used in reference to them, and it shocked them a little. In Kyrgyz culture, you are a girl before marriage, and a woman after. More bluntly, a girl is a virgin, and woman is a girl who has had sex. The fact that I used "women" in a way to describe them—and not in an offensive way—stuck with them. Later, when one of the young women was asked the lesson she learned that day, she replied, "I am not a girl; I am not a woman. I am a young woman."

Lesson #6: I need to watch what I say, because it has more gravity than I even realize. This is both good and bad. I had the pleasure of running around, taking pictures at each site. Half of the girls seemed to get the purpose of the day: to learn as much as possible from their mentors. For example, one girl was answering phones at the bank and running bank statements back and forth for signatures. Another girl was in a lab coat when I showed up at the hospital and later got to watch the birth of a baby. Another girl picked up the phone when I called the operator, since that's where she was working. Another girl was typing loan information into a computer for the microcredit organization she was placed at. Then there were the girls who I never found to take a picture of, since they took off to wander around the village immediately after they had finished their list of questions to ask their mentors. Then there were the girls who waited for their mentors who came into work late (one girl waited two hours). There were the girls who thought they would hate their sites, since they weren't their first choices, who came to appreciate the work done there and would like to work in similar settings one day. There were the girls who thought they would love where they were placed, but realized that the jobs were tougher than they thought, and they were really turned off by them.

Lesson #7: The girls had good and bad experiences for many different reasons. I need to learn to let that go and realize that they all learned something, no matter if they were working for two solid hours or waiting for two hours straight. After lunch, we met in a large room in the government building to give short presentations about each placement. The girls went nuts making visual aids, even though they were only allotted five minutes per presentation. Although some of the girls had bad experiences with their mentors, they began reporting that they had a good time.

Lesson #8: Students will lie when older authority figures (such as myself, my director, my counterpart, a teacher in the public school, etc.) are around so they don't offend anyone. I had to reiterate that I wanted the truth and wouldn't be offended if they said they didn't have a good time. One girl talked about how her mentor was late and commented on how much work could have been done in the time that she waited. Another girl was honest about how she will no longer pursue a career as a doctor after a conversation with her mentor about the difficulties of being a doctor and mother in Kyrgyzstan. Another girl commented on how she disliked the fact that all the court work and paperwork was done in Russian, since it's just another example of how Kyrgyz will be gone once she has grandkids. There were some very interesting presentations—some turned into debates; others were very humorous, like the one from a girl who watched a woman giving birth. Overall, the day went well; not as I expected, but well nonetheless.

I was going to visit the Internet site last weekend, but was prevented from doing so due to all volunteers being placed on "standfast." This time, we were instructed to stay at our sites, and to only go to work or stay at home, due to political protests in the capital. There had been protesting in various oblast capitals a few weeks ago, and at that time we were advised not to travel to the capitals. Nothing came of those protests, which were aimed at voicing the people's opinion that the current president is not doing his job, or at least not making good on promises he made when he was placed in office after last year's revolution.

Before last weekend's protests in Bishkek, HCNs were saying that they would take over the government building just like last year and kick out Bakiyev, the president, just like they did with Akayev. Others shot back that Akayev had been ready to leave; that's why he ran away, and that with only a year under his belt, Bakiyev will not run. In fact, they countered that he will use force and weapons to defend his position if necessary, which he himself has said. The protests were peaceful; however, HCNs are saying that protestors are giving Bakiyev one month, and if things don't change by then, they will storm the capitol building like last year.

This time around, while I am not afraid of violence breaking out in my village or oblast, I do take standfast and travel warnings more seriously. Last year, I was completely unprepared when the Peace Corps moved us into "consolidation" when the main government building was taken. I don't want to leave Kyrgyzstan yet. I have more work to do and to finish, work that I have been laying the groundwork for about twenty months. While I wait to see what the next month holds, I, as well as the rest of the volunteers in country, go about my daily business with a heightened awareness of how my time here is limited, thanks to a number of variables.

On a final note, I want to wish all of those who are graduating from SMU in just a week good luck in your future pursuits. You are in my thoughts and prayers!

Peace,

Jenny

May 7, 2006

When I first said hello, Jen wasn't sure who I was. She hesitated and then I had to say, "Jen, it's Mom." Unfortunately, I guess I sounded like Dad. A bad cold has dropped my voice about sixteen octaves. We had a laugh over that one. I told her that we've been doing yard work and spring cleaning. I ran across two spiders. I called them "Bert #1 and Bert #2" in keeping with her pet spider. She told us a while ago that even though he's huge, he doesn't scare her, so she gave him a name. It seems to help if she can see him in the corner. Then she knows he's not in her belongings. She had a chuckle about my Berts, but said seeing Bert is nothing compared to waking up and seeing a beetle moving across the floor.

"You would not believe how huge they are. I had to wake myself up, get out of bed, and get rid of him. They have terrible pinchers and you have to be careful so they don't grab on to you." I don't think I was really grasping it until she said, "Mom, I have watched a beetle push my shoe across the patio!" Then I was impressed. It still amazes me that this is the same person who used to scream and run from an itsy-bitsy spider. It's just a part of accepting and serving the culture. For example, even though her *banya* isn't functional, she goes there to wash her hair. Recently when she went, the door was blocked. There was a sheep inside. She didn't question anything, just walked away. Two days later, it wasn't there. She says nothing surprises her anymore.

Jen said she took care of the paperwork for her St. Mary's student loan deferment through the Peace Corps. Then she said, "Okay, keep talking... I'm going to the bathroom." I said, "What?" She said, "I've been having stomach problems so I'm just headed to the outhouse, but we can keep talking." I said, "Jeeeennnnnnnn!" She assured me, "It's not like I haven't done this before." I said, "EEEEEWWWWWWWW!" She joked that we probably get better reception when she's in there. There are very few things I don't want to know about her experience, but I think this would qualify.

Jen gave up pop for Lent and now she's making up for lost time. She said she has depleted the town. I'm pretty sure they don't have twelve packs with the EZ roll-out end or a suitcase of twenty-four cans. So one six-pack at a store doesn't go far. She admits that she's addicted. But the caffeine has helped with her busy schedule. The biggest event was Take Our Daughters to Work Day. I told her I loved the pictures she sent and she cheerfully said, "It was a success!" I was surprised (with all the changes and hardships she's had to endure) that she said it was the most stressful thing she has done in Kyrgyzstan. Maybe because they've talked about it since last summer and a lot of work went into it, but also because of the challenging attitudes of some of the people—and not just men in town, but also some of the girls. How exciting it must have been to be able to encourage them to be whatever they want. Maybe one of these girls will be the one to cure cancer because she was encouraged to shoot for the stars, instead of just shooting for making the best *plov* of the village.

Jen said it's been in the fifties, but she saw baby chicks and strawberries at the bazaar, so spring has arrived. That was the highlight of her trip to the city, because finding a reliable Internet connection was an adventure. She had to go to three sites before getting a decent reception and she cursed the whole time, saying, "Oh no—it's been three weeks and one standfast—you aren't going to fail me now."

Because I was feeling so rotten, we cut our visit short, but I had to ask her about something I read in her distribution email. She had talked about how she and her director went to the bank to get the money from her funded project and hauled it out in a large black bag. How safe is that, I wanted to know. Jen said that's how they do it. I then asked where they put all that cash. She said they're keeping it at her parents' house, because they are always there. I asked if she was worried that this Ajay and White Beard (a respectful term for elders) have all of their money in their mattress and could get wacked for the dough. She said, "This is how they do it, and it was just a matter of getting it done."

She is aware that people talk, especially when two women are walking down an alley with a big bag of money, but there is much protection from the fact that one of them is an American and attached to the government by the Peace Corps. I try to find comfort in that as well.

Love,

Karen

CHAPTER 22

A Surprise Visit

Tears ran down my face and onto my collar. I noticed the right side of my neck was more wet than the left. Then I realized it was because Jen's tears were mixing with mine. She said, "Mom, this is the last time we'll have to do this." I said, "I'm counting on it."

May 16, 2006

Around 9:00 p.m., Heidi said, "Mom, are you going to call Jennifer?" The best thing in the world is that all I have to do is just holler into the next room, "Jen, can you come here?" Some of you already know... we brought Jen home for Dominic's college graduation! What do you give a guy who already has a cell phone, laptop, and new truck? We decided to give him what he wanted the most, but knew he couldn't have: his sister. It was a total surprise to him and has been the gift that keeps on giving.

We picked up Jen at the airport on the afternoon of May 10th, a Wednesday. She was able to sleep more on these flights than when she came home for Christmas, so when she got off the plane, she looked refreshed, tan from all the outdoor holiday celebrations, and happy. It seemed strange to have a family event without Dominic knowing about it, but we've been working on this secret since March.

She recovered from her jet lag on Thursday, and on Friday, we headed down to Winona... in the rain. We set up camp... in the rain. Dominic and Sara came out to the campground... in the rain. We told them to close their eyes because we wanted to give Dominic his graduation gift. That's when Jen came out of the camper... in the rain. Dominic had a shocked look on his face. But Sara started screaming and dancing. Then Dominic hugged his sister and said, "Oh my God... Jen... How did you get here?" More hugs... in the rain. Even though the weather was not the best, it didn't seem to matter at that moment. It was the perfect gift.

Dominic and Sara did a great job as commencement speakers! Jen got lots of hugs from professors and students who were surprised to see her there. We moved Dominic out of the dorm and hung out around the campfire at the campground. Jen was telling us more about her trip home. She told us how she spent the night in the Almaty airport. She went off to a corner where there was an electrical outlet and worked on her computer and listened to music. She had been there ninety minutes when she saw two security police walking over to her, saying, "She is a foreigner, yes, she is foreign."

One was the good cop; one was the bad. In very loud, slow words, they asked why she wasn't sitting with everyone else. She explained that she needed the electrical outlet for her computer. They asked to see her ticket. She told them she had an e-ticket. *E* in Russian means "and." Again, he said, "Yes. And your ticket?" It was frustrating to Jen because they spoke in such terrible broken Russian to try to appease her, the foreigner. If they just spoke fluently, she would have understood them better.

Pointing to her Nalgene bottle, the bad cop asked, "What is that?" She told him it was water. He took it and shook it. Jen thought this was a strange way of determining if it was water or dangerous gasoline fuel. Then they asked if she had a bomb. Jen thought, "Sure... I've been working on my computer for ninety minutes, listening to music, and forgot to detonate it." She told them that she had no bomb and they were okay with that. That they took her simple no as the truth and their drug-sniffing dog was a poodle only added to the farce of security.

The only saving grace was that some ladies at the nearby shop kept staring at her because she is American. Kyrgyz people can stare and watch someone for hours and not see it as rude. Jen decided to use this to her benefit—at 2:00 a.m., she strategically put her stuff near them but in order to sleep and be safe she layed on top of her valuables and passport. Her bag was used as a pillow.

Even though Jen is back home, there are some Krygyz habits that are hard for her to shake. Heidi and Jen were going to the store the first evening she was here, so she walked outside. A minute later, she came back in the house and said, "I guess I need my shoes." She is so used to shoes never being allowed inside.

Another time, she threw some paper on the ground and Heidi looked at her and said, "Why are you littering?" Jen seemed confused and then realized it isn't like Pokrovka, where you throw things alongside the road wherever you see a little pile starting, since someone eventually comes along and burns it. She explained to Heidi that a country as poor as theirs does not have a sanitation department or garbagemen. They had a good laugh, but it shows how going from one country to the next doesn't mean you can switch over in an instant.

But Jen is doing great and eating like a horse, better than at Christmas when she was tentative about what would be okay for her stomach. It has been a blessing and so fun having her here when it wasn't really planned. It will help break up the time she has left, and we hope saying good-bye at the airport won't be as hard. That's what I keep telling myself.

Love,

Karen

May 23, 2006

Greetings! Many of you may already know that I took a surprise trip to the States. It was a ten-day whirlwind trip home, and I can't believe I am already heading back as I write to you during the second leg of my trip from Amsterdam to Almaty, KZ. But it was a good fix of home to keep me going for the remainder of my service.

I thought I would write about what I experienced, not the schedule I kept. There was a lot less culture shock this time around. For example, I didn't instinctively wait for the three-second delay when I talked to friends and family on the phone. And this time around, it only took a day for my appetite to catch up with me. As my mom can attest, I practically ate them out of house and home, which is completely opposite of my last visit. I did get stuck on a few things that surprised me though.

The first night I was home, my family surrounded me as I wrapped souvenirs that I had brought with me. I was getting more and more agitated and finally realized that it was the fact that I was surrounded by several conversations at once, all of which I *could* understand. I have gotten pretty good at just blocking out Russian conversations when I am tired or uninterested. This was different, and no matter how hard I tried I couldn't escape.

As I explained to my family, I usually have about five hours to myself every day when I just sit at home after work. Since I live alone, I usually take my time making dinner, then reading a book, writing emails, and maybe watching a movie. I live a very slow and concentrated life, so jumping into having to juggle more than one conversation that I can understand was a bit overwhelming at first.

At the commencement, I often forgot to offer my hand to someone when we first met. It's uncommon for me to shake hands in KG. I usually kiss women and girls on the cheeks when I greet them, and nod my head to men—that is, if they acknowledge me first. Sometimes a man will shake my hand, but usually it's because they don't know how to treat me. Am I a girl they can brush off, or am I a man, since I happen to be wearing pants that day and they know my culture is different?

There was also my habit of staring that became a slight problem. My sister reprimanded me during the commencement for rubbernecking to look at someone. In Kyrgyzstan, it's okay to stare, and since I am usually the focal point of stares, I tend to stare right back. I quickly was reminded that we don't do that in America.

I constantly got hung up with deferring the front seat of a vehicle. In Kyrgyzstan, I usually sit in the back, not only because I am a foreigner, but also because I am a girl. Men have priority for the front seat in any taxi or car. I didn't realize how engrained that mentality was until I almost crawled in the backseat and sat behind my sister who was driving when we were going shopping. We had a good laugh about it, because there were only the two of us in the car!

It was strange to order for myself in a restaurant and not have to clarify that the man I was with was not ordering for both of us. Usually in a Kyrgyz café, if a male volunteer accompanies me, the waitress gets very confused when I pipe up and say what I want.

Early in my trip, I was shocked to realize how strongly my response to the behavior of children in Kyrgyzstan has been engrained in me. As I was walking past two boys with a Nerf gun, I immediately tensed up and thought, "Please don't shoot me; please don't shoot me; please don't shoot me!" In Kyrgyzstan, boys are allowed to run amuck and face very little reprimand for bad behavior. The attitude "Boys will be boys" lets them get away with murder, like taunting foreigners and throwing rocks at them. I laughed at myself how I physically reacted: eyes down, pace quickened, and body tensed.

When arriving at a friend's house for the first time, I walked into the closet to hang up some of my clothes, and was so overwhelmed by the amount of clothes that was there that I turned around and walked out. As I explained, it's not you; it's me. I can fit all my clothes and shoes in two small suitcases, which is pretty abnormal for the average American. Talking about suitcases, I am starting to dread using mine to return to Kyrgyzstan.

Peace,

Jenny

May 23, 2006

The joy of having Jen home had to end on Friday night. Dan consoled her with the idea that her time left is only twenty or so Sunday phone calls from us. Makes it sound shorter if it's measured by Ma Bell. But her face was somber and distant. We tried to keep it light, but no matter what we did, she kept breaking down, which only made us do the same.

She even commented, "What is wrong with me? I know I have to go back." Jennifer has always been the stoic one, a strong woman for those around her. So uncontrolled signs of emotion or tears throw her for a loop. It is obvious she is not "choosing to be away" from us. She is just choosing to serve, and that happens to "take her away" from us.

As we got ready to take her to the airport, things were somber and the pouring rain outside did not make it any better. My insides were in turmoil and felt agitated by the pounding rain hitting the van as we drove. In contrast, it was so quiet at the airport, which made things even more intense, so I changed the subject and the conversation switched to her return schedule. She told us again how she would be going to Bishkek and then to Osh for a women's leadership conference. Sevara, her university student, has a family member in Bishkek that she would be staying with. But I really didn't listen, because my thoughts were more about OUR family.

I was glad that Sara was with us, as I knew that she would be a big help for Dominic. We all can use as much support as we can get. We stayed strong for her as she said good-bye. I even got her to smile. I stood and watched her walk until I couldn't see her anymore. The harsh rain continued as we drove home. The noise filled the dead space and I began to think about how the rain was a part of her trip on both ends: first, when we surprised the kids at the campground, and now bringing her to the airport. The heavens were crying both times, just for different reasons.

Even though Jen was not in Pokrovka, we made a Sunday call to her. She said she didn't see any protesting in Bishkek. And she slept pretty much the whole way from Minneapolis to Amsterdam. Then she had a four-hour layover, but there was a public lounge with reclining chairs and she nodded off there; but she didn't sleep from Amsterdam to Almaty. It took so long in the Kazakh customs, but she figured out that she could take the KLM shuttle to the Hyatt in Bishkek. Unfortunately, it didn't work. The shuttle took off without her. That meant she had to pay for a taxi. So there she was, standing in line with twenty Chinese tourists—but par for the course.

She has some leftover American germs and her voice is still hoarse, so she said people had a hard time understanding her Russian. She said, "It's bad enough that my Russian has a foreign accent, but then I sound like a man." She had trouble telling the taxi driver where to go, so she called Sevara on her cell and had him talk to her. When Jen finally got there, she started blurting out all they should do: "First, we need to get our tickets to Osh, and then go exchange our money." Sevara must have seen that Jen was still stuck in "American" mode and said, "No... first we will have some tea... then we will have a rest... and then we will get the tickets." With this reality check, Jen probably told herself, "Toto, we are not in Minnesota anymore."

Jen had brought home a DVD of an adaptation of a book that she and I had both read, so I told her that we watched it on Friday night. She said, "Did you watch it in Russian like I did?" I giggled and told Jen that she sounded good and seemed better than when she had to go back after Christmas. The silence on the other end told me that it was a dumb thing to say.

A teary and hoarse girl said, "Well, you know, it's so hard because it's such an abrupt change." Going from your comfortable home to a third-world country is change enough without being homesick. I told her I know how she feels, because one minute she was here and the next minute we were back from the airport to an empty house. She continued to cry and I reminded her how sad it would be if there were no tears.

It's hard to have the eleven-hour difference again. Now, when we are sleeping, she is up, and when she is up, we are sleeping. I told her that I woke up feeling sad, but that's okay, because it only means I miss someone I love. She said, "I don't like this part of coming home. I guess I just have to go through withdrawal again."

I told her that it would get better each day, and that the joy of coming home is worth all the hard parts right now. As if to convince herself, she told me, "I was just thinking that my last six months will go fast. Summer is the best time in the country and each month, there is a special thing. My renovation will be starting in June, in July I have a girl's camp, in August it is my and Ian's birthdays, in September we have our closing conference, and in October there is the Halloween concourse and the new volunteers arrive."

She shared that she was telling a friend's father about how much going home has reminded her of all that she misses out on by living in Kyrgyzstan. He then asked if she regretted her decision to join the Peace Corps. Her immediate and strong response was no. She told him that missing and regretting are two different things, and she can feel one without the other. While she misses Minnesota summers, talking to friends and family whenever she wants, driving, and the comforts of familiar food, she does not regret the decision she made two years ago to serve abroad. Deep down, we all know that the next six months will go quickly, but when your heart hurts, it's hard to see.

We talk every week, but that is not the same as being able to touch, to hold her and press our cheeks together and gently speak encouraging words. I just keep thinking about how we held each other at the airport. We have the best and longest hugs. As we said good-bye, the tears ran down my face and onto my collar. I noticed the right side of my neck was more wet than the left. Then I realized it was because Jen's tears were mixing with mine. She said, "Mom, this is the last time we'll have to do this." I said, "I'm counting on it."

Love,

Karen

CHAPTER 23

The Three Cs

Jennifer was about to present one of her talks at the CONFERENCE. Kathryn and Ian are done with school but have a few CLUBS planned in the summer. The busy CONCOURSE season won't begin until school starts in the fall.

May 28, 2006

A warden message about a protest scheduled for the weekend of the 26th in Bishkek got us worried about Jen traveling back to her village from the conference in Osh. Why does this always happen when she needs to travel? But I'm not going to obsess about it today; instead, I will choose to trust, something that is difficult to do, but better in the long run.

A quick call Friday night let us know that she was okay and knew about the warnings. There were two wardens attending the conference. Their warden John, from last year's consolidation, is done with his two years. Then Nicole took over, but she decided to go to India to serve because she wasn't too fond of Kyrgyzstan. Now they have Betsy, and she is doing an even better job! Jen's travel would be delayed, so she wouldn't be going through the off-limits area until Monday the 29th. She rushed me off because she was about to present one of the two talks she was scheduled to give at the conference. She was on in fifteen minutes. I told her I would light a candle for her and we said good-bye.

When we had our regular Sunday call, Jen said, "Mom, did that candle blow out or something? Because I had a heck of a time with my talk. The VCR machine wouldn't work, so I couldn't show the tape on human trafficking, and after struggles of switching machines, tapes, and technology, they bumped me back to after the tea break! Finally, I got a machine that worked and it went okay after that, but it was so frustrating." I had to come clean. I said, "Jen, I hate to tell you this, but I got distracted after our call and forgot to light the candle." "She said, "Mommmm... no wonder!"

We had a good chuckle, and then I asked if she was done with withdrawals from having been with us. She said that she is okay unless she thinks about it. And looking back on those first two days there... it sucked! But the family home of Sevara, where she stayed in Bishkek, was so nice. They gave her privacy and knew she was dealing with jet lag. She wasn't treated like a celebrity or stared at as a foreigner.

And a real treat was that Sevara's uncle came up to Jen later and asked in Russian, "Jennifer, where are you from? Tell me about you." In his hand he had a map of the United States and wanted her to point out where she came from. Jen tried to be creative with her Russian to point to Minnesota and say "Chas-kon-o-vich." Their hospitality gave her the boost she needed to prepare for the conference.

She asked the group of about thirty volunteers and university students, "Why do you think I am warning you about human trafficking?" Some girls replied, "You want us to be safe... so we don't fall into the trap of a free ride out of the country, and do what is best for us?" She told them, "Yes, but the most important part is that I need your help. I am only one person, but now that all of you have been given information, you can spread the word and that way, so many more can be helped." They thought that was cool, and one of the newer volunteers is interested in taking over this cause when Jen leaves.

I asked who had come from the farthest. She said, "I did..." Thinking how far south this was relative to her village, I was going to jokingly ask if she got the door prize when she finished her sentence: "I came all the way from America!" A part of my heart cried and the other part sang.

Jen is going to have Sevara come to Pokrovka to do a seminar for her GenGirls. When you start having guest hosts, you know the club is heading for the big time! Kathryn and Ian are done with school and have a few clubs planned in the summer, but both will be taking a month off in July. Ian is going traveling and Kathryn will be going home for her sister's wedding. The busy concourse season won't begin until school starts in the fall. Jen said she would be the only volunteer in the village. I asked if that would be okay. She said, "It will have to be."

But she has things going on at that time, so it will not seem as long. I told Jen I bet people will be extra nice to her when she gets back, because they didn't realize how much they would miss her. She just listened. Then I said, "Maybe even those mean ladies at the bank!" Jen said, "I doubt it," then giggled. But she got excited to tell me that she found 1,000 som in her coat. That is like us finding a twenty-dollar bill. She was so excited and wondered when she had hid it in that zipper compartment. It came at a good time.

While visiting Bethany, a TEFL volunteer, she was thankful for the extra spending money. Bethany needed to house-sit for some missionary friends, so Jen went along. The missionaries had been there for five years and had brought along their grandmother. She is eighty-seven years old! They call her "Grunt" or "Grandma Grunt," because she barks out orders, but Jen was so surprised at how enjoyable she was. She wanted them to have her cinnamon rolls and coffee; an even better treat was the house. The living conditions for missionaries around there are so much nicer than for Peace Corps volunteers. They get an American salary, as opposed to living allowances that reflect the pay in that area (which is poverty level) like Jen gets. The house had hot running water and flush toilets! The grandma saw them again at the church and asked, "How are my girls?"

In going back to Bishkek en route to Pokrovka, Jen had an extra day. She was able to collect her big suitcase from Sevara's house and say good-bye to the family. She gave them one of the bags of the bridge-mix candy that Grandma and Grandpa sent to her as a thank you. She still had one bag left for herself. She told us that she doesn't want to be selfish, but wants to honor the love in which the treat was sent. It is for her to enjoy however she likes.

She also spent time with her friend Melissa, who is "early outing" and starting grad school back home in the medical field. She was in Bishkek, getting ready to head home when Jen was there, too. Melissa's Partnership Program did not get totally funded. It was to renovate a park and also deal with public health. She had to give it over to the next incoming volunteer. Jen asked her how she felt. She said, "I feel like I'm sitting in a waiting room." She's not connected there anymore, but not yet home, either.

We packed tons of food from Grandma, Grandpa, and us in Jen's suitcase to save on shipping, so I didn't ask her if there was anything she needed. But she did say, "Mom, you know what I would like for my birthday? I would like a CD of Garrison Keillor's *Prairie Home Companion*." I wanted to say, "Who are you? And what have you done with my real daughter?" But I bit my lip. She went on to explain how "comforting" it is to listen to. "It is so Minnesotan and home," she said. "Bethany has a copy that I borrowed, and as I listened, I was so comforted by the Midwestern accents that I just drifted off to sleep." Any gift that rocks my baby to sleep is what I will send.

Love,

Karen

June 2, 2006

I need to tell you about the Osh Women's Leadership Conference, as well as my first Kyrgyz wedding! But business first.

If I could get away with it, all I would say is, "Wow." Liz and Bethany, two university TEFL volunteers in Osh, finally saw their dream of having this type of conference come to fruition. The idea came about last summer, with the hope of hosting it last fall. The conference was an amazing experience for participants and volunteers alike, and I am glad to have been a part of it. It was four full days of sessions from 9:00 a.m. to 4:30 p.m.. About forty girls participated, three of them from outside Osh Oblast, and about twelve volunteers kept the ship running. Sessions included a panel of visiting female volunteers, an Osh volunteer's eighty-one-year-old mother who was active in the New Hampshire legislature, and her daughters, who had come on a trip to Kyrgyzstan.

There was a session on political systems and parties, and how to organize a group/club. They showed the movie *Mona Lisa Smile*, with a follow-up group discussion. I gave my trafficking and small business presentations and there was a presentation on working in higher education. There were sessions with a vice rector of one of the Osh universities, as well as one by two Kyrgyz Peace Corps staff members. Also, there was a session in which the girls were able to break into small groups and think of a project they can do in their communities.

What I liked the most about the experience was the difference in energy between this conference and a girl's camp that I participated in last summer. In the camp, the volunteers were constantly the cheerleaders, pumping the girls up and getting them involved, making them feel comfortable, and trying to make sure that they were having a good time. With this conference, the girls were here to learn, and they were motivated to take as much away as possible—not because we were telling them they had to, but because they honestly wanted to. There were a number of girls who were already working with NGOs, involved on their campuses, or helping out with other camps/conferences, which all addressed some aspect of one or many of the sessions.

One topic that came up the most in a number of sessions was how to juggle being a wife, mother, and working professional in Kyrgyzstan. You have to realize that Kyrgyzstan is in many ways just like America in the 1950s. The idea of juggling all three is a new concept, especially that of the working mother. There are plenty of women I know who do juggle well, but they still face great social pressure to work and then do everything at home, or to quit their jobs, since work outside of the house is a man's job. I think the biggest lesson learned by the participants was that you can be strong, feminine, want to have a husband and family, and have a career. I didn't even know that this was the lesson we were teaching them, but it's what stood out to me as an idea that kept coming up in some way throughout the presentations.

Now, you may be wondering how an unmarried, just-out-of-college "girl" could have contributed to this lesson in particular. Well, in retrospect, I think there were two main lessons that I taught in my sessions that added to this topic. Just the fact that a girl was presenting about small business—the how and why of writing a business plan—was different for them. Yes, I like wearing pink and makeup, watching chick flicks, eating a combination of peanut butter and chocolate, and can stereotypically talk for hours. But I can also be knowledgeable about business and demand respect in the Kyrgyz workplace, despite having the "wrong gender." I don't have to act like a man because I do a "man's job."

After showing a video in the trafficking presentation, I asked, "Are you angry?! Women contribute to the continuation of this cycle of trafficking just as much as men. That makes me mad!" In an earlier session that day, a volunteer talked about how we need to change our perspectives on how a woman crying shows weakness and a man being aggressive shows strength. I wanted these girls to know that the anger, horror, disgust, or any strong emotion they were experiencing due to what they had just seen was good. Emotions can be crippling, but they can also motivate and energize. I wanted them to know, "Don't let yourself be labeled as a weak woman for being disgusted to the point of tears. Show your strength in being able to use your emotions to your advantage and as a wake-up call to action."

On a touristy note, the south was not excruciatingly hot yet and the amount of produce available in the market was awe-inspiring... well, at least for little old me from a village where we have to hunt to find carrots, even when they are in season.

I was able to climb Sulaiman Too Mountain, a holy site that you can see from almost anywhere in Osh. I frequented local volunteer hangouts and also got to make a trip out to Uzgen. It is a city with a 90 percent Uzbek population. I wanted to make good on the promise to visit my language teacher from training when her cherry trees where full of fruit. I was only about a week too early to pick the cherries myself from her trees!

Osh seemed like a city comparable to Bishkek. I looked at Bethany, my host for the week, and asked in awe, "Do you get to take a *marshutka* (public transportation) to work every day?" *Marshutkas* are something I only associate with Bishkek, and it seems so strange to do anything but walk to wherever you need to go. I seriously thought, "If there was a *marshutka* available to go from my house to Ian's, which is forty minutes away by foot, would I take it?" I really don't think so. I've just gotten so used to walking, it seems extremely strange that there are volunteers being driven to and from work, or from anywhere really. It's just a different Peace Corps experience—in the same country.

When I got back to my village, I stopped by Kathryn's house and her mom spilled the beans before Kathryn was able to; her host brother was getting married—that weekend! There are so many differences between American weddings and Kyrgyz weddings that I really don't know where to start. First of all, the bride and groom had dated for only a month. The decision to marry was made, and three days later, there was a wedding. Or at least we think there was, because we never actually saw the ceremony. I'll elaborate.

The party, as well as the ceremony, was held at the groom's parents' house. A *moldo*, or Islamic cleric, was asked to come to the house and marry the couple, but the partying started well before that. The groom's parents slaughtered two sheep for the feast. At noon when the slaughtering—or "cutting" as you say in Russian or Kyrgyz, so as to not disrespect the animal—began, men were already taking shots of vodka.

Four rooms in the house, basically all but two, were laid out with tables of food, cushions to sit on, and plates of salad, sweets, cake, and drinks. I'm proud to say I sliced cucumbers for the salads till my fingers were stained green. I'm also very proud of the fact that I was the one to wash out the bloody basins in which the sheep parts were kept until they were cooked. Yup, Jenny's gone native...

The groom and his buddies went to retrieve the bride, whose family, except for a few sisters, is not invited to the actual wedding. I was wondering why they hurried her into the house so quickly and why all the men standing outside were laughing and hugging. It seems it was a fake kidnapping to keep up with the "tradition" and make it an authentic wedding. Now, there are many marriages that begin by kidnapping the girl, and there are plenty that happen in a more American process, with dating and at least a few months until the big day. I had never heard of a fake kidnapping just to "keep up the tradition" except for cases in which the girl was pregnant and the wedding needed to happen quickly, or her parents wouldn't agree, so the groom simply stole her.

In this situation, the bride's aunts even came over to fake yell at Kathryn's family when they "took" their relative. It was all very confusing, and I am still waiting to talk to Kathryn's mom to find out the reasoning behind it. The bride arrived at 1:00 p.m., and was ushered into a back room where a curtain was hanging. A long time ago, the bride would sit behind the curtain for one month. To serve what purpose? I don't know. But now brides tend to stay behind the curtain only a day, and this bride only stayed behind the curtain as she changed into a dress that the groom's family provided and put on the wedding headscarf. Kathryn's grandmother joked that soon they won't have the curtain at weddings anymore. It is a tradition that is slowly fading out.

The role of the bride (her name is Malika, but everyone referred to her only as the *kellin* or servant, because she is now the property of her mother-in-law) in the rest of the activities was to sit in the corner of the back room and generally keep quiet, with her head bowed. Women came and went, eating food and drinking with her, but when an older woman came in, she had to remain silent with her head down. I commented to Kathryn that this was the one aspect of this wedding that bothered me, that she couldn't celebrate it with her groom and the rest of the people at the party. Perhaps it was because it was a "kidnapping" and that's the role she had to play, because I also know of Kyrgyz weddings in which the bride and groom sit side by side and enjoy the day together.

By about 5:00 p.m., the first round of dinner was served: some of the cooked sheep and potatoes, the traditional first course called *kurdok*. Then there was dancing and drinking. That lasted until about 9:00 p.m., with breaks for us girls to wash more dishes and refresh the tables for the constant flow of guests. Then there was the second meal, in which toasts were shared for the bride and groom, even though they may have been in one of the other rooms. I didn't get to toast, since I was sitting at a table of mostly men and they all go first.

More dancing and dishwashing followed, and by midnight, Kathryn and I were both exhausted, so we went to my place to find a quiet place to rest. We were glad we did, because the next day we found out that the party went at least until 3:00 a.m. We heard this from one of Kathryn's ten-year-old cousins, who said she didn't leave until then!

The rest of the month looks pretty quiet, but who knows... this is Kyrgyzstan.

I'll keep you posted!

Jenny

June 3, 2006

Before I could get out my Sunday letter, Jen got to the Internet site and connected with everyone first! I don't mind. Was a nice treat for her to have business with some volunteers that took her to Talas overnight. Meanwhile, she told us how she came back to Pokrovka and Liz, one of Jen's university TEFL friends, came with her. Liz is getting married to a Russian man and needed to get some paperwork filled out with the Peace Corps in Bishkek. They needed her to come back three days later, and she wasn't going back to Osh and then back up to Bishkek. So she came "visiting" with Jen.

Liz brought this new man home with her to the United States to meet her family at Christmas, but will be married in Osh and no real family is coming. Seemed strange to me, but maybe they will have a reception later back in America. Jen said that Liz thought her primitive living situation was cool. She was way too excited about getting water out of a well for the first time, and Liz announced that she loves peeing outside! Jen said, "Usually other volunteers feel so sorry for me, but Liz was having a great time." She needs to try it for two years and then see how fun it is. Jen said that Liz's home not only has hot running water and a bathroom, but an Internet connection! Jen thought she had died and gone to heaven when she visited. But she has said more than once, "If I lived in those easy conditions, it wouldn't feel like I was serving the poor. I would just be on a vacation where I miss my family."

There were three envelopes and one box waiting for Jen when she got back. It was one we sent her in April. I can't even remember everything we put in the box, but I know there was powdered milk, cereal, and Easter candy. Nothing like a chocolate bunny in June!

Jen asked if I could send some Terro, as she is having problems with grease ants in her kitchen. The Peace Corps will give them Raid, but she doesn't want to spray it around her food. I told her it's safe nowadays, and probably what she needs to keep the areas protected afterwards. She agreed and said, "I guess by the time the Terro would get here, I'd be overrun by the things." I wanted to break into "The ants go marching one by one, hurrah, hurrah," but thought that would be in poor taste. It's her first summer in her new place.

Jen talked about the wedding of Kathryn's host brother. They were invited to help, but then got the idea from the stressed-out mother of the groom that they better not, because they might do something the wrong way. But Jen was actually able to cut up cucumbers correctly. Imagine that.

Ian, Kathryn, and Jen used their cameras to help capture some special moments. What I can't believe is that in helping to wash dishes and replenish the food, Jen had to wash out the basin that held the butchered sheep parts. This, for a small-city girl who screamed bloody murder when she saw a spider in her room. Now she has a pet spider named Bert and washes bloody bowls! What is the world coming to? It's not something I thought she would gain from this experience, but I guess it's all part of the process. I asked, "How do they think that *besh bar mak* actually tastes good?" Jen said, "I don't know. It stinks so badly when they're cooking it. Then everyone begins to smell like it, so it's like I am eating it."

Jen said she had a sore throat. I told her it was all the germs she had from people kissing her upon her arrival. She laughed and said, "Some of them even asked, 'What is wrong with your voice?'" She was hoarse from our germs back here. But one lady quickly said, "You must have eaten too much ice cream while in America." (It's the whole "cold is evil" philosophy.) Jen joked that she wanted to tell her, "You're right: it's from ice cream, not from sinuses draining—I was binging on Dilly Bars and good thing I stopped, because I could have been in the hospital by morning!" We really shouldn't laugh at their beliefs.

Jen's biggest excitement is that construction on her Partnership Program project began while she was away. They've put bars on the windows at her work to prevent vandalism, and started knocking down walls in order to make one large room for the ladies to work in, instead of individual ones. Gulnara is responsible for hiring the workers, paying them, and providing receipts. Jen set up a budget and will complete the paperwork and report to the Peace Corps. They also started working on Kathryn's cafeteria by removing all the junk out of that area. She was so chipper as she relayed this info and is partly shocked that it has actually started. It should be interesting to see all the work take place.

She said good-bye to her friend Melissa, who headed back home. Melissa's mom said the last eighteen days were the hardest. Knowing that she was coming home for good, the time couldn't go fast enough. She told her daughter, "I just want to go to sleep and wake up, and you'll be here." Jen said, "Geeeeeeee, who does that sound like, Mom?" I pleaded the Fifth.

Love,

Karen

June 14, 2006

Jennifer may go to the Internet site this Saturday as a treat because Ian and Kathryn will be in Bishkek. Ian is doing some program travel and Kathryn has been invited by the family of one of her students to go on a horse trek. Jen said it will be an experience of a lifetime for her, because Kathryn loves hiking. We look forward to the pictures she will take of the country and share with Jen.

If she doesn't get to the Internet café this weekend, she will when she goes to Bishkek on June 30th to attend the embassy's Fourth of July celebration. From there, Ian will take off on his one-month vacation to visit volunteers at other destinations. Weeks later, Kathryn will go back home for her sister's wedding. We talked about how she may have quite the culture shock, as it has been twenty-two months since being in

America. We thought fifteen months was hard enough. This leaves Jen alone for a bit, but teachers have to take advantage of their time off.

Jen sounded down and it was due to her being sick (or "ill," as Kyrgyz people say). She has been running a temperature and the outhouse has been her best friend. Not sure what she has, but it is fly season; it's not good if flies get on your food and sit for too long. She doesn't have refrigeration, so she has to be careful, and prepare food from scratch daily. She has stomach pains and a headache, too, so it sounds like a virus she could get in America. However, that doesn't really help me feel better about not being there to take care of her. I wanted to travel through the phone lines so I could comfort her like I used to, no matter her age. But she is grown and so I tried to distract myself from any guilt.

One hard thing for her: she got a call at 10:00 p.m. on Sunday from her director, who wanted Jen to come to the office and take pictures of a shaddock (for the catalog) she had been working on because she had to take it to Bishkek in the morning. Jen explained that she wasn't feeling well, but Gulnara continued to give directions about what she needed to do. Jen then asked if Kathryn, who was over because she brought Jen crackers and a Sprite, could go in her place.

As soon as Kathryn got there, Gulnara asked in a gruff voice, "Why is Jennifer ill? What did she do? What did she eat—something cold?" The Kyrgyz have this obsession with "why." You can be sick, but they have to figure out why, for fear of the evil eye, and because of shame. Kyrgyz throw out ideas about what and who is to blame to each other and they usually say, "Yes, that is why!" but these dang Americans keep saying, "No, that is not true." Kathryn's host grandmother said, "It's because the sun touched Jennifer's head." Now that was a new one. Not sure if it means that she should wear a *kalpak* or what! Hate to think there is a problem with getting hot as well as cold. If I'm confused, I can't imagine how it must be for Jen.

We got disconnected while talking and I couldn't get her back on the line. I tried the next morning, but only got the Russian operator telling me to call back again. So we tried Monday night and got through. It was a good way to check if she was feeling better (I'm always a mom). Jen said she had broken her temperature but still felt a little punk.

To make her feel better, I told her we got a padded envelope from her in the mail that same day! I thought it was weird that she hadn't told us she was sending something, because the postage rates went up and are too high for her to mail much. I told her, "The package had thank-you notes in it." (Jen wrote them out at Christmas but accidently brought them back to Pokrovka with her, so we told her to mail them back and we would send them out.) After a lull, Jen said, "Mom, I sent that five months ago!" The kicker is that, in the meantime, our postage went up, so we're going to have to add a two-cents stamp to each note. The recipients will never know how much effort went into a simple thank you, but at least it gave us a good laugh.

Jen will be traveling to Issyk Kul to help facilitate a girl's camp, as she did last year. When she returns to Pokrovka she'll host K-14 volunteers who just arrived in the country. Jen is a K-12 and was visited by K-13s one year ago: Nick, Natalie, and Jen. Volunteers from the K-14 group will eventually replace Jen when she returns to America, but not necessarily the same people she will be hosting this time.

When Jen had her visit, it was with a current volunteer in Talas Oblast, even though she was supposed to be assigned to Issyk Kul Oblast at a children's orphanage. I wonder what Jen's experience would have been like if she had ended up somewhere other than Pokrovka. She surely would have missed out on her sewing ladies at History Sources, teaching at a school, having her own place, but most importantly, Aisalkyn. God has a plan and she was meant to be in Talas Oblast.

Love,

Karen

CHAPTER 24

It's What I Do

"My coworkers did not rest for two weeks up until the graduation, as they were making about ten prom dresses from scratch. No Saturdays or Sundays off. Just a continuous effort to handle consultations, orders, sewing, fittings, and more sewing. I could see in their eyes that graduation was a proud moment for them, as well as the students."

–Jen

June 22, 2006

Jen is feeling so much better. She is able to eat solid food with no problem. People commented that she looked like she lost weight again, and she told me, "That's because I lose weight from the top down and so it shows in my face." Hopefully, it won't get so bad that she loses those famous dimples.

When we were talking, I could hear some roosters outside and it was a reminder of how far away she is, with our night being her morning. I asked about them and she said they were pecking on her door. Then in a high-pitched, silly voice she said, "They are saying, 'Cluck, cluck... I want food... cluck, cluck!'" Silly girl. She doesn't even have enough for herself.

She was getting ready to leave for work, because she wanted to get there early to help Ian fax something. I asked why he couldn't do it himself. She said that it's a Russian machine and very confusing, and plus, she doesn't mind helping. She went out her door (the roosters got louder) and said, "Keep talking, Mom, while I walk." I said, "Hey, does that mean it's Take Your Mother to Work Day?" She chuckled.

Dan asked how the weather was, and she said hot, but the river is too cold to help out. She has her trusty fan and her place is cooler than when she lived with Venera, because it is more shaded. Jen said that Kathryn must be enjoying the outdoors on her horse trek. Jen called on Monday to confirm that Kathryn was leaving on Tuesday and the family said, "No, we are leaving today!" I guess she freaked out a bit, but scrambled and got ready in time, so she didn't miss out on going. Jen asked Ian when she would be coming back. He responded, "She didn't even know the exact day she was to leave; how would I know when she is coming back?" A dry sense of humor can really help at times.

Jen's country director from the Peace Corps came to visit on Wednesday to check on the renovation. Jen was also telling him about her girls' club and the different things they're doing, and he stopped her and said, "You ARE a really good volunteer." She told him how much that meant to her, because she was having a bad day and was sick all last week. Another good thing is that the construction is going gangbusters! When she was out sick (sorry, "ill"), she said walls were coming down and going up. I asked why it was going so quickly when their usual Kyrgyz way is slow. She said, "I have no idea," but sounded pleasantly surprised. They are actually planning a grand opening for late August or September, and to invite government officials; since the country director is so into it, Jen said they would definitely plan around his schedule.

It's nice when things go well, because it helps offset when they don't. Jen's landlord, Altynai, told her that her niece will be visiting and Jen needs to teach her English every day for a month, and sign a certificate that states that. It never ceases to amaze Jen how the culture "tells" people what they will do instead of "ask." But she just calmly told her she wouldn't have time to do that, with all that's going on at work. Altynai then said, "Okay, two hours a day." Jen said, "But that is not what the certificate says." "Okay, just one hour a day after you come home from work, because you never do anything at that time." Jen was frustrated that she wasn't getting it, but just kept telling her she couldn't. Altynai got mad and left.

On Saturday, after visiting the Internet site, Jen was doing her laundry and dumped her water down the driveway. Altynai came back and gruffly said, "Jennifer, don't dump your water there!" which seemed odd, because that's where they dump theirs. Then she came over to Jen's place and started yelling at her. "You never have tea with me, you never talk to me, and you think you are so much better than us; you think you are so rich. The other volunteer, Megan, used to drink tea and talk to me." Jen told us that Megan loved the "alcohol," so that probably explains the talking, but she also was a carouser, so go figure how she was so much better.

Jen said Altynai stopped saying hello to her in passing and when she would run into her at a store or wherever, she never acknowledged Jen, so she thought maybe she was embarrassed to let people see she has a boarder. Whatever. But Jen was so dumbfounded by her outburst and kept trying to let her know that all she was saying wasn't true. She kept referring to her as Ajay, which shows that she is the elder and deserves respect, but Jen is beginning to believe the rumors that the woman is crazy.

Altynai kept yelling. Jen was shaking and finally told her, "Since you are not going to listen to me, you can talk to my director." She called Gulnara and she came over right away. Gulnara talked to Altynai and told her that if she has a problem with Jen, she needs to tell her, because Jen doesn't know why she's upset. Gulnara also told her, "This is your war, Altynai, inside you." Jen was teary as she told me about it, but was so happy her director was there to help.

Gulnara reassured Jen that Altynai has her crazy moments and kept telling Jen how wonderful she is. She said, "Jennifer, you are so kind. You are so generous with the ladies when you make them copies of pictures you have taken or put money into the tea fund and you don't really drink it that much. You are so much more giving than my other daughters," meaning that Gulnara was a host mother for other female volunteers.

I told Jen that it was such a touching statement and she needs to hold onto that and not the weirdo landlord's antics. Jen's plan is to just be civil, to simply greet Altynai quickly when she sees her, and not to do anything that might be considered shameful. Fortunately, the good times outweigh the bad.

So the Sunday calls come in handy. Especially when it's Father's Day. It was a gift to Dad to hear her voice and I'm pretty sure it was a gift to her as well.

Love,

Karen

June 25, 2006

We're preparing for camping over the Fourth of July; it will be different to have a vacation without Jen. Thinking back to when we were camping for Dominic's graduation, even though Jen had jet lag, the weather was cold and rainy, and the camper didn't want to go up, we were together. I talked to her about how we would miss having her with us and she said, "Take lots of pictures and send me a CD. It's okay, Mom."

But even before we talked about the vacation, she just seemed down. She isn't going to Bishkek for the Fourth of July celebration as planned. I asked why, and she said, "I don't have the money." My first response was to offer to wire money, but Jen is too practical. She said that even though it would be fun, she doesn't want to tap into her July allowance now and then have to scrimp when she goes to the girls' camp in Issyk Kul. I wanted her to be able to do both (maybe that is an American thing) but she had it figured out.

I have been telling everyone who is interested to send Jen good wishes for her birthday, August 2nd. We will be sending a package soon so she gets it in time. Jen said that she wants to go to Taraz for her birthday in order to eat at a nice restaurant. Unfortunately, it sounds like Ian or Kathryn won't be available around that time, so I think that just adds to her feeling down. They put so much importance on their birthdays as a way to celebrate being American, I think she's disappointed. But schedules can change, so we will see.

Jen had Severa give her GenGirls a mini conference of what she brought back from the conference in Osh. She arrived on Sunday and they planned through the week. She said it was wonderful. She wished more girls could have attended, but many were busy working in the fields. Guess they'd be able to relate to our farm kids in America.

You may need to line up for an autograph from Jen. (I have been first in line for years.) She found out that a film crew from Washington will be coming in August to do a promotional video for the Peace Corps. They are targeting the Partnership Programs, including Jen's and eight other projects in Kyrgyzstan. The director is going to America to greet the new volunteers and travel back with them, so the visitors from Washington will be scheduled around that.

Jen found out that a married couple, Tacie and Nate, will be replacing her! When I heard that, I thought, "That's right; my daughter is so good that it takes two to do what she has done." After the visits they've had from volunteers, now the assignments are final. Tacie will take over at History Sources, since she has a business background, and Nate will replace Kathryn and teach. They both speak Russian and Kathryn was upset about that, but then realized that many classes have only Russian-speaking children, and that's why she was taking Russian classes on the side. And Russian is as important as English for the children to learn.

The shocker is that Ian's school is not getting a volunteer. This private school has not worked well with the Peace Corps, and so the Peace Corps officials are saying, "Okay, see how it is without one and maybe you will better appreciate our support next year." It makes Ian feel sad, because he sees the kids suffering for what the school administration lacks.

The neat thing is that the Peace Corps has Jen, Kathryn, and Ian helping find the new volunteers their housing. They go along with a representative and check it out from an American's standpoint. Jen didn't think a couple could exist in her small place: too many electrical problems and no heat in the kitchen. Not to mention that there's nothing that connects the two rooms. I still can't believe that Jen has to go outside whenever she needs to go from her bedroom to the kitchen—in minus-fifteen-degree weather.

It looks like they have selected a family to host Jen's replacements, friends of Gulnara and Baktigul that Jen met at Baktigul's birthday party. The man was very sweet and told her, "I will sit next to you and make sure your plate and cup are full." What surprised Jen was that he kept bringing her Pepsi (a luxury) instead of offering her alcohol. Jen even questioned Gulnara to see if she had prompted him and she said, "I think I told him that you don't drink, but that was a long time ago." Jen was touched that he remembered and hoped he would be the same with the new volunteers.

The couple will be having a site visit to see where they will live and work in late August and then move there in September. She thinks it looks like a good situation, but then she told me, "When I went for my site visit, Venera made fish and mashed potatoes. But we never had that again." I told Jen, "It's no different than when we have company over; we go the extra mile to make it special. But they will have to learn the reality of everything on their own... like you did." Then she joked that she surely wouldn't give them the advice Gulnara gave her with the landlady situation: "Jennifer, don't cry. It will be okay because you are young. Life gets so much worse than this." Somehow I think the new volunteers just might agree with that advice when visiting the outhouse for the first time.

So her replacement volunteers will be there in September and Jen is concerned that it is too much overlap and one or the other will be left hanging, but I think Jen will realize how neat it is and that she will love to have the extra support. She told us that the progress on her project continues, and they've even picked out a light yellow paint for the inside walls. I joked with her, "You mean they didn't choose the color aqua?" She said, "As I stare at the color of my front door, I'm sure aqua paint will be involved somewhere; I can guarantee that!" So much for getting her a turquoise necklace for her birthday.

Love,

Karen

July 1, 2006

I thought this would be a slow month, but I have been touched by some displays of generosity that have inspired, amazed, and energized me. Why are they so touching, you ask? In this country, people tend, for the most part, to be more concerned with what they will get out of a deal than how they can contribute to a cause. Prime example: when I was planning Take Our Daughters to Work Day I approached the directors of each school to ask them to dismiss girls from lessons so they could participate. Ian's director asked me, "What will I get out of this?" Luckily, my director was with me and immediately responded, "There is nothing in it for you, or me, or even Jennifer. What you should be asking is what's in it for the girls." Therefore, this month of generosity has greatly impacted me.

This month I suffered from a stomach bug, the likes of which I have not seen since my first bout of diarrhea upon arriving in country. This was the bug to end all bugs, and had me flat on my back for a few days. I avoided having to go into my kitchen at all costs. The source of this bug varied, depending on who you talked to. In Kyrgyzstan, people always have to know why you are ill. Not that it speeds up the recovery process any, but for some reason, knowing why you are ill is more important than actually finding a way to stop the illness. Kathryn's grandmother thought I had been touched by the evil eye, a power taken very seriously in Central Asia. That, or "the sun had touched" me, causing me to be ill. Any extreme in temperature can cause physical breakdown. Sitting on concrete that is too cold will cause women to become infertile. Being out in the sun will cause stomach flu. Eating ice cream was the source of my illness, according to another friend—which makes sense, since it falls within the "extreme temperature" reasoning.

My counterpart at work explained that when she stands out in the wind for too long, her stomach becomes ill soon after; therefore, I must have stood out in the elements for too long. I concluded that I must have been standing in the sun, on a windy day, eating ice cream—that's why I became so ill. (Side note: "sick" is a four-letter word in Kyrgyz; I have learned to avoid saying it, and just now realized I can hardly bring myself to type it.) In actuality, the source of my illness was probably my underestimating how quickly food can go bad in the summer heat. You see, I live without a refrigerator, which isn't a problem in the winter. In the summer it's another story, and I have since learned to be more careful with what I leave out for more than a few hours.

So where does the generosity lie in this entire convoluted story? Well, Kathryn's mom was very worried for me, and even warned that I could have gotten dysentery (and died, a point that she repeatedly and strongly emphasized!). When I went to Kathryn's the first time after falling ill, she sat me down and lectured me on how there was no need for me to be ill like that. Since she was an endorser of the poorly kept food theory, she offered their refrigerator to me, no holds barred. Anytime I wanted to keep leftovers there, or dairy products, I was welcome. They wouldn't touch anything, she insisted, and just wanted me to know that she didn't want me to become ill again. Kathryn's mom took me under her wing as a daughter as soon as I moved out on my own, this offer being just one of many instances of her kindness.

This past week has been busy with graduations at Ian's and Kathryn's schools, as well as a countywide ball for all the graduating seniors. Graduation ceremonies in Kyrgyzstan tend to resemble proms much more than the ceremony that Americans are accustomed to. Girls get dressed up in their biggest, puffiest (usually borrowed) fairy-tale dresses. Their hair often resembles the leaning Tower of Pisa, but with the added support of decorative bobby pins, an excess of hairspray that makes their hair look wet, and plenty of glitter. The boys all have the look of just having gotten a much too short haircut, or they forgo the haircut and simply use hairspray to add some fashion to their manes, which inevitably gives them a *Miami Vice* look. They also do their best mob-boss impersonations and don sometimes very oversized, hand-me-down, impressive suits.

At the lyceum, the graduation ceremony consisted of toasts from varying high-ranking officials, with intermittent waltzing, and at some random point, the handing out of diplomas. At the public school, there was less dancing—in fact, no dancing—because there were so many students who needed to receive diplomas; the proceedings were much more factory style. Get them through the doors and down the main stairs, and send them off to stand on the sidewalk with diplomas in hand as quickly as possible.

At both graduations, a DJ played Russian, Kyrgyz, and English music throughout the ceremony. At the lyceum, we had the pleasure of listening to a number of songs by 50 Cent before the ceremony (imagine kicking off your graduation with blaring music full of obscenities in a language you can't understand), and at the public school, Celine Dion wafted through the courtyard while some of the students received their diplomas. I can imagine how silly this all sounds—last year I had to bite my lip throughout the ceremonies in order to not burst out laughing at yet another ridiculous hairdo, or another attempt at one-upmanship of singing between high-ranking government officials.

This year I found myself looking at the various hairstyles and dresses, and appreciating the tasteful or creative ones. Also this year, I took great pride in pointing out each dress that was made by our office. I didn't know the girls who were wearing them, but I could identify the material that I had seen in our office. My coworkers did not rest for two weeks up until the graduation, as they were making about ten prom dresses from scratch. No Saturdays or Sundays off. Just a continuous effort to handle consultations, orders, sewing, fittings, and more sewing. I could see in their eyes that graduation was a proud moment for them, as well as for the students.

None of them had children, so to speak, in the ceremonies but their creations were greatly admired. An idea that inspired and impressed me was that of dress rental. My office agreed to make dresses for girls at rock-bottom prices, with the agreement that the girls would return them at the end of the festivities so the office could rent out the dresses to other girls in the future. The night of the public school graduation, my coworkers arrived before I did and noticed a girl in a handmade dress. As my director later told me, "Jennifer, her mother sewed it by hand because there was no sewing machine at home. It looked like she was wearing a sack." This girl was one of the *atleechnik* students, or excellent students. *Atleechnik* students have received only fives (A+s) the last two years of school and have done well in the two years prior to that. This girl was the cream of the crop, wearing a sack on her big day. One of the seamstresses remembered that there was one dress left in the office and my director approached the girl and offered to be her sponsor by letting her wear the dress for free that evening. Negotiating with her mother was a little difficult, since she had sewn for two days to make this dress, a labor of love. But the daughter convinced her mother to let her change, since everyone had seen the original dress already. The morning after graduation, the mother returned the dress and said her daughter had told her that she felt like the most beautiful girl in her class.

As you know, I presented at the Osh women's leadership conference in May. I brought a university student with me to represent Talas Oblast. Sevara was an Uzbek neighbor of mine when I lived on Kirova Street with a host family. She just completed her first year at university in Bishkek, where she officially studies psychology and attends English clubs to keep up her conversational and reading skills. I asked her if she would at all be interested in facilitating a similar leadership conference in Pokrovka, with my GenGirls, during the summer, and she jumped at the opportunity. With the craziness of graduation and necessary work to be done in the fields, we decided that a one-day seminar would be best suited for our community and began planning with Osh sessions in mind. The day began with a panel of three women, community leaders, speaking to the girls about their lives and how they came to be in their positions. One woman is Kathryn's counterpart, a very active English teacher (she teaches lessons at three schools) with a very active family.

My director also spoke, which seemed perfect, since people often tell her she's a man for having so much initiative and for speaking directly and honestly. Also, the vice-mayor spoke about how she climbed the ladder within the government system to get where she is. These women all have very different stories to share and currently live very different lives. The beauty in their openness was that it proved to the girls that leaders don't come from molds. It takes all types to be a leader, and sometimes the skills to be one are not cultivated until later in life. After the panel, Sevara presented on politics and political systems, a presentation borrowed directly from the Osh conference. There are few women in national government, mostly because women are not educated in politics, among other reasons. A healthy debate in Kyrgyz and Russian happened after this presentation as the girls discussed what type of system is best in their eyes.

After lunch, we watched the film *North Country*, the story of women working in a mining plant in Northern Minnesota in the late 1980s. The story focused on one woman and her decision to fight for equal rights in the workplace and the right to work without harassment. Her legal battle was the first ever class action sexual harassment lawsuit, which changed sexual harassment policies in the workplace, nationwide. A discussion about the movie followed, as did one about the leadership ideas that the girls had already discussed.

So where does the generosity come in?

In addition to the three speakers giving up their busy mornings to share with the girls about their lives, it came from Sevara. This hip, urban university student gave up a week of her summer to come back to little old Pokrovka to share knowledge with younger students. Earlier in the week, I joked with my director that Sevara was the boss; I was just her helper. I didn't realize how true this statement was until the actual day. Sevara kicked ass and took names later! I had no idea this girl was born to be a trainer, born to be in front of a large group of people. Professionalism, charisma, intelligence, and enthusiasm—you name it and this girl's got it! I watched as she maturely handled group discussions, encouraging quiet girls and reigning in the talkative ones. She thought of hypothetical situations on the spot to encourage debate and challenged the girls to think outside the box.

Most importantly, and most touching in my eyes, she shared her experiences over this past year of trying to find her place in the university and in the big city, and gently advised the girls on how to be intelligent, mature young women. I have a new hero in Kyrgyzstan. Her name is Sevara.

Peace,

Jenny

CHAPTER 25

The Robbery

Jen is looking at this process not so much for her justice, but to make things better for the next volunteer. We wouldn't have wanted her to walk into a situation like this when she was brand new. It's just like her to be loving and to put others first. But it still angers me, and I wish she didn't have to go through this. It helps to know that she's more mad than scared.

July 4, 2006

Hoping everyone had a nice Fourth of July! Jen did halfway across the world. She got a phone call at work and as Jen answered in Russian, Ian's host sister said, "I want to tell you a Happy July 4th." Ian had given them homework during the school year about our Independence Day and she had remembered that it was now. Jen was touched. Also, Gulnara gave her some candy. So Kathryn and Jen decided they better celebrate with tuna fish sandwiches, since the Kyrgyz people were making an attempt. (Their independence day is August 31st.) Then they simultaneously had a great idea. They just stared at each other and talked in incomplete sentences and said, "Let's get... watermelon. Yeah... watermelon... yeah... fourth of July... yeah, picnic." Not only did they enjoy the treat of watermelon, but they went swimming in the river. I asked if it was too cold and Jen said, "You just have to jump in and do it, and anyway, it takes an hour to walk there, so by that time, I'm ready for something cool."

Jen had a little holiday last weekend as well. She didn't go to Bishkek for the celebration, but decided she needed a break from the village and so at the last minute went to Talas. The ladies had Friday off because they had worked so hard for two weeks straight, so she decided to do the same. She stayed with one volunteer on Friday night and another on Saturday night. It was just what she needed as a pick-me-up. She enjoyed going to the Internet café, but was sad that she didn't get to Mass. She went there Saturday night and no one was there. So she went back Sunday morning and still, no one was around. Not sure why. That is common in Kyrgyzstan. But she will be going to Talas again this weekend to meet with a group that will be planning for the kids' camp in August. That's the annual camp for the whole Talas Oblast, the one that Jen was requesting embroidery floss for, to help make friendship bracelets. But the girls' camp at Issyk Kul is another story.

Last year Jen attended a girls' camp and loved it. So when they asked for volunteers again, she signed up. Then the leader sent an email that said there were twenty people willing to help, but he only needed six—and her name was not one of them. She was upset at first, because she thought they needed so much help, but then realized maybe there's a reason. That's when she got a call from her friend Liz in Osh about her wedding to a Russian man on July 15th. They are having a heck of a time with paperwork, but she wanted to invite Jen and even hinted at Jen being the maid of honor—but didn't want to pressure Jen to travel. Jen sees it as the choice she needs to make.

There was a terrible delay in our connection, so it was hard to know when to speak. Jen said she didn't know if it was a delay or if I was being silent. I quickly reminded her that I am never "silent" during our phone calls. She laughed and then a rooster crowed extremely loudly, so she said, "YOU are the one that needs to be quiet."

Jen happened to run into a boy named Nurgaza. He graduated from Ian's school the first June they were there and is a grad student at the university. He is certified as a seminar trainer, and he needs to run four trainings this summer. As he was explaining to Jen all that he had to do, she thought, "Ask and you shall receive." She told him, "Hey, I will help you! We can work on it at my office."

Jen was so peppy, and she got even more excited telling us that ever since she has gone swimming in the river, she's wanted to find an inflatable inner tube to float on. She has looked for something for over twenty-five months. At times she got hopeful, only to find out that the "tube" in question was just a kid's raft. But just last week she found one that fits! She even tried it on in the store. And she wonders why she gets stared at. But the best part is that it's decorated with animations from *101 Dalmatians*! Go figure. I asked, "Do you think it's an adult's?" She said, "Mom, it's *101 Dalmatians*. What do you think?" So she has this big kid tube and can't wait to try it out. I told her she will have to get a patch kit so she can repair it. She said, "Don't even talk about it popping... it will break my heart."

We told her all about our camping trip to the Black Hills and I said, "I sure missed having you with us." Long pause... long pause. I said, "Are you there?" She said, "Yeah... I was just thinking." Then I realized that she might be crying and that I better give her extra time. Then she wanted to know if I was there. The problem was the delay, not our emotions. We had a laugh about telephone lines versus tears. Thank goodness for both!

Love,

Karen

July 9, 2006

Jen told us her *101 Dalmatians* inner tube passed the test and she actually pretended she was back home, floating down the Apple River. But our call was mostly centered on a problem she's having. Over the past week, someone has been breaking into her house. It appears that they're getting in through her bedroom window. They stole the key to her kitchen one day and then some food out of the kitchen the next day. That she doesn't mind—everyone is hungry—but then her money was stolen.

Nearly 2,000 som were taken out of her computer case, yet her computer was still there. It became obvious that this was the work of some kids, because only they would be able to fit through her small window, which had been cracked. Jen ended up boarding it up, but decided she needed to do more. A call to the Peace Corps headquarters will get her money reimbursed, but she also had to inform the local police. When they first heard she was moving there, they had said to let them know if she needed any help. It was different this time.

They came over and at first seemed sympathetic, and told her that they were pretty sure it was her landlord's son. He is around eleven years old. He is home from boarding school, hanging with his buddies, and has been in trouble before; hence the reason he was sent to boarding school. He had been seen buying things (meats and cheeses, for example) that he usually couldn't afford.

All of a sudden, the mood seemed to turn, and it was as if the police were trying to find some fault with Jen. She thought maybe they were just expressing the attitude that because all Americans are so rich, the robbery was somehow okay. Then they started looking around the room and asking dumb questions. They talked about fingerprinting and about being in touch with a lawyer. But Jen knew that it was just big talk. Jen has learned why they are called militia more than police. One of them seemed nice enough, but the second-in-charge guy was rude enough to start eating some of her apricots and peanuts off of her table. Apparently, they like to show their power by intimidation, but Gulnara was there and that really helped. She said that Jen's lack of Kyrgyz language was to her benefit, because she could say things incorrectly and get away with it.

Then the atmosphere changed again, and they insinuated that Jen would have to prove that the kids break in when she leaves. They told her to write down her complaint in Russian. Jen said she didn't think she would do a good enough job for a legal form. Gulnara stepped in and said, "Do you think that you could go to America for one year and then write perfect English?" Jen was getting very frustrated and at one point she said, "I don't need your advice; I need you to do your job." One guy didn't even know what the name "Peace Corps" referred to. I have a funny feeling he will find out soon.

When Jen talked to the people at Peace Corps headquarters, she found them very kind. She said that whenever she enters the headquarter office, it's like going into the bar on the TV show Cheers: everybody knows your name. The man on the other end of the line said, "Jennifer, I am so sorry this has happened." Jen replied that it makes her so angry, because she came here to help and then gets treated like this. The man said, "Don't feel that way. You are making a difference. There just are bad people everywhere. Here and back home." They will be sending her money to replace what was stolen, as Jen can hardly live on her allowance the way it is. He also asked how she felt about moving.

Love,

Karen

July 11, 2006

Well, the one thing that I never wanted to happen during my service will soon happen—I'll be a statistic on our safety and security coordinator's (SSC) bimonthly report. Every two months, our SSC includes a report in the volunteer newsletter about what has happened to volunteers out in the field; basically, it includes anything that was reported to him due to a concern for safety. I will be included in this report because unfortunately, I was the recent victim of theft, which drastically affected my living situation. I'll start from the beginning.

Around the Fourth of July, I noticed things disappearing from my room. I didn't say anything to anyone because I thought I had forgotten to lock my room on one occasion and therefore the theft was my fault. Then I just thought I was losing my mind, as I would come home and notice sunflower seeds, something I don't eat, in my room, and things on my bookshelf out of order. I realized that if anyone was coming into my room, it was possibly through the small opened window, called a *fortitchka*, which I couldn't lock. I nailed a screen over the window as a deterrent instead of nailing it shut, so I could still have ventilation in my little room. After talking to Kathryn about my suspicion that someone had been coming into my room, she inspected my screen to find that it had been removed. "Check your money," she said. Two thousand som, or half of my living allowance, was gone. That's like fifty dollars in American money, but it's all I had left until the end of the month. This happened on a Saturday night. Because I had to wait until Monday to contact the Peace Corps or the local authorities, I nailed my window shut.

My director and I went to the militia office on Monday morning and told the second in command what happened. He looked at my director and said, "Two thousand what?" "Som," she replied. He seemed to be unimpressed, since he must have been working under the same misinformed assumption that you find in these parts; all Americans are filthy rich. When we told him where I lived and with whom, he said, "Oh, yeah; I know the family. It was her son who stole your money." My landlady's son already had a record at the police station. The commander promised that men would be sent to my house to fingerprint and check everything out. Two hours later, when they still hadn't shown up, I called the SSC and asked him to call the militia to impress upon them the importance of conducting an investigation. He said he would contact the highest-ranking militia official in the oblast immediately and that's when my director decided to use her connections.

Eventually, the process of reporting that had started at 9:00 a.m. was finishing at 4:00 p.m., with militia coming to my house and fingerprinting the window. I had been at work all day waiting for the militia and when we arrived at my place, I noticed that the things on my bookshelf were in disarray, a nail was removed from the larger window frame, and the glass was cracked. It was obvious that someone tried to get in, despite the fact that I had nailed the *fortitchka* shut, although one militia said it must have been the wind.

Earlier in the day, when I was writing up my own report and talking to the SSC, he had asked how I felt about moving, because it seemed unsafe for me to live in a place where my money had been stolen and the only suspect lived on the same property. I had agreed then, but the broken window fortified my decision. The militia proceeded to question me about details, looked over my room and the window, and asked me if I could fill out a report in Russian. I said no, and my director looked at the one officer who was giving me the most attitude and said, "Let's see you study English for a year and be able to fill out a police report fluently!"

My director proceeded to fill out the report, as the head guy told me I shouldn't have left my money in my room, basically implying it was my fault that this happened. After a day of running around, and an hour or so of being treated like I was the suspect, I had had it and snapped, "Do you have 2,000 som in your home? Yeah, I thought so. I don't need advice right now. I need you to do your job!"

I had to remind myself that in a third-world country, corruption is a problem at all levels, but none more so than in the militia and my frustrating experience was no exception. However, my director later told me that no one else would have been able to get away with talking to this guy like that. I am a girl and younger than he is. I should have been kowtowing to him like a good Kyrgyz girl. But I was able to avoid him yelling at me or other painful interactions because he knew I was fluent in Russian, not Kyrgyz. He wouldn't have been able to fully use his power of intimidation, like he wanted to. Lucky me.

Peace,

Jenny

July 12, 2006

Per Peace Corps instructions, Jen was told to pack her bags and move out. Her host family no longer fits the criteria and so they say that Jen must go. Kathryn was there and the biggest help. As they were getting things lined up for a taxi, the landlady came and started yelling that she should have been told first and not the police. She just wanted to take care of it secretly, but the police talked to the boy and he admitted to breaking in and stealing the money. She was demanding Jen clean everything beyond how it was when she moved in, but Jen just kept packing. She talked about giving Jen back half a month's pay that she already gave her, but Jen doubts that will happen. The Peace Corps told Jen to just clean and leave. So she did.

Gulnara was there and kept talking to Altynai as the girls hustled. Then Muktibek showed up. He is the guy Jen's replacements will be living with and he is so wonderful. Kathryn asked if he could transport her things, but first he said, "Wait; more importantly, how is Jennifer? Is she okay? Is she sad?" He hugged her and kept saying it was terrible that this had happened to her, that it wasn't her fault, and he would do anything to help her.

It was agreed that she would spend the night at Kathryn's and store her things at Gulnara's until she found a place to live. So Muktibek transported her belongings, and even though she offered to pay for the benzene (gasoline), he refused. One bad apple doesn't spoil the whole bunch.

Jen believes that the break-ins happened for a reason and even though it is bad timing to have to travel, she sees it as a plus to be away for a bit. With all that is going on, Gulnara is a good one to have on her side. She will make things happen. She said the police don't dare do anything shady now because it will cause such a scandal. Her follow-up trip to the militia office was uncomfortable, though; they were overly friendly to Jennifer and tried to insinuate that she owed them something. It made her skin crawl. They boasted about how they had caught the guy... like they said they would. Gulnara said "Enough!" and they left.

Regardless of these officials taking credit, Jen is focused on getting ready for a trip to Bishkek and then to the wedding. Jen is looking at this process not so much for her justice, but to make things better for the next volunteer. We wouldn't have wanted her to walk into a situation like this when she was brand new. It's just like Jen to be loving and to put others first. But it still angers me, and I wish she didn't have to go through this. It helps me to know that she said she's more angry than scared. Her things are not as important as her personal safety and she feels confident in that. And there are so many good people around her, so she isn't going to let a punk kid destroy that. And if we didn't have faith in the Peace Corps, we would not have been able to turn her over twenty-five months ago.

She says she's okay, despite it all. She will have a much-needed break from the village, and when the dust settles, she'll deal with finding new living quarters. And more importantly, she'll be getting back to the work she was put there to do in the first place. She continues to be an amazing woman.

Love,

Karen

July 23, 2006

We've had about four calls that finally add up to one Jen letter. The connections were terrible, which was so frustrating, since it was at a time when she needed to talk the most. With all the phone problems, we asked Grandma and Grandpa to try calling her because they have international dialing on their house phone. It was the same sketchy connection and Grandpa said he could sense the urgency in Jen's voice.

When we finally connected through a phone card that Sara purchased online, she was choked up with homesick tears. Jen said, "Crying was not on my list of things to do and that's pissing me off." We tried to reassure her that all the major changes she has gone through in the last weeks are bound to shake her up. She said, "I am okay during the week. I'm strong. But when I hear your voice, it makes me feel sad." She was hurting. We cried together for a bit and I found myself talking slower and louder, as if that would help.

All the changes have centered around the break-in and the wedding: one bad thing and one good thing. People usually say, "What do you want first, the good news or the bad news?" She had it the other way around.

We rehashed the list of all the wonderful people she has around her. Kathryn was a rock by her side. She calmed her down and was organized and focused. Muktibek was an angel in a red Volvo that day and soothed her with reassurances. Gulnara rescued her from the militia's corrupt ways. She put her foot down and demanded a resolution. Gulnara had the most to lose, but she didn't think twice about being in her corner. Jen agreed and gave a big sigh.

While trying to help her look on the bright side, my support was bordering on dredging it all up again, so I tried to think of something else to talk about, something happy to say. All I could come up with was to ask her about her *101 Dalmatians* floaty. She said, "He is doing fine. He is living in Kathryn's room on top of her tall bookcase for safekeeping and I plan to use him on August 13th when we go to the river." The distraction seemed to help.

Sometimes you just have to look "up" to feel better. In more ways than one.

Love,

Karen

CHAPTER 26

Moving Out... Again

Jennifer said, "It's the best situation and both Gulnara and I want this. I know Gulnara so well and we are comfortable with each other and each other's customs."

August 5, 2006

While Jen was traveling to Osh for Liz and Stas's wedding, she was given permission to live with Gulnara for her last four months there. It is not common to be hosted by your director, but with everything taken into consideration, the decision was made by the Peace Corps that Jen should live there for a trial period of one month. This gives each party an out, but Jen said, "It's the best situation and both Gulnara and I want this." After all they have been through together, it does seem right. Jen said, "It wouldn't be fair for a new family to have to adjust to an American living with them, nor me living with a new family. I know Gulnara so well and we are comfortable with each other and each other's customs." So true.

Jen had her things moved in and Gulnara has given her shelving on one wall of the kitchen for her food/cookware, as well as a shelf in the refrigerator. That's right—a refrigerator! Jen said she bought some juice and put it in the refrigerator and then when she came home from work, she was able to have COLD juice. Ahhhhhhhhhh! The things we take for granted. Also, there is some comfort with being in a family setting, with its noise and interaction.

Gulnara has two boys that are students of Kathryn's and are very well behaved. They are twelve and sixteen years old. Jen says that the sixteen-year-old, Semetei, is a bit squirrely, but cute. Another plus is that she can eat what she makes for herself or join the family. And her bedroom is huge.

Gulnara's husband was a terrible alcoholic, but because of her standing in the business community, she was able to keep her home with her children when the couple divorced. Gulnara's situation is similar to that of Jen's past host mother, Venera. Actually, Gulnara and Venera have been close friends for many years, but an odd thing happened last week. Jen came home from visiting and when she walked in, there was Venera sitting with Gulnara at the table, having tea! Gulnara greeted Jen and told her that there was water for tea if she wanted, and other treats. Then she dropped it.

That is weird in two ways. One—a Kyrgyz woman does not usually give you an option of what you can do. You are told what you will do and when. As Jen says, you are "whisked" around like a broom. But Gulnara is modern in her thinking and so she offers something to be hospitable and then lets you have your independence. The second weird thing is that Venera was at the table and was witness to how a hostess should treat a guest in her home. Offer them food! But we shouldn't complain. She did her best to be a good host mother.

Moving on to a good thing: the wedding. Jen said it was great! Liz and Stas met while working at the university and their first date was during the revolution last March. As the maid of honor, Jen saw her role as keeping things the way the bride wanted them. She had a list of things to do and was adamant about Liz having something old (a necklace), something new (her wedding ring), something borrowed (her dress), and something blue (her garter). Jen told her she could do Liz's hair, but Liz insisted on going to have it done. This would be impossible in Pokrovka. In Osh, the world is your oyster. Unfortunately, Liz was wearing a T-shirt, and when they got back to put her dress on, they couldn't lift the T-shirt off over Liz's head. Jen said, "We have to cut it off" (meaning the T-shirt!). And with shocked Kyrgyz women standing around, they did. (That was not the only time she has ever gotten shocked looks from Kyrgyz women.)

Then, when they were getting the dress on Liz, the zipper broke. The dress had a combination of a zipper and tie-ups, and Jen suggested they do the tie-ups first and then try to get the zipper to cooperate. The mother-in-law and sister didn't seem to care. One woman was pushing at Liz, one was pulling, and Jen was trying to reason things out. Finally, she was so frustrated that she said to one woman, loudly in Russian, "Just wait, Ajay—just wait!" The woman looked at her strangely, because Jen called her Ajay, which you say to an older Kyrgyz woman out of respect. But this lady didn't seem to like the connotation of being "older," no matter her nationality, so she walked away. But it all worked out. They fixed the zipper without her.

Jen is excited to see the pictures from the wedding; Liz is putting them on her website and it turns out that Jen was the only one taking pictures! What is the real job of a maid of honor, anyway? Jen began to wonder what they would have done without her. But that is an American way of thinking. Kyrgyz people tend to just enjoy the moment, and not worry about capturing it. They love having their pictures taken, but seldom do it for their families.

Jen enjoyed receiving earrings and a bracelet as a gift for being in the wedding, and really liked going to a waterfall on Sunday as a tourist. Her trip to Bishkek before the wedding was another tourist experience for her. When she arrived in the city, she thought it would be cheaper if she bought some fruit at a stand for her meal, but decided to sit down at a restaurant to eat. As she was leaving, two girls saw her backpack (a dead giveaway that she was American) and the pin on it that says, "I Love Chaska." (It was the pin that got lost in a snowdrift while she was on a seven-mile hike and later found.) They came up to her and said, "Are you American?" Jen said yes. She found out that they were from Elk River and Maple Grove, Minnesota, and were just visiting. What are the odds?

As Jen went to pay for her meal, one of the girls came over and just stared at her. Jen thought, "Okay, we are American and there are not many of us from Minnesota, but why are you looking at me?" when the girl burst out and said, "Are you Christian? Do you believe in Jesus Christ?" Jen said, "Oh, yes!" And they proceeded to talk about how hard it is to practice your faith so far away from home. I guess there was a reason that she was not supposed to skip a meal.

Kathryn's mother has been so gracious to Jen lately and even more so since Jen had to move. She offered Jen some *compote*, which is Kyrgyz for boiled fruit. She said, "You will eat it with us, the stewed fruit?" Jen's knowledge of Kyrgyz language is limited and sensed that the offer was a loving gesture, but was worried that *compote* was so close to our word "compost" that she should be cautious to accept; but she did in the end, and it obviously tasted much better than expected.

Staying informed about world events is such a challenge for her. She was doing her tutoring with Ian's host sister, Venera, and she was questioning her about the new war in Israel and Lebanon. Venera told her that she really doesn't pay attention to the news. Jen said, "You have to watch the news. I don't have a TV and you have to tell me what's going on!" Venera sensed the urgency in Jen's voice—Jen hasn't received her *Newsweek* magazine in a few weeks—and said, "I promise. I promise. I will watch what is going on and will talk to my parents to understand what is going on and tell you."

We let Jen know that a CD that was mailed by her on July 17th was received by us on July 22nd. We were flabbergasted! Not to mention that we didn't know she was sending anything, that the return address was Grandma and Grandpa's, and that it had an American postmark. Finally we figured out that she must have given it to Kathryn to take with her to mail from her U.S. address, as opposed to from Pokrovka. I told Jen we were so confused about getting this package in the mail and she just burst out with "Woooohoooooo" because she was glad it made it. I said the same thing as I started watching the CD.

The best part, which she never told us about, is a short film that a volunteer, Wilbur, made of the women's conference in Osh that she helped facilitate. It brought me to tears after the first minute. It was breathtaking to see these girls coming from all parts of Kyrgyzstan to learn about how they could make a difference in their world. It was such a treat to see Jen in every other frame of the film, made up of both still photos and video, all set to wonderful music.

Other volunteers keep telling Wilbur that he needs to do this video stuff as a profession. The neat part was that John, who was in her study group in the early days, just happened to have his mother (who is eighty-one), his aunt, and a friend visiting from America. They were asked to be part of the panel discussion, because one was a lawyer and the other two are professional women in America. The girls loved them! You're never too old for educating.

Connecting with Jen was very frustrating. We ended up trying to call her fifteen times on her cell phone and had terrible connections, so she finally said to try Kathryn's landline. I asked if she was there to *banya* and if so, didn't Gulnara have one? She said she just went there to visit, even though Kathryn was gone, and thought the extra phone option would be good. Gulnara does have a *banya*, but it is under repair. Aren't they all? Just thinking of the one that had sheep stored in it.

It seems there are two ways to shower. One involves standing with a cloth around you as a stall. You put water in the metal tank above you in the morning so it will heat up enough during the day for you to shower that night, when you then let the hot water out via the nozzle slowly, so as not to run out in just a few minutes. Or the much nicer *banya* which is heated by coal and you can use water right away and there's usually a wooden room with a bench where you sit and wash yourself. Jen has had this type but most often does her "bucket bathing."

Her walk to work now takes about twenty minutes instead of seven but, funny thing is, it seems to take Gulnara over thirty minutes, since she needs to stop and talk to people on her way. Jen thinks that this is a good thing. Gulnara's influence in the community has helped her in so many ways. The renovation for their project continues to thrive! It is obvious that Gulnara's business sense has played a big role. However, the cafeteria project of Kathryn's that Gulnara helped with has been slow going. They have only put bars on the windows as instructed, but the director has the sense that school has not started yet and it's vacation time, so why work now? In America, we take advantage of the downtime of summer to get ready for the school year. But there is a different mentality there and Jen accepts it, though she is glad her project has followed more of an American way of doing things.

While Jen was in Osh for the wedding, Gulnara ordered new tables and chairs for the area of the building where they'll teach sewing techniques. She just needs to find a way to get them hauled to Pokrovka. Can you imagine?

The new volunteers had their site visits, but Jen didn't host anyone because of her living situation. She attended a Saturday night picnic with everyone, though. They had Kyrgyz food and a guy asked her how to eat the flat bread. She got so excited and thought, "I am actually teaching someone how to eat this type of bread. There was a point when I didn't know how to break bread." I asked what she meant and she said that she told him to tear off the outer ring, and then to use the inside like a pocket for his onions and potato. They don't have sliced loaves like we do, with sliced cheese and sliced bologna. It reminded her of how far she has come.

Love,

Karen

August 8, 2006

In a way, it feels as if I am coming full circle, living with the woman who has given the most of herself, her time, energy, support, and understanding. And it's kind of nice to have family around me again. Just the hum of people living and going about their business is comforting. My director has two sons, Semetei (sixteen) and Ernur (twelve). Semetei speaks English well and is fun to tease. Ernur is a bookworm and still a silly little kid. The other day, he was playing hide-and-seek with the puppy whose name is Oomka, or the Russian equivalent of Little Smarty. Both my director and I think the dog's name should be Little Crazy! I was getting water at the well and yelled to the dog, who had lost track of Ernur, "Oomka, Ernur's over there! Go get him; he's got lots of meat!" I was thinking pockets full of sheep or horse. But Ernur yelled back, as he ran away from the dog, "No, no! Jennifer, I have only bones!" It took me a second to realize that he wasn't talking about animal bones, but his own. You see, Ernur is pretty much a brown skeleton. I couldn't stop laughing and neither could Semetei or Gulnara when I told them Ernur's witty retorts.

In the midst of all the upheaval was the wedding of my good friend Liz and her Russian boyfriend, Stas. They had been dating for over a year and decided to get married in country. Liz had said that she wanted me to be her bridesmaid, but didn't expect me to travel there. But when she sent me a text with the date of the big day, the decision wasn't hard to make. I was her "maid of steel" as she claims, and I was so glad that I went down, despite everything that was going on in my neck of the woods. I've learned that there usually is something that comes along when you need it the most. So the wedding was one of two fun things that helped take my mind off all that had happened.

The other was celebrating August 2, 2006. My second birthday in country went swimmingly—literally—on one of the days. Turning twenty-four turned into a three-day marathon, which started with a picnic at the river with some GenGirls; then bacon and eggs with my favorite guys, Erich and Ian, and Uzgen *plov* with the women at work.

Albina, Kathryn's best student whom I have been tutoring while Kathryn is on vacation, asked if some of the GenGirls could take me on a picnic to the river. I of course agreed and we turned the event into a potluck affair. When I arrived at Albina's house with the other girls—Albina lives closest to the river—her mother was hurrying around, packing utensils and plates. I thought we were just going to make sandwiches, so I asked why we needed forks, spoons, and platters. She said it was for the *dim-domah*, a cooked pot of cabbage, carrots, potatoes, and some meat, which she had promised to make for me about a month ago when I said I had never heard of it or eaten it. My eyes got big as everything clicked. I said, "Ajay, will you go swimming with us?!" She started laughing and said of course and was just tickled pink that she was going on an excursion as if she were one of the girls.

It was a fun day of taking turns riding my *101 Dalmatians* inner tube down the flowing river, eating, and relaxing. The highlight for me was being referred to as "my daughter" by Albina's mom and "Jennifer *ap-chay*," or "big sister," by the girls.

Bacon and eggs may not sound like a big deal when you live in the first world, but it was the ideal birthday treat on Wednesday. Erich came out from Kirovka village (a village thirty minutes away, the village nearest Pokrovka that has volunteers) and the three of us got together for lunch. Good friends have been religiously sending me precooked bacon since pork products are difficult to come by in a Muslim country; it's especially hard in an area where there are few Russians. I've come to realize that bacon tastes best when shared, so we ripped into one of the seventy-two piece packages that came as a birthday present. The highlight of lunch was the fact that the boys made it and I was even served first. That's not common here, since I am "just a girl" and should be cooking and serving the boys before I help myself.

But lunch with the boys was fun, and making lunch for the women at work was even more fun. I brought back Uzgen rice, special red rice, from the south as a thank you for some folks, and in order to make lunch for the women at work. It's custom here for the birthday person to bring in lunch the day of his or her birthday. Last year I did this begrudgingly, since I am accustomed to the American tradition of getting pampered as the birthday girl on my big day, but this year it was a labor of love. I really wanted to treat these ladies who give me so much of their time, friendship, and understanding.

This year, I was brave and decided to make a typically Kyrgyz meal, consisting of eggplant appetizers, salad, treats, and watermelon. I have to admit that the most I did to make the *plov* (fried rice) was buy the rice and clean the carrots and raisins. My director did everything else, so I would not ruin the Uzgen rice on my maiden voyage of *plov* making. The highlight of bringing lunch to work was that I got to ride in a *kamaz*, or big rig truck, to work with the pot of *plov* on my lap. Just as we were preparing to go to the office, a *kamaz* of appliances for the cafeteria project arrived from Bishkek, and the driver offered to take us to the office so we wouldn't have to walk twenty minutes carrying a steaming pot of rice.

As I told my mom on the phone, birthdays here aren't bad for volunteers. You're a celebrity of sorts; therefore, I celebrated much more that I would have in America.

Peace,

Jenny

August 11, 2006

Jen said it was a great birthday, better than the one in country last year. Being a celebrity was okay with her this time. As Jen said, "Well, why not. There is only one of me and hundreds of them, so my birthday is a big deal." She told us of people coming out of the woodwork, giving her things. Ian gave her five DVDs as a "chick flick" pack. His host sister, Venera, helped make a Kyrgyz potholder and cosmetic bag for her. Gulnara bought a watermelon for her guests. Erich brought some candy and sunglasses from his girlfriend. The women at work bought her a four-hundred-unit phone card that will last her until September. She got flowers from so many others, and Kathryn's mom had her over for dinner and a special cake. Venera gave her chocolate and some cool, bright pink cups with constellations on them. The GenGirls took her on a picnic and some of them gave her little trinkets as presents. Kathryn left a card behind for Albina to give to her, and it's a beautiful painted scene that she will frame when she comes home. Some volunteers from Talas found out it was her birthday and so they said they would celebrate with her at the café, after the camp meeting on Saturday.

Also, she got calls from some Peace Corps headquarters friends about a gift waiting for her. Jen says that headquarters is a place where you can bring things like clothes, household items, or books to drop off for others or to shop for something you need. A book was waiting for her there with a note attached that read, "Make sure this book gets to Jenny Lawrence." It is called *Children of God Go Bowling* and the author is from St. Paul, Minnesota, but grew up in Chaska and makes so many references to the town in her story. I may check that out myself.

Jen's bacon-and-egg birthday party with Erich and Ian was a treat. And they also had "Kyrgyz daiquiris." Erich's host brother got married and someone gave them a blender, which is a bizarre gift in itself, since most didn't know how to use it. But it was perfect for Erich, since he gets "care" packages of booze sent from home. He had some rum and they decided to make cocktails in the martini glasses that Uncle Paul and Aunt Patty sent. They weren't sure what to add to it, with their limited resources. Jen said, "Anyway you look at it, we can't screw it up," so they put in juices, even from watermelon, and threw in some ice cream! They poured Jen's first to keep it a virgin, and then added rum. (In my opinion, the rum would be necessary to make that combination pleasing.)

I have to say, it bothers me a bit that packages of alcohol get to Erich without a scratch, but one of Jen's birthday packages was definitely tampered with. I got so angry when Jen told me that she didn't get all that I thought we had sent. Jen said she did at first, too, but then let it go, because it had been awhile since it had happened. That's not how most of us in America would take this kind of thing. The good news is that her birthday card and the portable CD player were still there. (She has gone without reliable music while walking since May.) But other things were missing, which is so frustrating. So here's a word to the wise: write down what you send, like Grandma and Grandpa always do, so you know when what you sent eventually arrives. There is one more padded envelope that she hasn't gotten yet, so maybe all things are accounted for. The bright side is that it probably is the last time we will need to send anything. I hope that whoever opened her birthday package is enjoying the Little Debbie oatmeal pies and Kotex!

Jen found out her group could have an early out in November without losing any of their benefits. People immediately sent in a "request for departure" for November 2, 2006. I think headquarters is being flexible because of the greater overlap of volunteers; they arrived in country in June instead of September so that the teachers can start at the beginning of the school year. Jen also requested to early out, but was turned down because so many had applied for the same date. She said she didn't mind. She will be busy showing the new couple the ropes.

She may end up leaving anywhere between November 6th and 10th. Then she has her three-day "out processing" in Bishkek. She plans to travel to France to see Jessy, and spend time in New York seeing Melissa and Uncle Doug and Aunt Diana. She figures she will get home around November 22th, just in time for turkey! We are counting the days!

As we were ending our call, I heard Jen chewing. She said she was enjoying her cornflakes. She casually said, "Sometimes they are pink-milk cornflakes." I thought, "What? Should I ask what kind of cows that comes from?" Then she explained that she makes milk using powdered milk and distilled water from her Nalgene bottle, and sometimes the day before, she's made some Kool-Aid in there. The powder often gets stuck in the cracks and comes out in the next batch, which is sometimes milk.

Makes sense when you don't have a dishwasher, running water, or sink for that matter, to help you totally rinse things out. Never would have thought that having the right colored milk, consistently, would be one of the perks of coming home.

Love,

Karen

CHAPTER 27

The Grand Opening

"Hello, dear guests. Thank you for coming to our ceremony. My name is Jennifer Lawrence. I am a Peace Corps volunteer and a worker at History Sources. This day is very important to everyone here, but it also is important for my family and friends in America. They helped sponsor this project, and without these people, this renovation would not have been possible."

—FROM JEN'S SPEECH ON THE OPENING OF THE
POKROVKA BUSINESS CENTER

August 25, 2006

The week that Jen was in camp was such a treat. She had access to the Internet every day, and so each morning at work I rushed to turn on my computer to see if she was there. She was. Each night, she emailed us to let us know how the day went—those were my early morning greetings. Maybe that is not a big deal to some, but for us it was "to die for!"

Throughout the week, she did a lot of running around to keep things going smoothly. When they had an art project, she helped set up for the meal. And when they had the meal, she would clean up the art supplies and get the volleyball all laid out. She would help clean up from one project, and when the next project didn't need her, sneak away to the Internet café that was downstairs. She lost seven pounds during the week because they fed the kids first, and then the volunteers got the leftovers. We hope to hear more stories about the kids, and Jen told us that Wilbur was there to take video. When he showed what he had filmed during his first two days of shooting to the group, Jen cried and the kids screamed. She said, "They have never seen themselves on TV or in any kind of film and it blew them away." I can't wait to see it as well.

During camp, Jen's feet were killing her because her tennis shoes are on their last legs. With her last pair, she had to resort to duct tape before we could send her new ones. Guess she is just going to tough it out until coming home, but my suggestion to future volunteers is this: bring two pairs of tennis shoes from the get-go!

They celebrated Ian's birthday and Kathryn gave him a foot massage as a present. Jen piped up and said, "Hey, you were gone for my birthday... I want a gift of a back massage!" I guess Kathryn has a gift that keeps on giving.

When Jen got back, she said Gulnara was just terrific. She knew Jen would want to have downtime. Even with her cousin visiting, Gulnara didn't try to make Jen have tea with them. Jen said, "She understands and let me be a hibernating bear. I slept for four hours."

Jen told me that one day she was on her phone and Semetei needed to get into a cabinet that is in her room; she motioned to him and said, "Go ahead." This boy is a great student and knows English, but looked confused and said, "What does that mean?" It does make you think of how weird our phrases can be. But yet, she said, "He is the only Kyrgyz person who calls me Jenny. They have a hard time pronouncing long vowels, so it is easier to just say Jennifer." But Kathryn's host dad calls her "Jen'ya," and she likes that.

Love,

Karen

September 12, 2006

We've had a few quick phone calls over the past two weeks with Jen. A volunteer said her dad told her that something bad had happened to St. Paul, Minnesota. So Jen called in a panic, and we didn't know what the bad thing could possibly be. We told her that the Minnesota State Fair was going on, but if there had been an explosion or something bad, we would have heard about it. We told her that it could have been a St. Paul in some other state. But the next time we talked, we found out the volunteer's dad was an insurance man and was terribly busy with all the claims from the huge damaging hail we'd had that week. This little misunderstanding reinforces the need for volunteers to get accurate information from home when they are so far away. But our quick calls were also due to Jen's health. She got the famous "Kyrgyz flu."

It is surprising that after all this time, she could still run into something that could affect her as much as her illness did when she first came into the country. This time she's had trouble getting to the outhouse in time, and has also been running a fever. Kathryn had some of the same symptoms and so Jen thought it was a virus rather than food poisoning. And when her replacement volunteer, Tacie, also was sick, too, it made sense. But true to form, Tacie had to succumb to "You must have had something cold" and "You didn't wear a jacket." When Tacie was sipping on Sprite, and her host mom said, "Sprite does not work in this country—you must have tea," Jen told Tacie, "Get used to it."

When Jen wasn't feeling well, she was slow getting out of bed and so Gulnara checked on her. When Jen told her that she wasn't feeling good—Jen's voice sounded gruff because she just woke up—Gulnara said, "Is it your voice?" Jen said, "No, my stomach." Her immediate response was, "Do you want to eat?" Jen says it still amazes her that when there is illness, this culture is obsessed with cold and food.

Unfortunately, what ended up seeming like a simple flu turned out to be a bacterial infection. When things just didn't improve and she missed almost a week of work, she called the Peace Corps doctor. Jen was advised to call the warden and get a dose of antibiotics. This was a relief and a confirmation that she wasn't being a baby. When we talked to her last, she had just had some real food—Spam and some string beans—but she was so upset that, as terrible as her stomach felt, she just kept craving food. She said she had fantasized about things she hadn't thought about in two years, like white bread, bologna, and mayo. She kept internally yelling at herself, "Why? Why? Soon that food will be mine!"

She didn't want to miss work with all that is going on. The construction is coming to completion and the ribbon-cutting ceremony is being planned. The linoleum (a luxury) was being laid, the trim needed to follow, and the furniture was ordered. It was delivered to Gulnara's house, and now needed to be brought to the office by donkey cart. Everyone was just shopping and relaxing on Sunday, since there would be so much to do on Monday to get ready for Tuesday. Jen still has that "American" mentality of worrying about being ready by the planned date, which has already been announced to the mayor and country director. She's also stuck with the mentality that you work first and play later.

At any rate, she told Gulnara, "We need to know NOW if we can't make it. We don't call them the night before and say... sorry." Gulnara may be a bit overwhelmed with everything going on. The stoves that are to go into Kathryn's school's cafeteria are also being stored at Gulnara's until they can be properly installed at the school. And the school is already using them (in Gulnara's house!) to bake rolls for some of the children's breakfasts and all of the children's tea breaks. This makes for a lot of activity at Gulnara's!

Jen said the smell of baking bread has been heavenly to wake up to, but a mouse is not! Jen has such wonderful new living quarters, but the baked items have been drawing in other creatures. As she was watching TV one night, one ran across the room. I tried to make light of the situation and asked her if she was going to name him, like she did with the big spider she called Bert. She quickly said, "NO, I'm not naming him, because I don't want him to stay!" She told Semetei, "Get him." He just smiled.

There are two nice white walls in the cafeteria and Kathryn has decided to do a mural. She is very talented in art and talked about wanting to leave a legacy behind. She will have the time to work on it, with Nate (Tacie's husband) taking over the teaching for her, but now has to figure out how to get the funds for the paint.

I asked Jen what else was going on and Jen said, "Not much," and then piped up with "Hey, I've had the experience of riding in a Kyrgyz ambulance." As a resident advisor in college, Jen had ridden in ambulances a few times, but somehow I knew this must have been different.

She explained that it had been Independence Day there, and so they took the new recruits to a hippodrome in Talas to see a horse show. Lucky for us (and for Jen), God was looking out for her, because the bleacher row in which she was sitting collapsed. Melinda, a one-year volunteer from Talas, fell fifteen feet to the ground. Others, including Jen, grabbed the side and stayed up. Jen said that she looked down and saw Melinda lying there and thought she was dead. Jen took out her cell phone and called Peace Corps headquarters and their doctor. Upon hearing what had happened, the doctor drove four hours from Bishkek to be there. In the meantime, an ambulance came to take care of Melinda, and Jen offered to go with her to the hospital. Melinda is married to another American volunteer, but their Kyrgyz and Russian aren't the best, so Jen asked if they needed someone to help with translation. They agreed and Jen jumped in.

The ride truly was an experience. First of all, the driver was a madman. They hit every bump and valley in the road in a vehicle that didn't have shocks. Jen yelled in Russian, "Slow down, slow down! She's not dying and we don't want her to before we get to the hospital." Melinda kept asking what had happened and was saying that her arm hurt. Jen tried to explain about the fall, but Melinda just looked at her and kept saying, "What happened? My arm is killing me."

About the fifth or sixth time they had this conversation, the medical man started preparing a shot. Jen remembered that they were told to never allow or accept a shot of local medicine. The only exception was if it were to be administered by a Peace Corps doctor. Jen started screaming in Russian that Melinda would not take the shot and then she stuck out her hand to block his needle. After it was all said and done, she realized that she could have gotten the shot in her hand (and who knows what it was), but at the time, she didn't think of that. She did think about how it would look in the Kyrgyz newspaper: Peace Corps volunteer killed at a local horse show! She had already risked generating enough publicity, being the Peace Corps volunteer who was vandalized in a small village!

Finally, a nurse took Melinda back to Bishkek to be treated, where they evaluated her with an injured arm and a concussion. People kept telling Jen that she was lucky. Melinda was lucky. She was very lucky. Jen wanted to scream, "Don't you see? It is not luck! This is an example of how God was taking care of us!" She ended up asking Erich if he would talk to her about it, because it was so frustrating to her to see the lack of faith in the face of such a scary situation.

I think Jen is ready to come home to her community of religious support. She asks for prayers for the ribbon-cutting ceremony to be on time. Gulnara told her that she will do whatever it takes to get it ready, and then will sleep for a week. Jen agreed, but has been busy preparing the speech she has to give at both of the grand opening ceremonies. She has Semetei helping to make sure her Russian is correct. As she practiced with him, he began to giggle. That's when she realized there were a few things they needed to work on, plus she needed to put some picture boards together. But she knows the longest speech will be for her History Sources. Then she will do a speech for the cafeteria. She said she is trying to impress how important it is for the kids to have good nutrition in order to be able to learn better. She's not sure how well this will be accepted.

I told her, "Why don't you share with them about the time you participated in an event of being homeless and slept in a cardboard box, in the cold, in the college courtyard, and also decided to fast. After being hungry, cold, and without good sleep, you had a hard time looking at your watch and making sense of what time it was. Remember how you realized that homeless people are not lazy or stupid? They are just deprived of what is necessary to function."

I waited for her to thank me for this angle for her talk, but instead she said, "Mom, they would think I was crazy to suggest that someone from 'rich' America would purposely go without food!" I guess I could understand that, but yet my so-called rich daughter went hungry so many times when she didn't have to. Instead, I told her I would light a candle and knew her speech would be wonderful.

Jen told Ian that the ribbon-cutting ceremony will be like all the important moments in her life... in America... all put together. It will be like her dance recital, high school graduation, and college honors all in one day. Unfortunately, her replacement will be in Bishkek for some training; she wished she could be there. But Jen is thankful that Tacie is going to take over the GenGirls, and more importantly, that the Gen-Girls are just as excited. I told her that they want the girl empowerment to continue as much as she does.

I could hear how proud she feels about all that she's accomplished. Knowing that makes her being away from us for two years and three months all worthwhile. Only sixty-nine more days! But who's counting?

Love,

Karen

September 17, 2006

My two main projects for the duration of my service, the business/training center funded by Partnership Project and a new school cafeteria funded by a SPA grant, are finally complete. It was a stressful few days leading up to the opening ceremony. The trim on the floor was not finished, and neither was the electrical in the center. The tables for the training room didn't arrive until the day before, and I wasn't able to move my office until the evening before the ceremony. In true Kyrgyz fashion, nothing was ready until the last minute, and again true to Kyrgyz fashion, everything was miraculously pulled together eventually.

The morning of the ceremony, I wanted to help make salads for the cafeteria ceremony, or help paint the exterior of the building once more to cover the bricks, but no one would let me help. Part of Kyrgyz culture is being very particular about how chores are done. I think everyone thought it would be easier if I just sat on the sidelines, although I tried my hardest to find something to do by following the women at work around like a forlorn puppy dog. Since they wouldn't let me help, I took the opportunity to corner people doing chores and forced them to listen to my speeches. It was good practice and helped me get the intonation and pronunciation in Russian spot on.

The speech for the center was the more important of the two for me personally. I will write it out so you can see why:

Hello, dear guests. Thank you for coming to our ceremony.
My name is Jennifer Lawrence, I am a Peace Corps volunteer

and a worker at History Sources fund. This day is very important for everyone. For Manas county and History Sources. But it is also a very important day for my family and friends in America, because they sponsored this project. Without these people, this project would not have been possible. If these people were here, they would wish you all the best for this project. In two months, my contract to live in the Kyrgyz Republic finishes. I hope that this center will last until my next visit. Thank you for listening.

It sounds a little choppy in English, but it flowed really well in Russian, and I translated for the volunteers after every sentence, since the other six volunteers in attendance were all Kyrgyz speakers. My director's son helped me translate from English to Russian so it would be smooth and understandable, unlike my broken Russian.

The country director, as well as his assistant and my program manager, came from Bishkek to attend the ceremonies, as did a handful of volunteers from the oblast. The mayor, local government officials, other NGO workers, and business people were all in attendance. After a number of speeches from my director, the country director, the mayor, business people, and me, the red ribbon was cut and everyone checked out the center. Then a quick fashion show displayed the best work of the women in the sewing center before we all walked to the public school. The walkway to the school was lined with students in grades one through three, waving ribbons, clapping, and singing. In the cafeteria, tables were set with fruit, salads, cookies, and drinks. Kyrgyz people love toasting, so once again there was toasting and speeches.

Erich and I spoke on behalf of the volunteers. I commented on how I agreed to write the grant application because nutrition is important for development and education. Erich commented on how wonderful the school and cafeteria are. Finally, the sheep's head was presented to the country director. He carved up the head and distributed pieces to other honored guests. I asked him in advance to give me the eyeball, which he did and I ate. People gave my director money as they toasted her and my hard work, which is a tradition when opening a new facility. They had done the same when they renovated the local library.

After the ceremony and the meal wrapped up, all the volunteers went to Talas to have dinner with the country director. It was a great day and the ceremonies went extremely well! I have to admit that I slept like a rock that night. My director joked that we wouldn't go back to work until the following Monday. But as usual, we were back in the office a day after the ceremonies. No rest for the wicked.

Peace,

Jenny

September 23, 2006

It has been cold and rainy in Jen's village and even though it's in the fifties, they've already had frost. We were hoping she would have a warmer fall, but at least she doesn't have to endure another harsh Kyrgyz winter. The rodents must feel the same way. Now she has two mice who want to live with her. She may try again to get some poison soon, since there is no such thing as a mousetrap in the country.

Jen has lost ten pounds from her recent bout of bacterial diarrhea. She had lost weight from the camp and then gained a bit back, but I'm not as worried as usual about her weight since she will be home soon and Thanksgiving dinner will be waiting for her. Just thinking of this brought back memories of how she gained twelve pounds while home last Christmas. Speaking of food, how does Jen think she will gain weight over there when she eats a sheep's eyeball? Yes, you heard me right. More details to follow.

We called Jen from Grandma and Grandpa's house and she was on the speakerphone. She told us how the grand opening had turned out and she recited her speech at the ceremony in Russian from memory. It was so cool to listen to her and I could just picture her in front of the crowd. I can't wait to see pictures from the celebration. Right before the ceremony, she ran into Melinda, the volunteer who fell off the bleachers, and was touched that she traveled all the way from Talas to be at the ceremony. Jen was concerned it would be hard for her and asked how she was feeling. Melinda just stared back at her and said, "Va-va-va-vooooom! I've never seen you so dressed up. You go, girl!"

Jen realized that she must have looked pretty different, since she usually doesn't wear makeup, straighten her hair, or wear fancy clothes. I think she is beautiful without all that, but sometimes a girl gets to go the extra mile. She deserved feeling special at the opening ceremonies. And that is where the sheep's eye comes in. The Peace Corps country director was there, and since he is like a celebrity, he was given the honor of being presented the sheep's head. To me, that would be like punishing the guest of honor, but oh well. Even though Jen did all the hard work and was the main speaker, she wouldn't be seen as the guest of honor. There was a man present, after all. After two-plus years, Jen still gets upset with that mentality, so she decided to make it work for her. She told the director that she would like to eat the eyeball. Other volunteers had done it and she wanted to do the same. With all she had accomplished, he had no problem fulfilling her request.

The sheep's head arrived. Its lower jaw had been cut off prior to cooking, so as to be able to get at the meat better and to get at the eye socket more easily. When Jen saw the sheep's head, she panicked and started to wonder, how does one go about eating an eyeball? With eyeball in hand, she raced around, asking. Sure enough, she found out there is a right and wrong way to do it. You don't just pop it up in the air and catch it in your mouth like a grape. You have to cut through and remove the mushy iris and eat the firmer inside part. I still can't believe she did this without any spices or lots of alcohol. And she wasn't on *Fear Factor* to win a prize! As Melinda said, "You go, girl!"

Here is an excerpt from an email Jennifer sent regarding the monumental honor of eating a sheep's eyeball:

Below are the most commonly asked questions when a person eats a sheep's eye.

(1) Why was there a sheep's eye to eat in the first place? Most people know that *besh bar mak* is the traditional Kyrgyz dish that is basically boiled sheep's meat served over cooked noodles. This is the dish you serve in order to show your guests you honor and respect them, because the more money you spend (meat is expen-

sive) the more you respect your guests. The head is also boiled, whole, and served to the oldest or most honored guest. At the ribbon-cutting ceremony, the Peace Corps country director, who I had invited out for the opening ceremonies, was the most honored guest. The person who is served the head is in charge of cutting up parts and distributing them to other guests.

(2) What does eating the eye symbolize in Kyrgyz culture? Every part of the head symbolizes something, and the eye is no different. The eye is given to the guest you want to be friends with, or whom you'd like to "see again." The head is given to special guests, or old people to whom you want to show respect. The fore-leg is given for services rendered. This part of the sheep is usually given to the daughter-in-law (kellin, or household slave), since she does most of the housework. The ear is given to young boys so they will listen to their mothers. The roof of the mouth is given to brides or young women so that they will be good at embroidery (the ridges of the mouth are said to resemble embroidery). The brain and tongue are also eaten, but I do not know the symbolism of these two parts.

(3) Was it your choice to eat the eye? Yes, as strange as it sounds, I wanted to eat the eye. Lately I have been brave in trying traditional food and drink, such as fermented mare's milk (kumis) and a corn drink (jarma). They haven't turned out to be all that bad, but perhaps that's just because I no longer have standards for what's gross and what's not. I want to experience these things before I leave, and the sheep's eye was one thing I had not experienced that I really wanted to. It seemed like good timing, the day in which I was most honored for my work in the community, to share in something that is seen as an honor: partaking of eating the sheep's head.

(4) What technique did you use when consuming the eye? Since the eye is boiled, the iris, or center, becomes dark mush. You open the white membrane, scoop out the iris, and then enjoy! The best technique, as told to me by another volunteer, is to chew it three times and then swallow it whole. I also took a gulp of aerated

water to help it slide down. I gagged a few times only because it was a lot to get down at once, in one swallow.

(5) What did the eye taste like? It really didn't taste like anything at all. Some would assume that it tastes as vile as some of the cuts of meat that you get here, but it had no flavor. When they served the *besh bar mak* after I ate the eyeball, the smell of the meat made me want to throw up. However, the eye did not. It was hard to get down due to the size and texture, but not the smell or taste.

(6) Does the eye actually look like an eye? No, the eye is not a perfectly preserved eye staring up at you from the palm of your hand. It's a white ball with fat and other tissue around it. The iris is cooked and basically a puddle of mush in the middle, which you don't see until you open up the white part. You probably wouldn't even know it was an eye if you didn't ask.

(7) Do you regret eating a sheep's eye? No, it was a test of the strength of my will, not the strength of my stomach. I told one of my site mates that I was going to do it and I did. I wanted to make good on my word. Sounds silly, but I can now leave Kyrgyzstan not feeling like I've missed out on anything.

(8) How did Kyrgyz people react when they heard you ate the eye? When some of my GenGirls heard that I ate the eye, they were impressed, because I didn't vomit, and because they themselves have never eaten the eye. As I explained before, the most honored or oldest guest usually does the honors, and usually that's a man, if not a really old woman. The GenGirls are too young to be honored in such a way, although one girl had gotten the ear once. It seemed so silly to be in a group of girls and to be the only one who had eaten an eye. I am a foreigner and don't fully appreciate the culinary value of the eye and basically had to choke it down. Meanwhile, there are girls who, because of their age and gender, are envious of something that I did with a cringe on my face.

(9) How did people back home react? Disbelief that I would want to eat an eye. Also, people really can't understand how being offered the eye truly is an honor and why I would willingly eat something that we consider to be inedible and disgusting. I really don't know how to explain my decision to people back home, but

volunteers seem to get it to a certain degree, even if they wouldn't do the same thing themselves.

Peace,

Jenny

September 23, 2006

Jen will be going to an Internet café on Sunday because new and old volunteers are meeting in the Talas area to have lunch together. The soon-to-depart volunteers will bring anything they have in excess and want to give away to the newbies. It helps both parties. Jen has always believed in "living simply so others can simply live." Then she will be traveling to Bishkek on Tuesday to take care of final paperwork on the construction project. I told her she will be living high on the hog, having access to the Internet all the time.

The next task is planning their going-away party. The local tradition of having to do your own party is similar to the local tradition of having to bring food for everyone else on your birthday. Ian, Kathryn, and Jen are going to each invite twenty people, so there will be about sixty and the party will be by invitation only. They want to eliminate the fiasco that would certainly result if the whole village showed up and they didn't have enough food. There would be much shame. The whole village will have a chance for their good-byes as well, but they want this party for themselves and their closest people. Ian will take care of getting and preparing the sheep, Kathryn is doing the cakes (her host mom is a pro), Jen will do salads, and they will buy the rest. It will be in October sometime.

As much as she's counting the days, Jen will find leaving Kyrgyzstan difficult. It's been an adventure she will never regret or forget and no one can take that away from her.

Priceless.

Love,

Karen

CHAPTER 28

The Changing of the Guard

Tacie told Jennifer, "I feel bad because I get to walk into something that has already succeeded from so much hard work and where so many goals have already been accomplished. When you started, the center didn't even have a desk for you to sit at. There was no phone, no computer, no fax, or copy machine. It doesn't seem right to have such an established program handed over to me."

September 23, 2006

Ten new volunteers will be coming to Talas Oblast, and three Californians will be taking over Pokrovka for the next two years. That's right; after spending two years fighting the notion that everyone lives near Hollywood and knows Arnold Schwarzenegger, we will be replaced by three volunteers from California. A Russian speaking couple, Tacie and Nate, will replace Kathryn and me. They have been married for a year and seem really enthusiastic, but at the same time have a very realistic outlook about what the next two years will involve. Amanda, a Kyrgyz-speaking volunteer, will replace Ian at the lyceum. Amanda has teaching experience and seems eager to learn the Kyrgyz language. I feel extremely blessed to be replaced by Tacie. She already seems to be a hardworking, dedicated volunteer who is interested in integrating into the community and making a lasting impact on people's lives. Plus, she and Nate are just a lot of fun to be around. The next month should be a good mix of transferring knowledge and skills, as well as having fun during my last weeks in the village.

While the new volunteers were here, we celebrated the fifteenth anniversary of Kyrgyzstan's independence, as well as First Bell, or the first day of the new school year, which is a holiday. On Independence Day, we all met in Talas and decided to go out to the Hippodrome to watch some traditional horse games and have a picnic. One of the traditional games is played much like soccer, only the teams are on horses and they try to get a headless and hooveless sheep carcass into a pit at either end of the field. We joked that it was American day at the Hippodrome, since there was a group of thirteen of us there. That is rare.

Peace,

Jenny

October 8, 2006

We have been collecting a few calls from Jen to finally send out a letter. I asked Jen if she was going to bring her cell phone home and she said no. At first I worried about her traveling home without it, but then realized that she will be going to places where there are friends and family... and modern technology that she didn't have before. She said that she would like to give or sell the phone to someone, just as it came to her. It has been a godsend.

Erich took on the challenge to run from village to village before his time of service was over. He was a runner in high school and college, so he knew very well how to train for the fifteen miles from Kirovka to Pokrovka. That would be like half of a marathon. Jen was so enthusiastic about the whole thing and reminded him that he would be running through a mountain pass, which not many other marathoners have encountered. The three Pokrovkans followed Erich in a car with cameras, water, and a medical kit. Besides some pesky dogs chasing him for about a kilometer, Erich had a smooth, but at times grueling, run. The official time was just under two hours from the taxi stand at the edge of Kirovka to the taxi stand at the center of Pokrovka.

He was greeted with flowers and a big spaghetti meal, as volunteers from Talas as well as the new volunteers from Pokrovka came out to congratulate Erich on his successful run. He said it gave him something to aspire to, but that he would never do it again. In the next breath, though, he said that he wants to make the run a tradition, continuing throughout all the next generation of volunteers. I can just picture the despair from the non-joggers that get assigned to Kirovka.

The threesome decided to celebrate their second-year anniversary in the country by making a cake. They used two Jiffy cake mixes and some chocolate frosting that they bought as a luxury in Bishkek. The final touch was coconut shavings on top. They toasted their time in Kyrgyzstan and as they ate, they thought they had died and gone to heaven.

Tacie comes to work with Jen every day and they have a system. One half of the day, they each do their own things. For Tacie, that means studying Russian. The other half of the day, they work together. For Jen, it is exhausting. She said her brain is so tired at the end of the day from showing Tacie the ropes and teaching Russian at the same time. Headquarters had the right idea to get Tacie and Nate there early, even though the volunteers didn't think they wanted to have such an overlap of time together. Even now Jen is scrambling to get it all in.

One day, she had to stop and calm herself and say, "This is a marathon, not a sprint." I wanted to tell her how familiar that sounds. I seem to remember her using those same words to me when I was constantly offering her all kinds of food in her first forty-eight hours home at Christmas. But I bit my tongue and was just grateful that Jen has a wonderful replacement and she can greatly help Tacie with the two years that lie ahead.

Tacie told Jennifer, "I feel bad because I get to walk into something that has already succeeded from so much hard work and where so many goals have already been accomplished. When you started, the center didn't even have a desk for you to sit at. There was no phone, no computer, no fax, or copy machine. It doesn't seem right to have such an established program handed over to me." Jen is modest, but I agreed!

More importantly, I am just so thankful that everything has come together in time for Jen to be able to finalize and celebrate her success. After all the hardships she has been through, she deserves this reward. But Jen quickly defended Tacie to say that she will have to be in charge of organizing the new facility and arranging sewing conferences and gatherings. I bit my tongue again and wanted to say, "But that's the fun part."

They are planning their going-away party for October 27th and 28th, not to interfere with the Halloween concourse the school has. But their biggest highlight to date has been their COS (close of service) conference that was held in Issyk Kul resort. Jen said one of the challenges was the twelve-hour *marshutka* ride, during which she didn't have water. But the beautiful scenery and sunsets made up for that.

I asked if they discussed the transition of going from volunteering abroad to civilian life and she said yes. They will also have more out-processing for days before they leave. She recalled how they talked about how volunteers can be nervous when reconnecting with family and friends. She said she wanted to scream, "What do you mean?" They said it is possible, that once you get beyond the conversation about your service, you might be at odds for a lack of words. Jen said she wanted to blurt out, "Are you kidding?"

But those are issues that Jen may or may not experience. She said it was really hard saying good-bye to other volunteers and staff, and we honored that.

Her biggest trouble at the COS was with her dental visit! She found out she has four cavities! This from the person with the best teeth in our family. She had one cavity when she was eleven and then the Peace Corps medical team made her get a small one fixed before she left. Four cavities? I THINK I KNOW WHY! It could be from the poor nutrition: the lack of calcium and the presence of so many starchy breads. But Jen is blaming it on drinking Coke whenever she could get her hands on it and not brushing her teeth afterwards.

Whatever the case, she has to get them filled before she leaves. They are small and on the surface, but can only be done one at a time. Go figure. Kathryn had a few, too, and told Jen to just look at it as a free trip to Bishkek and the Internet café. She goes on Sunday, Monday, and Tuesday and then the fourth filling will be done during her out-processing November 4th. They also are going to fit her for a mouth guard because of her TMJ. It's nice to have all that taken care of, but unfortunately she doesn't have much time left.

Another adventure has been the mouse in her house! She noticed that it had nibbled at the poison she bought, but then saw it running around again. She called on Semetai to help. He just laughs at her. Nobody else has seen this mouse but Jen, so Gulnara calls it the "imaginary" mouse. They put the cat in her room all day to help the situation, but the mouse was still there, so Semetai thought it was getting in through a vent. They duct-taped it shut.

Then Jen heard, "Squeak, squeak, squeak." She thought, "Crap... I trapped him into my room!" She doesn't know the Russian word for "squeak," so she tried to explain it to Gulnara and Semetei by making an "eek, eek, eek" noise every time she got to that part in the sentence. Again, Gulnara and Semetei laughed. When Jen was trying to tell Ian and Kathryn about it, she started making the sound again and then said, "Oh, for crying out loud; I know the English word for 'squeak'!" She said, "I'm sorry. I just wanted to tell you that I saw him go into a crack in the wall, so we taped over it." We will see how that goes.

Another bit of Kyrgyz animal trouble involved their dog. It had puppies. Jen doesn't know how, because it looks like it suffers from anorexia. When food is scarce, animals are the last to get food—not like the fancy dogs in America. The dog gave birth under a tree by the well. It would growl a terribly scary growl when anyone came by, so the family was unable to get water for a day. That meant no *banya*, clean up, or extra drinking water.

The trip to take the new volunteers to Taraz involved a small group. It was only Jen, Kathryn, and Will. Ian's dad is a part of the Rotary and got computers donated and Ian was going to pick them up. Nate was ill with stomach problems, so Tacie stayed with him. And Valerie (the one who is replacing Ian) was having health issues. She has proven to be the "token" weirdo of the new group of volunteers that just arrived. She comes on so strong to be liked and they have caught her in so many lies. She has terrible Kyrgyz-speaking skills (how can she teach?) because she was always missing language lessons with lots of excuses.

This week, they said she had a blood clot in her leg and was restrict-ed to bed in Bishkek. She called and asked Ian to bring a bag and some reading material. He asked Tacie to go with him to her host family's house, not wanting to go through a girl's stuff, but then got another call telling him that plans have changed—the Peace Corps is sending her home! Pack everything. Jen hated to admit it, but she was so thankful her replacement worked out to be Tacie and not Valerie. Headquarters must have sensed a problem as well, because they are sending her home. The blood clot would heal itself over time with bed rest and they couldn't justify her laying around instead of serving. And if it got worse she would be close to medical treatment. . If she wants to come back, she needs to apply all over again.

This leaves Ian's school without the volunteer they thought they had. But they weren't very cooperative in the past and it was sketchy if they would get another volunteer at all. Jen says she feels sorrier for the family that was hosting her. They had gone through training and preparations to, not to mention there's the extra income they would have gotten from hosting her.

When we called Jen this Sunday, she sounded sleepy. I asked if she was awake. She said, "I'm awake... in spirit. Not in body." She has had busy weeks and now all her paperwork has been faxed to headquarters and final. But it's still busy... a good busy.

Her latest excitement was the birthday package she got from Uncle Paul and Aunt Patty. She said it was awesome! It took so long to arrive, but was in perfect condition. Lately, so many volunteer packages have been opened. Strange things have been taken, like a container of cocoa, and one pod from a canister of Crystal Light.

Nate and Tacie also got packages, and so they decided to have a "chip and dip" night. They are going to combine any chips they got in the packages. Since Kathryn was going to Talas to fill out some paperwork, it became her critical job to get sour cream. The result will be a true trea-sure: they'll take vegetarian bouillon cubes, crush them up, and mix with the sour cream to create a dip! She can hardly wait.

Jen always wants to know what's going on back home, so we told her about the Twins being in the playoffs. We didn't tell her the results. We told her about going to the Crohn's and Colitis walk at the Mall of America in support of Grandpa, our nephew, and his aunt. She told us to let Ryan know that she walks about five miles a day and so she will donate her Friday schedule to the cause.

We've learned how hard it must be to be away when important things are happening back home, but she is very creative in finding a way to still be connected. In five more weeks, she won't have to!

Love,

Karen

October 22, 2006

We talked to Jen while she was in Bishkek having her teeth taken care of. In the morning, she showered in a real shower—ahhhh—and was rushing to get to the dentist. She worried that they would be upset with her because her hair might still be wet, and the evil eye would get her and make her ill. Then she thought, "What the heck? What am I thinking? I'm in a more cultured area, so I shouldn't have to worry about that stuff." But she did have a slight cold and hoped it wouldn't turn into a sinus infection again. Nothing is going to stop her from getting on that plane on November 7th.

We got interrupted by her saying, "Hello... oh... oh... okay." I told her I was waiting to hear some Russian and she said, "No, just boring English. Ian is here." Since school is on vacation, he is looking to get some headphones and speakers for the new computers that were donated. Actually, he came along for moral support, since Jen found out she would have Novocain, because two fillings were next to each other. Jen was nervous about it, but Ian was more concerned that she would come out of there with four gold teeth, like all the other Kyrgyz women have. Jen reassured him that her fillings would be white, even though her dentist is a Kyrgyz doctor used by the Peace Corps. They also approved her getting a mouth guard once she gets back home, so I need to make her a dentist appointment soon.

She has decided to leave most of her kitchen things behind because she wants the married couple to have it better than she did. They already asked her what that "R2D2 thing" was, and when Jen explained that it was a washing machine capsule, they said, "WE HAVE DIBS!" Since it wouldn't be easy bringing it home, nor will she need it once back in America, Jen got Aunt Sue's permission to give it away. So Jen told them, "ENJOY!"

Since her dental work was taken care of more quickly than expected, she wouldn't need to arrive in Bishkek until the 5th instead of the 4th. My heart thinks about the person or situation in Pokrovka that might need that extra day with her. She will have access to the Internet then and see about selling her phone. Semetei said he wants to buy it, but Jen asked him where he would get the 800 som. I'm sure her mind flashed to the landlord's boy who suddenly showed up with an expensive sausage to eat. He said, "I will have it." I guess we will see what Gulnara thinks about this.

The mural at Kathryn's school is finished. It only took five days! Jen helped with a lot of the background painting. Kathryn planned to use some of her own money to get the paint, but got to Talas only to find that the Western Union was not open (it was a Saturday). But then Jen remembered that three former volunteers from Talas had wanted to send funds for a summer camp but hadn't gotten the money in on time. So she contacted them and took them up on their offer in order to buy paint, brushes, buckets, and other supplies needed for the mural. It finally worked out and Jen said it was wonderful!

Since a pillar dissects the wall on which she wanted to paint the mural, Kathryn decided to do two separate murals; however, they would be linked together. The left picture is Kyrgyz scenery with mountains, animals, and a yurt. They are joined together by a night sky and day sky. There is a bird on the Kyrgyz side that turns into a dove on the other side and a star, which is the Peace Corps symbol. It joins the east and the west. How absolutely beautiful! It got lots of praise from teachers, government officials, and students alike. I can't wait for the pictures.

They had their Halloween concourse and Jen found out that bobbing for apples is hard! But a bigger problem was getting all the kids there for the celebration. Ian had arranged for a bus to go to a few villages—Pokrovka, Bakai Ata, etc.—to pick up kids. He would be charged 1,700 som. Then the day before, the driver said it would be 2,000 som. Maybe he heard it was Ian's last concourse, so he decided to overcharge the rich American. As the story goes, the driver refused to pick up just eight people at the first stop, saying it wasn't enough to drive to Talas. They tried to explain that there would be more, but it ended up that Ian had to get another driver. That didn't work out either, so he had to get four taxis to get twenty-eight kids to this concourse and it ended up costing them 4,000 som! Jen gave some of her money, and Ian and Kathryn did, too. They arrived late, but didn't want the kids to miss out on the festivities. They also paid for the taxi drivers to stay the day. Jen held onto their paperwork so the driver wouldn't leave without the students on board.

Apparently, one of the drivers was bored, so during the day he took apart his engine and then put it back together, only to find out... it wouldn't run. The three other taxis took the kids back, but Jen didn't want to leave Tacie and Nate with this dilemma, since they don't speak the language well enough. Jen, Ian, and Kathryn ended up pushing the taxi onto the main road so they could get towed by another taxi. They tied a rope around the taxi to get towed, and as they were finally moving down the road, a cop pulled them over. After much discussion, they continued. Then the rope broke. They tied it again. They drove on and the rope broke again. But they retied it and got there. Puts a whole new meaning to AAA.

After all this, I hated to even ask. "What did you dress up as?" But I'm glad I did. She said that the three of them went as an American flag! Ian was the pole. He dressed in grey and they cut out a section of a basketball so that he could wear it like a hat and covered it with duct-tape. His head was the top of the pole. Jen had a blue shirt and red pants. She had stars taped on her top and white stripes on her legs. Kathryn was all red and white stripes. She said, "We pretty much had to walk together to make it work, but the fun part was when we figured out a way to make it look like the flag was waving in the breeze." Don't want to know, but can't wait for the pictures. Tacie dressed up as a Jennifer. She had a sign on that said, "I am a K-12. I am leaving. I don't care." She had some of Jen's things and folders from work, too. It was humorous.

Ian had a teacher conference and got some surprising news. Since Valerie was sent home, the director announced that she thinks Ian should stay until next May. She implied that if he really cares about the school system, he will do this. She said, "Our school system is bad and our teachers aren't good." Ian pretended to be touched, but saw it as a pushy administrator wanting to get her way. He just said, "You'd have to convince my parents that I shouldn't come home." People shouted out, "Then talk to your parents."

Ian showed up at Jen's nearly in tears and said he needed a hug. He explained all that went on and said, "I just wanted to serve and leave quietly. One person alone can't change a corrupt education system." Jen said that she wanted to march back to that meeting and say, "Is your poor educational system Ian's fault? Why don't you try harder to do something about it? If all you people really love him, you will let him go home." It just gave me another reason to give thanks for all Jen has done, the wonderful replacement she has in Tacie, and the valuable time she has had with her before she leaves her behind.

Dan asked if the ladies in the sewing center like Tacie or if they are having problems accepting her. Jen thought about it for a while and said that she noticed that when Tacie goes out, they ask, "Where is she?" and "Where did she go?" Jen thinks that this is a good sign. They care about what she does. Also, she sweeps. Jen said that she never did that, but when Tacie gets bored of studying or helping, she sweeps the sewing rooms. The ladies like that. And she survived her first lunch with them. It just brings me back to the experiences Jen had when she first started, with her minimal language skills and without any help or insight as to what she should or should not do. Tacie is in good hands and we know Jen wouldn't have it any other way.

We wanted to make sure that Jen realized that we only have one more Sunday call; then our phone bill will dance the JIG! It truly is the final countdown, and Jen doesn't know it, but Sara and I created a paper loop chain with the days left. We even included fancier loops for when she reaches France and when she reaches New York. We have it hanging in the living room. It is the colors of the Kyrgyz flag, symbolizing her leaving there, little by little.

I asked Jen about Ian's and Kathryn's plans once they get home. Kathryn said she is just going to focus on taking care of her mom, who is having hip surgery. And Ian plans on eating burritos on his parent's couch for a month. Wouldn't mind if Jen did the couch thing, but somehow I think she will be more anxious to get back into her old world.

Pray for Jen's safe travel home.

Love,

Karen

CHAPTER 29

A Last Time for Everything

As she sheds tears of sadness, we will shed tears of joy. Kyrgyzstan's loss is our gain. On September 15, 2004, I didn't think I could survive until November 19, 2006. In some ways, it seems just like yesterday that we were saying good-bye at the airport. But yet, it seems like a lifetime ago. Her Kyrgyzstan lifetime.

October 27, 2006

My final email from Kyrgyzstan. It seems unreal and a relief at the same time. It's time to come home. But it has already proven very difficult to say good-bye to loved ones here.

Nate hit the ground running by taking over all of Kathryn's lessons from the start. Overall, the kids have really responded well to him, as my coworkers and the GenGirls have with Tacie. It's good to know that Pokrovka is in good hands for the next two years with volunteers who are hardworking and genuinely care about the well being of projects and programs that we have worked two years to implement.

I enjoyed our COS (close of service) conference at the end of September. Out of the sixty-five volunteers who started in our group, thirty-six were left. It was a good feeling to be in the group of "survivors," as one volunteer put it. A lot of time was spent catching up as well as saying good-bye. Good information was shared between volunteers and staff as we prepare to transition back into the developed world. What I appreciated the most was just knowing what hoops we would have to jump through before leaving. I had to make sure that both of my grants had been closed out and that there were no problems with the budgets.

Long ago, the three of us decided to throw one big going-away party together. Since we know each other's families and coworkers and have many of the same friends, it seemed only natural that we would all celebrate together. On Saturday, October 28th, about forty of our friends, families, and coworkers gathered to send us off. We had local music and a slideshow of pictures from the past two years when the first guests arrived. With Rosa, my counterpart, as our master of ceremonies, the toasts and gift-giving were constant as people nibbled salad, bread, *borsok*, and cake. There was dancing, *besh bar mak, dancing*, picture-taking, and more dancing before the night was done. Of the gifts I got, most were knickknacks I will have to leave behind. But the best was a head scarf to wear at my wedding and a beautiful *kalpak* for my husband. My office made two *tushuks*, or cushions, for the bride and groom to sit on. Kathryn's mom gave me two hand-sewn pillow covers with Kyrgyz designs. These were true gifts from the heart that already have spots in my suitcase.

The serious good-byes began the morning Kathryn left the village, a few days before me. It struck me that Kathryn's leaving was the beginning of the end of this amazingly hard and amazingly good journey that Kathryn, Ian, and I had been on for the past two years. After Kathryn drove away, Ian and I had tea and breakfast with her mom. Kathryn's mom told us, "It is okay; you'll see her again. But we will be far away from her." Kathryn's mom was talking as if Kathryn were dead, but in reality, it was as if she died to them. God only knows if their paths will meet again in the future.

The good-byes continued that afternoon when the GenGirls threw a going-away party/concert/disco for me. There were a lot of tears, a lot of food, and a lot of dancing. It was bittersweet to say good-bye, because I know the girls will be in Tacie's capable hands. I took our last meeting as an opportunity to come full circle. During the first meeting of GenGirls, I had them divide pieces of paper in half and write one list of things they could do, like be mothers, sing, speak English, etc. And on the other half they wrote the things they could not do. I then had them tear the paper in half and tear up the list of things they couldn't do and told them to only focus on what they could do. We did the same activity one last time and I explained to the girls that this was the most important lesson I could leave them: that they should focus on the positive.

My final day at work was low-key, with a good-bye meal put together by Zareena, Mika, and Baktigul, my coworkers. My director seemed to be getting emotional as the end of the day neared and I prepared to leave. I surprisingly did not have a hard time leaving the office for the last time, which I think is due to the fact that I have Tacie to carry on the work that I started and make Pokrovka even better. Having a replacement as wonderful as Tacie really made leaving History Sources much easier than if I had left without one. I am so lucky to have someone who genuinely cares about the organization, the people, and the culture to take my place.

My final good-bye or "tearfest" ended at the Almaty airport in Kazakhstan, when I walked down the glassed in runway to my KLM flight to Amsterdam. My last view of Central Asia was of the Kazakh mountains at sunrise, a truly beautiful and memorable scene to cap off my two years of service. I can't imagine a better image to be burned into my memory.

I am constantly in the midst of good-byes and with each one comes a varying level of difficulty and a new realization about myself: what this person has meant to me and how they have personally added to my growth as an individual and to my experience as a volunteer. As a wise friend recently wrote, there is a "grieving in leaving." I guess I agree. If it weren't difficult to leave—if I didn't grieve a little—then what were the past two years all about?

Love,

Jenny

October 29, 2006

This is your last call! LAST CALL! Grab a beer quick! It's OUR last call!

Seriously, we may be sending along a few updates, but Sunday was our last scheduled call to Kyrgyzstan. When Jen answered, I started hollering in the background, "Last call... it's last call... bar's closing... last call." I started to laugh and then heard her I-can't-believe-you-just-did-that giggle. Then the oh-my-gosh giggle. And I could feel her big smile. I said, "Did you remember that this was our last call?" She answered, "Well, you only told me about fifty times." Okay; whatever. It was fun to joke about it, but also sad in an odd way. This was the last time we would be calling a third-world country. I will kind of miss that little Russian operator.

Jen was so excited when I told her that we went to the Peace Corps exhibit at the University of Minnesota and how great it was to see her picture on the wall. They chose the picture of Jen with Kadim, Madim, and Aisalkyn by the snowman they had built. When I told her, Jen screamed! She said that was her favorite. It's amazing that all this came from an open house that Heidi and I went to about six months after Jen left. The exhibit is free and open to the public. It will be there until December 15th. Jen can't wait to go see it. I told her I would take her picture... by her picture. Then came her I-can't-believe-you-just-said-that giggle.

I asked how the going-away party went. Her voice escalated about ten decibels and she said, "Excuse my language... but it KICKED ASS! It was amazing; it was amazing that we pulled it off." Swear word aside, all I felt was thankful that all of Jen's efforts were being rewarded. It turned out the way they wanted it. Even Ian's director, who is so persnickety, said, "It was a true Kyrgyz party." So in true Kyrgyz fashion, it had to be an adventure with many chains of events.

Kathryn's mother accompanied them to the bazaar in Taraz, where they bought everything necessary for three salads, cakes, *borsok* (traditional fried diamonds of dough), noodles for *besh bar mak*, napkins, drinks, etc. It was an exhausting trip, and she doesn't know how they would have managed without Kathryn's mom's food knowledge and bargaining skills. Ian was in charge of the sheep. He even helped butcher it. They had a cook lined up, but realized that they didn't have a *kazaan* (a wok-like pan to cook with). Finally they located the *kazaan*. So... they had the cook, they had the *kazaan*, but there was no meat. The sheep hadn't arrived yet. Then the cook decided to leave. Finally, the sheep arrived. So they had a kazaan, they had the sheep, but they had no cook. He had gone up to Jen and said, "I am leaving. I hope you are not offended." I can just see her frantically running around, not having much empathy for this guy. She snapped back, "I am offended... so good-bye." Not the best way to address a male. But the saga continues.

Jen talked to the ladies in the cafeteria and found someone who agreed to do the cooking, but they didn't have any wood to make the fire to cook the sheep. So... now they had a cook, they had a *kazaan*, they had the meat, but no wood. To add to that, the lady who was supposed to bring the plates didn't show. Jen was freaking out, but Ian seemed cool. He said, "You know, every time these people have a party, it always seems to work out," so he wasn't concerned. Must be a guy thing. Somehow, the wood was located and the fire was started and someone else got plates.

Jen said they had three tables full of food. It was unreal. There were about forty-five people there who ate and were very satisfied. Kathryn got to eat the eyeball, as she had hoped to do before they left. As it turned out, her host dad was the oldest in attendance, so he was presented the head. This worked perfect for him to be able to offer the eyeball to her. The sheep was huge and so she had to eat the eyeball in three pieces. Jen was so thankful that once she swallowed it, she was done and didn't have to do it the way Kathryn did by having to take bites out of it!

So many people gave them gifts. Venera and the kids were there and they gave her a *kalpak* for her future husband. They got mushroom salt and pepper shakers, which were interesting. Since most people live very modestly, re-gifting is common. Some of the strange trinkets they received are going to Tacie and Nate, and they can use them at the school or clubs as prizes. They will be selective as to who gets what, so there aren't any hurt feelings. Tacie and Nate had the three over for dinner and gave them each a gift of cash. They knew it would be the best thing to travel with, and would allow them to get souvenirs. They shared how they loved that their time overlapped and appreciated all their help. Jen joked that they were really scared because they didn't know what kind of characters they would have to overlap with! They all had a good laugh.

Jen said the GenGirl group last Wednesday had twenty or more girls in attendance. She was so happy because they talked about the terrible practice of bride kidnapping. They all filled out contracts, brought them home, and the parents signed them as well. They are agreeing as a family that they do not wish, nor will take part in, any bride kidnapping traditions. All of them returned their contracts. The times, they are a' changing. But Jen said that it probably wouldn't be until the next generation, when these girls are mothers with daughters, that there will be real change. I wonder if Jen truly realizes how she has been and will be a big part of that.

I started to tell Jen about a new movie called *Borat* that is about a Kazakhstan guy who comes to America. Ironically, we got cut off, and when I finally got back through to her, she said, "Hello... ah... ah... well, true to form, I am in the outhouse." We have joked about getting the best reception when I tag along with her during our phone calls in the early morning. Puts a whole new meaning to the phrase, "Come walk with me, come talk with me." So I start again to tell her about this silly movie and she squealed on the other end, telling me how she had read about it in her *Newsweek*. She said that the Kazakh government was appalled at the picture and how it depicted their country. Jen said, "Please! I'm sure it is dead-on right. They just don't want to admit it." She plans to go to the theater when she gets home to see it. I'm sure it will be more enjoyable and relatable to her than it will be for the other hundred people in the theater.

Jen will be leaving Pokrovka on the 5th and headed to Bishkek. Erich and Gulnara have business in Bishkek, so they are traveling with her, which is nice for two reasons. One, it will give Jen a bit more time with them, and two, it gives her extra protection. As I write this letter, there is a huge protest going on in Bishkek's square. Over 5,000 people from the opposing party are trying to get the current president ousted. He hasn't lived up to the promises he made a year and half ago to implement more democratic ways. So far, it is peaceful, but people are pitching tents and staying until they are heard. Hopefully this won't interfere with Jen being able to leave as planned. Someone told her that if the Peace Corps purchased the ticket, they could delay or change travel dates, but since she purchased it, they really can't hold her. And she is leaving the country, not just having program travel or vacation. These are the things I keep telling myself so it doesn't get scary. She's come this far... don't mess with us NOW!

On the 6th, she will be at the headquarters all day and go through the process of being signed off in all areas and checked out. She heads to Almaty the evening of the 6th and leaves on the 7th, headed to Jessy in Paris, France! Then to New York on the 13th, and then Chaska, Minnesota, on the 19th! Keep her safe travel in your prayers.

As Jen has been preparing to leave, she has been sorting through her things. She asked if we could mail her winter coat to Doug and Diana's in New York (our last package to her) because she is going to leave her ski jacket behind. She plans on giving it to Baktigul. She is the one with gold teeth who had asked if she could touch an American dollar bill. In her packing chores, Jen ran across our 2004 Christmas newsletter. At the time she had been gone about three months. She told me that she sat and reread it and couldn't believe how different things were then.

In the letter, I described her primitive living conditions. She thought back. It was hard. The food was weird, she was having such stomach problems, and she was dropping weight quickly. The only way to reach her was by the unreliable landline in her host family's home. Calling her required us learning some Russian and placing lots of trust and hope on the phone lines and electricity. If they were down, we couldn't talk. If she traveled, we couldn't call. Three months later, she was consolidated because of the revolution and we couldn't call. It's amazing how things changed so much over her time there, yet pretty much stayed the same.

Jen said that Nate and Tacie each have a cell phone and sometimes Tacie's mom calls just to say a quick hello. Jen told Tacie, "If your mom had to rely on a landline and couldn't get through for a week or so, she would go nuts! My mom did... many times." I think running across that letter showed her how far she has come, how strong she is now, and all that she has accomplished. Knowledge is power.

Before we said good-bye, I told her to make her last week a good one. It is the only last week she will ever have. I asked her if leaving Pokrovka is kind of bittersweet. She said, "That's a good word for it." As she sheds tears of sadness, we will shed tears of joy. Kyrgyzstan's loss is our gain.

On September 15, 2004, I didn't think I could survive until November 19, 2006. In some ways, it seems just like yesterday and we were saying good-bye at the airport. But yet, it seems like a lifetime ago. Her

Kyrgyzstan lifetime. Thank you to all our friends and family who have walked with us during this journey. And God bless America.

When Jen was eleven years old, we were at my parent's house for Christmas and we asked if anyone had a New Year's wish. She quickly answered, "World peace." It seemed kind of strange at the time, but I guess this passion and focus has been a long time coming.

I'm thankful that I was finally open to her serving in this way. I'm thankful that I was able to share her with the world and survive it. I'm thankful for all the people she has touched, both in Kyrgyzstan and in America. It's not just THAT she served, but HOW she served.

We continue to pray for world peace.

Love,

Karen

How... I Am Me, Because of You

KAREN: Because Jennifer was able to take such a huge leap of faith by leaving all she knew to serve our world, I have also become brave in trying new things. Writing this book is the biggest one.

I've learned to trust my instincts, like she did. If something keeps "nudging" you, it's okay to listen and follow your heart, even if it isn't popular or doesn't make any sense. I decided to nudge back and took a risk to become an author. Jennifer's story was the stepping-stone that I was waiting for, and one of those "God winks" that she talks about. My life was so full of what I "should" do. I finally got brave enough and re-placed it with what I "could" do.

By documenting her adventures, I realized that I'm able to accept and support things that I don't necessarily want or agree with. Jennifer's journey was a perfect, yet difficult example of how we all have to truly let go and rely on faith in God. The type of faith that believes and trusts in what cannot be seen. Although I was her mother, He would be the one taking care of her.

Before she left, we heard some song lyrics that touched both of us. It talked about having a heart filled with dreams and having the faith that gives you courage, to dare to do great things. Jen said she thought of me when it said something about how I would let my love, help her find her wings. As a mother, I would have tears as she took off, but I would cheer when she flew.

That became true and now I have a grandson with a Kyrgyz name— Bek, which means "strong." He is just like his mother.

JENNIFER: In the summer of 2013 my husband, Travis, was leading a youth group to experience World Youth Day in Rio de Janeiro, Brazil. Saying good-bye was extremely difficult because his travels took him so far away. But it would only be for ten days, so I needed to stay strong as a wife and mother.

I dropped off our son Bekett at day care the morning Travis left, and as I headed to work I heard the most unsettling news. A bomb threat was being resolved at one of the locations where my husband was scheduled to be. Travis was still in the air flying from Texas to Brazil and did not know about the security threat. I felt helpless knowing about the unrest in his destination even before he arrived there.

In that moment, I truly realized the depth of what my parents lived through for the two years I served in the Peace Corps. My thoughts immediately switched from Brazil to the feelings they must have dealt with when hearing bad news, more than once, before I was even aware. Now that I am a parent, I am in awe of their sacrifice and truly understand just how hard it must have been for them to trust and "let go."

Life would be easier if I could keep Bekett safe and loved, within arm's reach at all times. But my mom and dad taught me that true parenting is part educating and part empowering. I am me because of who they are. I want Bekett to be able to grow and develop as an individual, just as I was able to do by serving in the Peace Corps. He can't have those life experiences unless I am brave and eventually let go... just as my parents did. I hope to be as strong for Bekett as they were for me.

If I Knew Then
What I Know Now

KAREN: If I knew then what I know now, I would have treated Jennifer's decision to serve more seriously. I would have respected her choice and remembered that she knows what she wants and wants what she knows. She doesn't rush into things, and had made very smart decisions up until that point, so why did I question the opportunity for her to make a difference in the world?

Choosing the Peace Corps made sense, and it's a wonderful organization, but the mother part of me was very protective and leery of the idea. At times, I trivialized it and hoped she would change her mind. I judged that she wasn't capable, and believed that she had no idea of what she was getting into. I regret being so judgmental.

This was something I couldn't comprehend and I didn't feel in charge, which was very scary to me. There were no words of wisdom out there from people going through the same struggles. We were on our own. But that shouldn't have stopped me from reaching out to any agency or family support system that could have helped. That extra effort could have gone a long way.

I had to be honest with myself and admit that if I truly knew my child like I say I do, I needed to trust her unconditionally. I tend to want everything to go smoothly and have it all figured out ahead of time.

Then I can feel in control and decide if it's right or wrong. But that is not trusting; that is manipulating. When I'd barrage her with questions, I could sense I was offending her, and she would push away. So I tried to convince myself that maybe it was best that she didn't know every nitty-gritty detail, good or bad. This was her adventure. I had to let go of my agenda, and I learned the hard way that holding my tongue allows me to speak volumes.

Prayer is a constant, but don't hesitate to do whatever it takes to lift your spirit. I would read the same book Jen just finished or watch a movie she suggested. I found that I could feel closer to Jen by attempting to emulate her challenges. I had a deeper appreciation for water, so I didn't let the faucet run aimlessly while brushing my teeth. I was grateful for the warmth of a heated room, so I kept the thermostat a bit lower than usual. I didn't overeat in hopes that she had a decent amount of food that day. As a mother, my heart ached knowing I couldn't help her when she was thirsty, hungry, or cold. But it was through these hardships that I was able to see how she was truly "called" to serve with such determination, strength, and grace. I realized that a mother's hug lasts long after she lets go.

JENNIFER: First of all, I would have better prepared my parents for my journey. I could have invited them to attend informational meetings with me instead of just gathering all the helpful information for myself. Not that it would have been easier to say good-bye, but I could have made it more of a shared experience. Knowledge is truly powerful.

If I were to serve in the Peace Corps again, I would spend less time worrying about my inability to speak Russian fluently and more time engaging in conversations to improve my language skills. Looking back, I wasted five months of service because I judged that I couldn't speak Russian "good enough." Serving is not about perfection; it's about doing your best and finding what your "good enough" is. In total immersion language learning, you truly do receive an A for effort.

Hindsight is 20/20, but now I realize I should have spent more time in my village just walking around, engaging in conversations with community members, and going guesting upon the invitation of friends. In general, I wish I had spent more time with the natives of my host country. You can call it networking, but I call it relationship building, which is the keystone of bridging the gaps for future peace.

While some Peace Corps volunteers distance themselves from friends and family during their service, I heavily relied on mine for support. Limited communication can sometimes help to totally immerse in the culture and maximize the experience, but I felt compelled to share everything I was going through. Once I returned home, my family knew the details of the past two years of my life. It lessened the sorrows and doubled the joys. And when my service was done, my family could immediately identify with me and we didn't have to spend too much time trying to catch up.

Coming home is bittersweet. It will be hard. What I suggest is this: take some time to settle in, but don't disengage. I found myself retreating into a book when activity buzzed around me. I was so used to being alone, quiet time, and tuning out what I didn't understand. My stomach gave me some troubles and the abundance of food everywhere was disturbing. But within a few weeks, I got a job and became busy myself. However, I realized I needed to connect with someone who could relate to serving abroad so I contacted the local RPCV (Returned Peace Corps Volunteer) group. It was a godsend.

Don't be afraid to talk to your coworkers, or even speak at information nights and share your story. Tell them about the wonderful aspects of your service, but be honest about the challenges. My mom and I continue to attend these events and we both enjoy passing on any words of wisdom that we needed the most at that time. Sharing your story can ease your transition back into the first world by bringing your past into the present.

HELPFUL HINTS

- Don't believe everything you read online about the culture of your host country. Be prepared and educated, but be open-minded about the people you will meet and the experiences you will have.

- Remember, you are just a guest. You are not there to change their ways nor should you adopt them so deeply that you lose your American identity.

- When sending mail, expect letters to take two weeks and packages four weeks. Be prepared if they don't arrive at all. A box of long johns and boots arrived in time for the Fourth of July!

- When sending letters, number them so the recipient isn't confused when they receive information non-sequentially. The same applies for letters or emails you receive that share how they are struggling. We would immediately panic and try to contact Jen to "fix" it, but by the time we could connect, the trouble has passed.

- Use feminine hygiene products as packing material when mailing boxes. They are extremely expensive in country and a deterrent to your contents being tampered with. It is also helpful to lay personal undergarments on top of the care package. We used an old pair of Jen's underwear that she left behind. It is superstitious for Europeans to touch a stranger's personal items, so they will pass on pilfering through the box.

- Use duct tape when sealing packages. It is not available in third-world countries, so it can't be removed and replaced easily. Keep an inventory of what is being sent. We asked Jennifer if she enjoyed the Discman in the last package and she didn't know what we were talking about. Someone in customs is enjoying the music.

- If you need to send cash, do not put it in a card or envelope. That is the first place curious postal workers will look. Jennifer got our birthday card, but not the twenty dollars that was inside. The next time, I stuck the money in a sock and it worked!

- Decorate the outside of the box with religious symbols, like Christian sayings or stickers. We even just hand-drew angels and crosses all over the brown paper wrapping and it arrived quicker and safer. It also appears to be more effective when using red ink to do so.

- Try not to complain to your loved one about how things are done in their country, or the lack of situations being handled. They are just as frustrated, and drawing attention to it only makes it seem worse. At times, Jennifer seemed hurt when I would try to interfere with what was out of her control, anyway.

- When leaving home, utilize space in your suitcase by packing peanut butter, canned meat, and extra tennis shoes rather than toiletries. And when returning home, give away your belongings. It will be less to carry and will greatly help those you are leaving behind. It is a win-win situation.

ABOUT THE AUTHORS

Karen Lawrence resides in Chaska, MN with her husband of thirty-six years, Dan, who was her biggest supporter while on this journey to write her first book.

She feels blessed that her three children and their spouses live nearby, and that their home tends to be the gathering spot for everyone. Gardening with flowers is her hobby and she still enjoys speaking at Peace Corps events with Jennifer. But Karen's biggest joy is having grandchildren.

She helps out with her two granddaughters, and takes care of her four-year-old grandson with the Kyrgyz name, Bekett, every Friday. Some day Bekett will be able to read this story and realize the sacrifice they all made when his Mom said, "Yes…I will serve."

Jennifer Nelson lives in Robbinsdale, MN with her husband of five years, Travis, and their four-year-old son, Bekett.

After returning from the Peace Corps, Jennifer fell into the field of volunteer management for nonprofits. This career has proven to be a perfect fit, and she loves that her work enables compassionate folks to give back to their community.

In her spare time, Jennifer enjoys cooking, baking, and sharing her creative side by preserving family memories in scrapbooks. Her total recall and editing skills were very crucial in supporting her mom's dream of publishing this book. More importantly, she is very busy raising a possible second-generation Peace Corps volunteer.

Photo credit Bill and Sue Corby

Jennifer and Karen keep their story alive by attending Peace Corps events and talking to others that may say, "Yes, I will serve."